Farm M

CW00449878

Farm

Machinery

A. G. HARRIS
Principal, Harper Adams Agricultural College

T. B. MUCKLE
National College of Agricultural Engineering, Silsoe

J. A. SHAW
Training Development Adviser, Agricultural Training Board

SECOND EDITION

OXFORD UNIVERSITY PRESS

Oxford University Press, Walton Street, Oxford OX2 6DP

OXFORD LONDON GLASGOW
NEW YORK TORONTO MELBOURNE WELLINGTON
IBADAN NAIROBI DAR ES SALAAM CAPE TOWN
KUALA LUMPUR SINGAPORE JAKARTA HONG KONG TOKYO
DELHI BOMBAY CALCUTTA MADRAS KARACHI

First edition 1965
Reprinted (with revisions) 1966
Second edition 1974
Reprinted 1978

Printed in Great Britain by
Hazell Watson & Viney Ltd., Aylesbury, Bucks

Preface

The ever-increasing rate of development and technological change in modern farming imposes greater demands on the knowledge and skills of those working in the industry. It is no longer sufficient to acquire the various skills in a routine manner, it is also essential to understand the principles which underlie them in order to acquire and adapt to new techniques as they develop. This is particularly true for those in contact with the increasing range of complex and sophisticated machinery and equipment involved in animal and crop production if the machinery and equipment is to be used effectively. It has been our intention in this book to deal primarily with these principles and to relate them to the everyday situation encountered on the farm.

In such a vast subject it has been necessary to select material, and we have been guided in this by our knowledge of the essential needs of those operating farm machinery and equipment. For the student, the material adequately covers the requirements of part-time and full-time craft-level courses and also technician-level courses, providing intelligent reference is made to current manufacturers' literature and instruction manuals. Mention has been made throughout the text of normal safety precautions and, where relevant, safety regulations which concern the operator.

The main aim in preparing this second edition has been to introduce metric units. The opportunity has been taken to revise and up-date the text and many of the illustrations, as well as to include an additional chapter on Materials Handling and new sections on fault-finding in Chapters 11 and 12.

A. G. HARRIS
T. B. MUCKLE
J. A. SHAW

October, 1973

Contents

1. MECHANICS — 1
2. HEAT — 14
3. ELECTRICITY — 20
4. MATERIALS — 29
5. TOOLS AND PARTS OF MACHINES — 40
6. THE INTERNAL COMBUSTION ENGINE — 62
7. FUEL SYSTEMS — 73
8. THE ELECTRICAL SYSTEM — 81
9. LUBRICATING SYSTEMS — 91
10. THE COOLING SYSTEM — 100
11. THE FARM TRACTOR — 105
12. PLOUGHS AND PLOUGHING — 126
13. CULTIVATING EQUIPMENT — 155
14. FERTILIZER DISTRIBUTORS AND SEEDING EQUIPMENT — 173
15. FIELD CROP SPRAYERS — 193
16. HARVESTING EQUIPMENT — 208
17. GRAIN DRYING, STORAGE AND PROCESSING — 246
18. DAIRY EQUIPMENT — 257
19. MATERIALS HANDLING — 268
Index — 279

Acknowledgements

The authors gratefully acknowledge the assistance of the following organizations which provided material for the figures listed.

Bamfords Limited. Figs. 114 (a), 117.

David Brown (Tractors) Ltd. Fig. 71.

Evers and Wall Ltd. Fig. 102

Farmer's Weekly. Figs. 82, 85, 86, 114 (b), 115, 120.

Fullwood and Bland. Fig. 134.

Gascoigne, Gush and Dent Ltd. Fig. 131 (a) and (b).

International Havester Company of Great Britain Ltd. Figs. 42, 46, 93.

Johnson's (Engineering) Ltd. Fig. 123.

Massey-Ferguson (U.K.) Ltd. Figs. 59, 69, 70, 80, 81, 83, 91, 107, 113, 116, 121, and the frontispiece.

Sperry New Holland Ltd. Figs. 118, 119.

Ransomes, Sims & Jeffries Ltd. Figs. 64, 68, 72(a),72(b), 76, 95, 96.

Salopian – Kenneth Hudson Ltd. Fig. 90.

Sisis Equipment Ltd. Fig. 89 (b).

Stanhay (Ashford) Ltd. Fig. 98.

E. A. Webb Ltd. Figs. 87, 97.

The Controller of Her Majesty's Stationery Office has also kindly granted permission for the reproduction of the diagrams shown in: Figs. 99–101, 103–6, 122, 125–7, 129, 130.

1. Mechanics

Energy

Have you ever wondered how horses are able to pull carts, how men are able to carry sacks of corn, how dogs are able to run quickly or how a tractor drives a baler? To perform these tasks it is necessary for the horse, or the man or the dog to have food and to rest at intervals but, providing the tractor is supplied with fuel, it is able to work continuously. It is this food and fuel which provides them with the ability to do work. We call this ability to do work *energy*.

Although energy exists in many forms, they all, apart from atomic energy, originate from the light and heat radiated from the sun. A good example of this is the fuel used to drive our tractors, cars or aeroplanes. It is thought that, many thousands of years ago, plant and animal organisms in the seas were covered by mud deposits sealing them from the access of air. These residues gradually decomposed in the absence of air, forming crude oil. This crude oil is now pumped out of the ground and refined, to give various fuels to drive our tractors, cars and aeroplanes. Thus the light and heat energy absorbed by these organisms thousands of years ago is being used in a different form today.

This also illustrates another important property of energy: it can never be used up or lost, but merely changed from one form to another. It would be appropriate here to consider some of the forms of energy that have frequent application in our farm equipment. The diesel tractor provides a suitable example. First, it is necessary to start the tractor. The chemical reaction or *chemical* energy in the battery produces *electrical* energy to drive the starter motor. The starter motor turns the engine, a form of *mechanical* energy, compressing the air in the cylinders until sufficient *heat* energy is produced to ignite the fuel as it is injected, causing the piston to move back down the cylinder—*mechanical* energy. It is this mechanical energy which drives the tractor and enables it to pull implements.

We divide energy into two forms. The first is called *kinetic* energy—the energy due to motion or movement. For instance, water rushing over a waterfall or a tractor pulling a load of corn along the road is said to have kinetic energy. But if this same tractor was stationary at the top of a hill, it would then have *potential* energy, because by merely releasing the hand-brake it would move down the hill. This is the second form of mechanical energy and in fact is the energy due to the position of the object. Water being held by a dam possesses potential energy. When it reaches the level of the sluice gates or pours over the top, this potential energy is transformed into kinetic energy.

Force

We often speak of 'force of gravity'. We know if a stone is thrown into the air it will return to the ground under force of gravity. What exactly is a force? It is defined as that which changes or tends to change a body's state of rest or uniform motion.

One of the most simple examples of force seen on the farm is the direct pull or push which the tractor exerts on an implement drawbar when travelling forwards or reversing. In this case, the state of rest of the implement is changed to a state of motion by the force of the tractor. If a man tried to pull a heavy implement, it is quite possible that he would be unable to do so but he would still be exerting a force on the implement, even though insufficient to move it. This force would only 'tend' to change the state of rest.

Force is also necessary to reduce motion. For instance, a tractor driver may need to slow down as he approaches a steep downward slope with a heavy load. He does this by applying his brakes. The force applied through the brake shoes to the brake drum slows down the tractor by converting the energy of motion to heat energy. If the load were very heavy, then the force exerted by the load pushing the tractor forward down the slope might be greater than the maximum force exerted by the brakes in trying to hold back the load, causing the tractor to gain speed. Nevertheless, the brakes would still be exerting a force.

So far we have only mentioned forces that move in straight lines, pulling, pushing or lifting. Force can also cause a turning movement. When tightening or undoing a nut, a direct pull or push is exerted on the free end of a spanner, whilst the other end turns the nut.

It is necessary to know the units which are used to measure force. The direct pull or force exerted by a tractor on a trailer or on a trailed implement, such as a set of disc harrows or rolls,

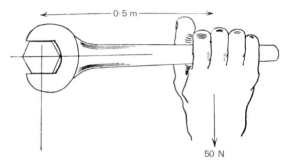

Fig. 1. Torque

is measured in *newtons* (N) and is commonly called the *draft* or *drawbar pull*. A medium-sized wheeled tractor can exert a draft of about 20 000 N, and a tracklayer tractor about 45 000 N. Similarly, a turning force is measured in *newtons*, but in this case it is common to refer to the turning force multiplied by the distance between the force and the centre of rotation; this is known as *torque*. Torque is measured in newton metres (Nm).

In Fig. 1 the torque would be:

$$0.5 \text{ m} \times 50 \text{ N} = 25 \text{ Nm}.$$

In practice, this means that if a nut is very tight, we can usually undo it in one of three ways:

1. by exerting our force at right angles to the spanner;
2. by increasing the force at the end of the spanner;
3. by applying the same force and lengthening the spanner.

Mass and weight

The amount or size of a body is called the *mass*. This mass when at rest exerts a force. This force has in the past been called the *weight*. However, due to the fact that the earth is not completely round but slightly flattened at the Poles the effect of gravity varies on different parts of the earth's surface. Therefore the force, or weight, exerted by a mass will vary, but the mass itself will remain constant. As an example, a sack of potatoes will have the same mass in any part of the world even though the force it exerts may vary slightly—the correct description of the amount of potatoes is to say that they have a mass of x kg. The weight is no longer used. In order to calculate the force in newtons resulting from a mass in kilograms, the mass is multiplied by 9·81. In the example of the sack of potatoes we will assume its mass is 50 kg. Therefore, the force it exerts is $50 \times 9 \cdot 81 = 490 \cdot 5$ N.

Work

In mechanical terms, when a force moves through a distance, *work* is done, the amount of work being measured by multiplying the force in newtons by the distance moved in the direction of the force in metres. The basic unit of measurement of work is a *joule* (J). One joule of work is done when a force of one newton is moved through a distance of one metre. For example, if a man lifts a 25 kg sack (force $= 25 \times 9 \cdot 81 = 245 \cdot 25$ N) from the floor through 2 m on to his shoulder, the work done is $245 \cdot 25$ N $\times$ 2 m $= 490$ Nm (or J).

It is important to remember that, for work to be done, the force must move through a distance, and in this respect the mechanical term 'work' differs from the normal interpretation of the word. In the above example, the man could stand quite still with the sack on his shoulder and, although he would become physically tired by exerting a force on the sack to maintain its position, no mechanical work would be done whilst the sack (force) remained stationary. Work would be done when he returned the sack to the floor.

In testing and comparing some new cultivating equipment, it is often necessary to measure the force required to pull the implement in order to calculate the work to be done by the tractor. This can be done by placing a traction dynamometer, which acts like a spring balance, between the drawbar of the tractor and the implement, and measures the force required to move the implement. When this force is multiplied by the distance travelled, the amount of work done is obtained.

Where an object is lifted, the force required results from the mass of the object. This is not so when an implement or trailer is being pulled, where the force required is related to the resistance to movement. A trailer loaded with three tonnes of potatoes will need only sufficient force applied to overcome the resistance of the wheels to the ground and of the axle bearings. The former will obviously be much less on firm ground than in muddy conditions. This also explains why we refer to some soils as 'heavy' and others as 'light', because the heavy soils require a much greater force to pull an implement through them than do the lighter soils.

Power

Power is the rate of doing work and may be measured in units which we call *watts* (W); one watt being a rate of work equivalent to one newton–metre (Nm) or joule (J) per second (s). Our cars and tractors are often classified on their power, e.g. a medium power tractor is one which is capable of producing 25 to 35 kW. This power rating given to a tractor is the *brake power*, and it is measured when the tractor is stationary by driving, directly from the engine, a machine designed to measure power (absorption dynamometer). The watt as a unit of power replaces the old unit of *horse-power*. One horse-power is equivalent to 746 W and to convert horse-power rating to watts the horse-power should be multiplied by 746. In practice it is more common to multiply by 0·746 to convert horse-power to kilowatts to avoid high numbers. For example an existing 60 brake horse-power tractor would be 44·8 kW.

Brake power, therefore, indicates the capacity of an engine to produce work. Under field conditions, not all this power will be available to pull implements, because some of it is needed to propel the tractor forward and overcome the resistance of the bearings and the soil on the wheels of the tractor. To take an example of a 40 kW tractor moving across a field at about 3 km/h, it may take about 5 kW to move the tractor, leaving 35 kW to pull an implement. This power available to haul an implement is called *drawbar* power. Many of our implements such as forage harvesters are driven by the tractor through the power take-off shaft (p.t.o.). Therefore, in addition to pulling the implement, some of the available power is needed to drive it as well. When a stationary machine is being driven from the p.t.o., all the power—apart from that lost through friction in the transmission—is available for driving the machine.

The more easily a tractor can move itself along, for instance on a hard surface, the more drawbar power will be available. On heavy wet land much power is absorbed in moving the tractor, leaving less power available at the drawbar. This is why heavy-land farmers need higher-powered tractors than light-land farmers.

It has already been mentioned that it is possible to measure the pull at the tractor drawbar by putting a dynamometer between the implement and the tractor. If the distance covered and the time taken is also measured, the drawbar power exerted can be calculated. To pull a set of discs in heavy soil may require a pull or force of 10 000 N, and if the tractor moves 1 m in 1 s, then (10 000 N × 1 m) of work will be done. Therefore, the drawbar power =

$$10\ 000\ \text{W or } 10\ \text{kW}.$$

Machines

A machine is a device used to change the size or direction of a force, to make the most use of the work being done.

The lever

The simplest form of machine is the lever, e.g. a tyre lever or a long pole, for raising heavy objects (Fig. 2).

It would be very difficult for a man to lift a mass of 200 kg, but by using a lever as in Fig. 2, he would be able to lift it quite easily, because the lever would multiply the size of the force applied and also alter its direction. It is possible to calculate

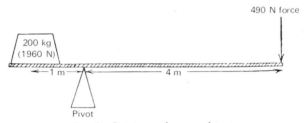

Fig. 2. Raising a heavy object

the extent to which a lever increases the size of force applied and this is related to the distance of the force and the distance of the mass from the pivot.

In Fig. 2, if the free end of the lever, which is 4 m from the pivot, is pressed down with a force of 490 N, then this exerts a turning force or torque at the pivot of 4 m × 490 N = 1960 Nm. At the other end of the lever, the mass is also exerting a force of 1960 N × 1 m = 1960 Nm. As the turning force in each direction is of equal size, the mass is balanced and remains stationary, but a slightly-increased force exerted by the man causes the mass to lift. The downward force applied by the man is converted to an upward force by the lever.

It might appear that the man has gained something for nothing. Closer study shows that this is not the case, because the work done by the man equals the work done on the mass. Work = force×distance and, with the lever arranged as in Fig. 2, it is necessary to move it down 1 m to raise the mass 0·25 m. Therefore, the work done by the man is 490 N×1 m = 490 J to raise the mass 0·25 m. Alternatively, the work done on the weight is 1960 N×0·25 m = 490 J. This means that the amount of work done by the man at his end of the lever is in fact the same as the amount of work done on the weight if friction at the pivot is neglected.

However, despite the fact that equal work is done at both ends of the lever, the man is able to reduce his physical effort by taking 'advantage' of the lever. The extent of his advantage can be measured and is known as the *mechanical advantage*. We do this by dividing the *load* by the *effort* which gives the formula:

$$\text{mechanical advantage} = \frac{\text{load}}{\text{effort}}.$$

The mechanical advantage in our example:

$$\frac{1960 \text{ N}}{490 \text{ N}} = 4.$$

Mechanical advantage is a ratio and is therefore expressed as a number without units. It is sometimes necessary to consider the movement of the effort in comparison with that of the load. This is known as the *velocity ratio*. In our example this would be $1 \div \frac{1}{4} = 4$. Like mechanical advantage, velocity ratio is expressed as a number without units.

The *efficiency* of a machine is found by dividing the work put out by the work put in, i.e.

$$\text{efficiency} = \frac{\text{work obtained from machine}}{\text{work applied to machine}}.$$

This is usually expressed as a percentage by multiplying by 100. With the lever, efficiency is very high, in fact 100%, because the work put out = work put in.

In the example chosen:

$$\text{efficiency} = \frac{1960 \text{ N} \times 1 \text{ m} \times 100}{490 \text{ N} \times 4 \text{ m}}$$

$$= \frac{1960 \text{ J} \times 100}{1960 \text{ J}} = 100\%$$

In any machine where there are shafts rotating in bearings, some of the power put into the machine is used in overcoming the resistance of these bearings. This resistance is known as *friction*. Because of this, the actual efficiency of machines is always less than 100%.

Hydraulics

The principle of levers is widely used in modern tractors for lifting purposes such as tipping trailers, fore-end loaders and mounted implements. The force required for lifting is transmitted through a liquid and we usually refer to the liquid as the hydraulic fluid. The force to operate the lever is increased as a result of a small piston, fitting closely in a cylinder full of oil, forcing the oil through a pipe to a larger cylinder also containing a close-fitting piston (Fig. 3).

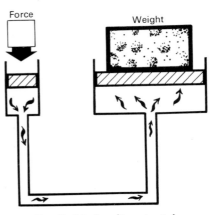

Fig. 3. Hydraulic principle

If the area of the small piston is 10 mm² and the force on it 30 N, the pressure transmitted to the large piston is equal to force/area, i.e. $30 \text{ N}/10 \text{ mm}^2 = 3 \text{ N/mm}^2$. If the area of the large piston is 40 mm², the total force exerted on the piston is force per unit area × area of the large piston = $3 \text{ N/mm}^2 \times$

40 mm^2 = 120 N. Therefore, the mechanical advantage is equal to resulting force/initial force = 120/30 or 4.

It is sometimes necessary to compare the distance moved by the effort with the distance moved by the load. The ratio of these two distances is called the *velocity ratio* which has the formula:

$$\text{velocity ratio} = \frac{\text{distance moved by effort}}{\text{distance moved by load}}$$

In the example in Fig. 3 the small piston would need to move 4 mm to move the large piston 1 mm and thus the velocity ratio is 4. As with other machines, friction—in this case between the piston and cylinder wall—prevents the efficiency from reaching 100%. Therefore, it can be seen that the principles are the same as with mechanical levers and on many machines, such as the fore-end loader, both hydraulic and mechanical levers are used.

Pulleys

So far we have considered only the lever, but other simple machines are in frequent use on farms and will serve further to illustrate these fundamentals. Pulleys are often used to lift heavy loads. If a rope is passed round a single pulley, as in Fig. 4, then a man must exert a force equal to the load he wishes to raise.

If two pulleys are used, as in Fig. 5, then to raise the load 1 m the operator must shorten each of the two ropes supporting the bottom pulley by 1 m. The velocity ratio would then be:

$$\frac{\text{distance moved by effort}}{\text{distance moved by load}} = \frac{2 \text{ m}}{1 \text{ m}} = 2.$$

The mechanical advantage, assuming no loss through friction on the pulley bearings, would also be 2, that is, an effort of 100 N would lift a load of 200 N.

The maximum effort an operator can exert vertically downwards is that resulting from his mass. Therefore, if the operator

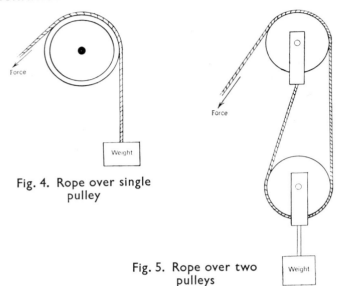

Fig. 4. Rope over single
pulley

Fig. 5. Rope over two
pulleys

has a mass of 75 kg, we can now calculate the greatest load he
could raise using the pulley arrangement in Fig. 5.

$$\text{The mechanical advantage} = \frac{\text{load}}{\text{effort}} = 2$$

$$\begin{aligned}
\text{therefore load} &= 2 \times \text{effort (force due to man's mass)} \\
&= 2 \times 75 \times 9 \cdot 81 \\
&= 1471 \cdot 5 \text{ N.}
\end{aligned}$$

This force represents a mass of $1471 \cdot 5/9 \cdot 81 = 150$ kg. If he
wishes a greater load, then he would have to use more pulleys
giving a larger mechanical advantage.

The screw

The screw or the nut and bolt is also a simple machine. The
principle involved is best illustrated with the screw jack, used
for lifting cars or tractors. When using a jack, one full turn on

the handle causes the threaded vertical part to turn one revolution, raising the load the distance between two threads, as shown in Fig. 6.

The work done by the operator is the circumference of the circle described in turning the handle through one revolution ×

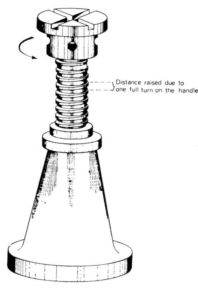

Distance raised due to one full turn on the handle

Fig. 6. Screw jack

the effort. The work put out by the jack is equal to the load multiplied by the distance raised. Therefore, using a large handle or a fine thread on the vertical part of the jack reduces the effort.

Gears

Gears are used to increase or decrease the speed and torque of shafts when power is being transmitted, as in the tractor gearbox, where the gears alter the speed of the rear wheels, even though the engine speed may remain constant. Names are given to these gears: the driving gear being called the *driver* and the one being driven, the *driven* (Fig. 7).

To take an example, we will assume the driver has 10 teeth and the driven has 50 teeth. The driver would need to make 5 revolutions to turn the driven 1 revolution, giving a velocity ratio of 5 and also a mechanical advantage of 5, assuming no loss through friction. Where the driver and the driven have an equal number of teeth, the velocity ratio is 1. This explains why a tractor in bottom gear can pull heavier loads than when it is in top gear, because the driver selected in the gearbox has fewer teeth and therefore a greater mechanical advantage than when the tractor is in top gear. The lower the gear, the wider the velocity ratio, and therefore the slower the tractor

Fig. 7. Gears. Where *A* is the driving and *B* the driven gear, the speed of gear *B* is increased relative to the speed of gear *A*. Where *B* is the driving and *A* the driven gear, the speed of gear *A* is decreased relative to the speed of gear *B*.

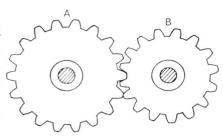

moves forward at a constant engine speed. It is important to realize that, when using two gears meshed together, the direction of drive is reversed.

Belt and chain drives

These are used to transmit power from one shaft to another some distance apart. Like gears, they may increase or decrease the speed of rotation. The velocity ratio in this case is calculated by comparing the diameters of the pulleys or sprockets. We usually refer to the wheels driven by belts as *pulleys*, and those driven by chains as *sprockets*. If an 0·6 m diameter pulley is turning at 100 revolutions per minute (rev/min) and driving an 0·2 m pulley, the velocity ratio is:

$$\frac{\text{diameter of the driving pulley}}{\text{diameter of the driven pulley}} = \frac{0·6}{0·2} = 3.$$

From this, the speed of the driven pulley can be determined since the velocity ratio is 3, so the small pulley must be turning 3 times as fast as the large pulley, i.e. 300 rev/min.

Unlike gears, the direction of rotation using belts and chains is the same on both shafts unless the belt is crossed, in which case the direction of rotation is reversed.

2. Heat

In the previous chapter we mentioned that the heat from the sun is one of the original sources of energy. It is of direct importance in farming to make the seeds germinate in the soil and the crops ripen. *Heat energy*, produced from different sources, is used for drying grain, warming water in the dairy and many other purposes in modern farming. It is therefore important to understand some of the fundamental principles of heat energy.

Heat can be added to or removed from liquids, solids and gases, and affects each of these in two ways.

1. A change in heat energy causes a change in *size*. The iron hoop on a wooden waggon wheel is a good example of this. When its temperature is raised, it increases in size (expands) and can thus be easily fitted over the wheel. As it cools, it decreases in size (contracts) and becomes a tight fit on the wheel.

2. A change in heat energy may cause a change of *state*. For example, if sufficient heat energy is added to water, it boils and turns from liquid into vapour (steam).

At the point at which water and other substances change their state, their temperature remains constant. Yet for this change to occur, further heat energy must be added. This heat energy is known as *latent heat*. Similarly, latent heat must be added to change ice into water, and taken away if steam is to be turned into boiling water (condensed) or water into ice. The effect of water *expanding* on freezing in water pipes and car and tractor radiators is frequently seen when the ice starts to thaw and the water leaks through the cracks caused by the expanding ice.

Temperature

The degree of heat that matter possesses is called the *temperature* and can be measured with a thermometer. Different types of thermometer are found in practice, but the most common type consists of a glass tube having a fine hole through its length (capillary tube), drawn out into a bulb at one end and sealed at the other, air having been removed prior to sealing. The bulb contains either mercury or alcohol and, as the temperature increases, these liquids expand, forcing their way through the fine capillary or hole. Similarly, when the temperature decreases, these liquids contract or shrink back along the capillary to the bulb. If a scale is marked on or beside the tube, it is possible to note the point reached by the liquid and therefore the temperature of the matter.

The temperature scale which we use in this country is *Celsius*, in keeping with the Continental countries. Celsius is usually abbreviated to a captial C and the scale itself is divided into units or degrees. Degrees are signified by a small circle after the number, e.g. 45°C. The freezing point of water is 0°C and temperatures lower than this are recorded as a minus figure, e.g. −6°C, six degrees below the freezing point of water. There are 100 Celsius degrees between the freezing point and boiling point of water and, therefore, the latter is 100°C.

Expansion and contraction

It has already been stated that a change in heat often results in a change in size of any particular body and, generally speaking, adding heat causes expansion whilst the removal of heat or cooling causes contraction. The notable exception to this is water, which expands on freezing. Different solids, liquids and gases expand by different amounts when heated through the same temperature range. This is a very important factor when designing equipment made of different materials which are likely to reach quite high temperatures, because the differing expansion rates of the materials could set up quite considerable stresses within the machine, unless suitable allowances are made. For instance, the pistons in a car or tractor engine are often made from aluminium whilst the cylinder barrels in which the pistons move are of cast iron. Aluminium expands more than cast iron and therefore the piston should be quite a slack fit when cold, to allow free movement at the normal running temperature. Glass in aluminium frames in a greenhouse is another example.

Expansion and contraction also occurs with a change in state, when energy is added or subtracted, in the form of latent heat, as in the case of water freezing. When a liquid changes to a gas, considerable expansion occurs, a large volume of gas being obtained from a smaller volume of liquid. If a gas is heated and cannot expand, its pressure rises. Conversely, if a gas is compressed, its temperature rises.

Heat transference

Heat will flow from a body at high temperature to one of lower temperature, until both are at the same temperature. This transfer occurs in different ways.

Conduction

When a pan of water is warmed on an electric ring, the metal of the pan is in direct contact with the ring, and the heat flows from the ring through the pan to the water. Similarly, when the end of a metal rod is placed in a fire, the heat gradually flows along the length of the rod. This type of heat transference is known as *conduction*. Materials which allow heat to pass easily through them are called *thermal conductors*. Metals are good conductors of heat. Materials such as asbestos, wool or timber resist the transfer movement of heat and are called *thermal insulators*. These insulating materials vary in their resistance to heat movement and are important in the construction of livestock buildings, where it is necessary to maintain an even temperature, and also for covering (lagging) hot water pipes to keep the heat in, and exposed cold water pipes to keep them from freezing. Most milk coolers work on the principle of conduction, heat being taken through the metal of which the cooler is constructed and carried away by the cool liquid circulating inside the cooler.

Convection

When liquids or gases are heated, they expand and become less dense causing them to rise and the cool liquid or gas falls to the lowest point. Movement by heat in this way is known as *convection*. The heat produced in a tractor engine is conducted through the cylinder walls to the cooling water. As the water is warmed, it rises and returns to the radiator for cooling, before returning to the lower part of the engine, although in modern tractor engines this movement is aided with a pump.

Radiation

The third type of heat transference is *radiation* and arises from the heat waves given off by a warm or hot object. The heat that we feel from the sun reaches us by radiation, as does the heat from an electric or coal fire. Waves of radiant heat travel in straight lines and can therefore be cut by an insulating material. Radiant heat waves pass through a vacuum, but may be absorbed by bodies whose temperature is thereby raised. Some materials reflect heat waves and are therefore called reflectors. Radiant heat waves will also pass through certain materials, such as glass and water. Thus they pass through the panes in a glass-house and warm the soil and plants inside. The heat accumulates inside and the temperature rises above that outside the glass-house. Black bodies or painted surfaces, other than white, absorb most of the heat rays. White bodies are good reflectors of heat. Dark or matt surfaces absorb more radiant heat than light or shiny surfaces. We wear dark clothes in winter time to keep as warm as possible and light clothes in the summer to keep cool. Similarly, dark-coloured soils warm up more quickly in the spring than do light-coloured soils.

Refrigeration

Refrigeration is the process of removing heat, thereby maintaining rooms and substances at a lower temperature than they would otherwise have been. The equipment used for this purpose is called a *refrigeration plant.*

The most common type of plant used where there is electric power available is called *a vapour compression plant* (Fig. 8).

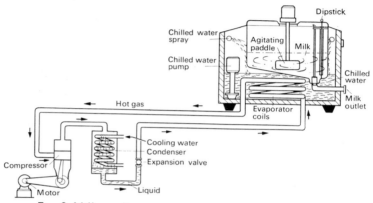

Fig. 8 Milk cooling system using vapour compression

An electrically driven compressor increases the pressure of a gas known as the *refrigerant,* causing its temperature to rise. The compressed gas then passes through a condenser, similar to a tractor radiator, and is cooled by air or water. This cooling causes the gas to become a liquid at high pressure, by removing the latent heat. The liquid is then allowed to expand through a valve, into an evaporator. In expanding, the liquid reduces its pressure, boils and changes into a gas. In changing its state, it takes in the latent heat it lost when it was condensed. This latent heat is provided by conduction through the walls of the evaporator from a liquid, usually brine, which is in constant circulation around the evaporator. The brine is then the active cooling agent, the gas returning to the compressor to continue the cycle.

Relative humidity

The amount of water vapour which can be absorbed by the air depends on the air temperature. The higher the temperature the greater the quantity which can be absorbed. When air can absorb no further vapour, we say that it is *saturated*. This situation occurs at night when the air cools. The relative humidity increases as temperature falls, until saturation occurs. If the temperature drops lower, the air can no longer hold the water, which is deposited on the ground as dew. The term relative humidity (r.h.) is used to measure the amount of moisture in the air when compared with a fully saturated air at that temperature. Thus air at r.h. of 50% contains half the maximum water vapour possible. If the air were heated, the r.h. may fall to 25% because we are comparing it with saturated air at a higher temperature, and it has already been stated that the higher the temperature the greater the maximum quantity of water vapour which can be absorbed.

3. Electricity

The days of poorly lit farm buildings are quickly disappearing, as the supply of mains electricity stretches out from the more populated areas into the countryside, making working conditions much more pleasant in the dark winter mornings and evenings. The benefits of electricity are so obvious that many farmers, at present beyond the reach of a mains electricity supply, instal equipment to generate their own supply of electricity. When thinking of electricity, we usually think first of electric light, but electrical energy on farms is now widely used as a source of heat, for drying grain or keeping young animals warm, and also as a source of power in electric motors for driving many different pieces of stationary farm equipment, such as grinders and food mixers.

Conduction and insulation

To make full and safe use of electricity, we must first understand how electricity is transmitted through wires from the generators to the point where it is required. Some materials, such as copper, steel and aluminium, allow electricity to flow easily through them and we call these materials good *conductors* of electricity. Other materials, such as rubber and porcelain, are very poor conductors of electricity and we refer to these as *insulators*. Therefore the wires carrying the electricity will usually consist of a copper core covered by an insulating material.

Amperes and volts

Electricity flowing through a wire is very similar to water flowing in a pipe. We can measure the flow of electricity or *current* in a wire, and the units of flow are called *amperes* (A), frequently abbreviated to *amps*. The flow of electricity in a wire, as with water in a pipe, results from 'pressure' at its source. This pressure is measured in *volts* (V), and the pressure of our normal mains supply will either be about 220/240 V or 400/440 V. Just as for any fixed pressure the flow of water in a pipe depends on its length and diameter, so the flow or current depends on the length and diameter of the wire—the longer and thinner the wire, the greater the resistance to flow. Poor conductors also increase resistance to flow. This resistance to flow causes heating in the wire, and it is important in wiring equipment to have the correct size of wire to carry sufficient current without overheating, a factor which needs consideration in electrical extensions in farm buildings. On the other hand we make use of this factor when we want to turn electrical energy into heat energy by inserting a wire of poor conducting ability, and probably of a smaller diameter, to increase resistance and thus produce heat, as in the bar of an electric fire. Similarly, light is produced in a bulb by a length of wire getting white hot in the bulb. Resistance is measured in units called *ohms* (Ω), and is equivalent to the voltage divided by the amps.

Watts (W)

When electrical energy is used to light a bulb, heat a coil or drive a motor, work is performed. In an earlier chapter we referred to the rate of doing work as power, and the unit of power as the watt (W). The amount of power (in watts) being used by an electrical device on a particular task is the voltage multiplied by the number of amps flowing through the device, i.e. amps × volts = watts. When buying electric light bulbs, we might ask for a 60 W or 100 W bulb depending on the intensity of light we require, the latter being much brighter because it absorbs more power. The bar on an electric fire is often rated at 1000 W and, therefore, if the supply pressure is 240 V, the current would be:

$$\text{amps (A)} \times \text{volts (V)} = \text{watts (W)}$$

$$\text{therefore } \frac{\text{watts (W)}}{\text{volts (V)}} = \text{amps (A)}$$

$$\text{therefore } \frac{1000}{240} = 4\cdot16 \text{ amps (A)}$$

Similarly for an electric motor taking a current of 10 A at 240 V the amount of power used would be:

$$\text{amps (A)} \times \text{volts (V)} = \text{watts (W)}$$
$$10 \text{ A} \times 240 \text{ V} = 2400 \text{ W}$$

In practice, the power produced will be less than this, due to electrical losses in the motor and friction of the bearings; but electric motors do have a high degree of efficiency with 75 to 90% of the power put in being delivered at the pulley.

The watt is a very small unit and in practice we usually speak of 1000 watts (kW) as a basic unit. The cost of electricity to the consumer is based on *kilowatt–hours* (kWh) called units, each being equivalent to a power of 1 kilowatt consumed for a period of 1 hour. This can be illustrated by three simple examples:

1. A 100W bulb will burn for 10 hours on 1 unit.
2. An electric fire with two 1000 W bars will burn for $\frac{1}{2}$ hour on 1 unit.
3. A 5 kW electric motor will consume 5 units in 1 hour.

Circuit

For electricity to flow in an electrical device, it must be connected to a source of electrical 'pressure' by supply and return wires, which complete a circuit. This will apply on any scale, whether it is the large circuit from and to the generating station, or the smaller circuit from the mains supply around the farm buildings and back to the mains. The electrical circuit can be made or broken by the use of a switch which is a convenient

and safe means of joining or breaking the supply wire. In Fig.
9 (a) the current which is regarded as flowing from positive to
negative is cut off when the switch is in position A but lights
the bulb when in position B.

If another bulb is added it may be wired in series as in Fig.
9 (b) or in parallel as in Fig. 9 (c). In a series connection it is

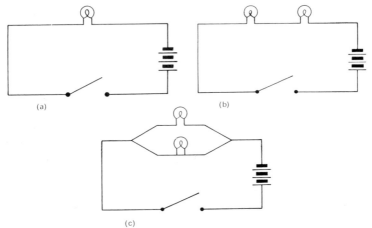

Fig. 9. (a) A Simple circuit, (b) A Series circuit, (c) A Parallel circuit

impossible to operate each bulb independently, the current
flowing through each bulb in turn. If one bulb should fail the
circuit would be broken. If further bulbs are added in series
there would be progressively less light from bulbs further away
from the current source. In Fig. 9 (c) the voltage across each
branch is equal and each branch can operate independently of
the other. A pair of tractor headlamps is a good example of
components which would be wired by a parallel connection.

Fuse

It is most important always to include a safety mechanism or
fuse in an electrical circuit. This fuse consists of a piece of wire
of such material and of such dimension that it will carry the

normal current without becoming overheated. If the current becomes excessive through some fault developing, then the fuse will melt and cut off the supply. Fuses incorporated in circuits carrying 220/240 V can easily be repaired, but it is of *vital importance* to replace the fuse with a wire of the correct size to carry the current required for the circuit. Before replacing the fuse, the supply of electricity should be switched off at the main and the circuit inspected to determine the cause of the fuse 'blowing.' The following are a few common causes.

1. Overload on the circuit because too many lights, heaters or other pieces of equipment have been connected. This is not uncommon where larger and more bulbs are used to improve lighting or where extra leads are taken to outlying buildings. Where a fuse has blown from this cause the fuse wire has a 'clean' break with a narrow gap.

2. A short circuit ('short') between two wires where the insulating covering has worn off or perished causing the current to by-pass its normal route: a common fault in badly connected plugs or in cable which is frequently being moved (such as that on inspection lights and portable power tools). A short circuit may also result from dampness acting as a conductor and from wiring which has become wet. Where a fuse has blown from this cause there are usually more definite signs of intense heat, such as blackening of the holder, a wide gap, and beads on the broken ends of the wire.

Generation of electricity

To understand electricity completely, it is necessary to study the behaviour of atoms, but it is sufficient for the reader to know that it is produced whenever a magnet is moved in a coil of wire. This is illustrated simply in Fig. 10, where by moving the magnet up and down a current is produced in the coil. This basic principle is involved when electricity is generated by the dynamo on a car or tractor, and also by the large generators at power stations.

The electrical current generated at power stations differs

from that produced by dynamos in many farm installations or on cars and tractors. In a power station it is convenient to use a generator (alternator) which produces a current that flows through the circuit first in one direction and then in the other, because 'pressure' of this type of current can easily be boosted

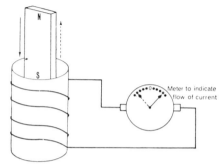

Fig. 10. Magnet and coil

for transmission over long distances. This change in direction is quite rapid and in fact usually occurs 50 times each second. This type of current is known as *alternating* current (a.c.) Dynamos produce an electric current which flows in one direction only. This is known as *direct* current (d.c.) and this, not a.c., is necessary where the electricity generated has to be stored —as in a tractor battery.

Transmission

Electricity is transmitted from power stations at very high voltages owing to the long distances that it has to be conveyed. The National Grid, for instance, works at 132 000 V, the Super Grid at 275 000 V, whilst other transmission systems operate at 33 000 V or 11 000 V. These voltages are much too high for normal farm use and that is why one frequently finds the frustrating case of a farm with pylons carrying a high-voltage supply over the fields, but no electricity available for use on the farm. Where high-voltage cables cross a farm, great care is required not to touch them with high loads or with aluminium ladders, as anyone in contact with or near these objects would be electrocuted.

Three-phase and single-phase

To reduce these high voltages, it is necessary to instal a transformer. This is expensive and is usually done near a centre of population where the consumption of electricity warrants the cost. The current from these transformer stations may be conveyed to the farm by two, three or four cables. Two cables imply a *single-phase* supply, three cables a *three-phase* supply and where four cables are present, three of which carry the current, the fourth being a neutral or return wire, it is possible to have both single- and three-phase supply.

The 'pressure' in a single-phase supply is 220/240 V, whereas in a three-phase supply it is 400/440 V. This higher voltage in the three-phase supply, whilst being fully used by large electric motors, is not needed for normal lighting and heating and, for these purposes, only one of the three current-carrying wires and the neutral wire are used. This combination is then single-phase, giving a voltage of 220/240 V. In outlying districts, single-phase supply is quite common as the amount of electricity consumed does not warrant the higher cost of a three-phase transformer, despite certain advantages of three-phase supply to both the Electricity Authority and the farmer. One of the main advantages of three-phase current to the farmer is that where large electric motors (3 hp or more) are required, three-phase motors are simpler, cheaper and more reliable than single-phase motors.

Earthing

One type of safety precaution, the fuse, has already been mentioned. Another safety precaution which is essential on all supplies being used for power is an earth wire. This wire leads from an appliance to either a copper or iron water pipe (but not a gas pipe) running underground, or a copper plate driven into the ground. Then, if the insulation of the wiring in the appliance becomes faulty, the current can flow direct to earth through the earth wire and back to the transformer and so minimize the shock that a person who touched a metallic part of the appliance would receive. If no earth wire were present, then the current would pass through the person to earth, unless he were fortunate enough to be wearing thick rubber boots and not holding a conducting material in contact with the ground in his other hand. Efficient earth wires are of great importance in damp conditions where 'shorting' is likely to occur.

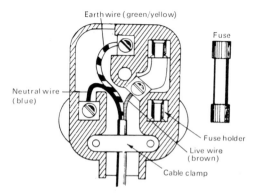

Fig. 11. Three-pin plug

Small appliances can conveniently be earthed by using three-core cables and three-pin plugs, the earth circuit continuing from the plug through the cable to link with a central earthing point, where an automatic earth trip switch may be installed which cuts off the electricity supply in the event of a leakage to earth. To ensure that earthing can occur, the plug must be wired correctly, the right wires being attached to the right terminals. The three wires in a three-core cable are coloured, by convention, green/yellow, brown and blue. The green/yellow or earth wire must be connected to the terminal marked 'E', the brown or live wire to the terminal marked 'L', and the blue or neutral wire to the terminal marked 'N'. Whilst this colour code applies to all new equipment, it is important to realize that older electrical equipment has a different colour code (green—earth wire, red—live wire, black—neutral wire).

In removing the insulation material from the wires to expose the copper for attaching to the terminal, care must be taken not to reduce the number of copper strands in the wires. When this does occur, the current has to pass through a wire of smaller effective diameter, causing heating in the plug. Many three-pin plugs now contain a fuse attached to the live terminal in addition to the fuse in the main circuit (Fig. 11).

When electrical faults occur, the layman is often tempted to rectify them without fully realizing the possible dangers. All wiring and installations should be made by a competent elec-

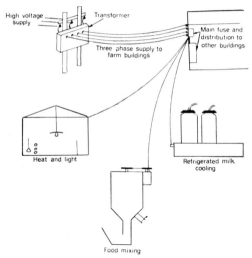

Fig. 12. Electricity on the farm

trician, the layman confining his activities to fitting a fuse or wiring a plug on single-phase supplies. He should never touch three-phase supplies. (See Fig. 12.)

4. Materials

Many different materials are used in the manufacture of agricultural machinery. Each material is chosen for its particular characteristics. Some parts of machines have to withstand wear or abrasion, and are therefore made from hardened steel or cast iron, whilst other parts may need to resist corrosion and for this purpose stainless steel and plastics are frequently used. In addition to these characteristics, the relative initial and maintenance costs, as well as the weight of the materials, also have to be considered.

In selecting materials, the manufacturer must have a knowledge of the characteristics of the materials and the *stresses* and *strains* that are imposed on the materials when the machine is at work, to ensure that they are capable of performing the task for which they are designed.

Stress

Whenever a material is subjected to an external force, such as a blow from a hammer, internal forces are set up within the material to oppose the external forces and resist a change in shape. The effect of these external forces is known as *stress* and if the stress set up is too high for the particular material, permanent distortion or fracture may occur. The external forces can be divided into three groups:

1. *Tensile forces*, which tend to stretch the material.

2. *Compressive forces*, which tend to reduce the dimension of the material in the direction in which the force is applied.

3. *Shearing forces*, which tend to cause one part of the material to slide over the piece next to it.

The ability of a material to withstand these stresses is referred to as its *strength*. We therefore recognize three types of strength.

1. *Tensile strength*. This is the ability of a material to resist stresses which tend to stretch the material. Copper has a low tensile strength, as shown by the way that telephone wires stretch when weighed down with snow. The steel cables carrying a suspension bridge have a much higher tensile strength.

2. *Compressive strength*. The ability of a material to withstand compression without distortion, cracking or breaking. Chisels used for cutting metal have to be able to withstand compressive loads each time we strike the chisel with the hammer.

3. *Shear strength*. The ability to withstand shearing forces is important in all shaft drives, such as the p.t.o. on the farm tractor, for materials with a low shear strength would soon twist or shear. Materials of low shear strength have their uses, for example in the rivets which hold a section to the knife of a mowing machine. The rivets easily shear when the section is tapped sharply with a hammer.

Strain

Strain is the increase or decrease in unit length of a material due to an applied force. Therefore, whenever a material is subjected to stress, it is also strained. Materials differ in the amount of force they can withstand before becoming permanently 'strained'. Up to a certain point, known as the yield point or elastic limit, materials regain their original shape when the force is removed, but beyond this point they become permanently strained.

The wire used in many farm fences is easily strained beyond the elastic limit when a stress is placed on it, and therefore periodic tightening has to be carried out. The material used in springs, such as those which close the valves of an engine, is able to withstand high stresses, without permanent straining, regaining its original length immediately the stress is removed.

Characteristics of materials

Before describing the individual materials, it is necessary to explain some of the terms used to indicate their characteristics.

Hardness

The ability to withstand abrasion, cutting and indentation, such as marking with a centre punch.

Ductility

The property of a metal which allows it to be drawn into wire by a tensile force.

Malleability

The ability of a metal to remain extended in *all* directions when subject to a compressive force.

Brittleness

The property of a metal which causes it to break rather than bend.

Toughness

The ability of a metal to withstand shock loads without permanent deformation or breaking.

Joining of metals

It is often necessary to join metals together. Several processes are available, some of the commonest are briefly described.

Soldering

The joining of the metals by a process using a compound called solder, which is described later.

Brazing

Similar to soldering, but carried out at a higher temperature and producing a stronger joint.

Welding

This can be divided into two main processes:

1. *Fusion welding.* In this process, two similar metals are heated until they melt and fuse together, and a similar type of metal is fused into the joint to give extra strength.

2. *Bronze welding.* By this process, different metals can be joined. The metals are heated to below their melting points and bronze is added to each to form the joint. It does not produce such strength as fusion welding, but the lower temperature used causes less distortion.

METALS

The metals used in the construction of farm machinery can broadly be classified into two groups. These are *ferrous* and *non-ferrous*.

Ferrous metals

Ferrous metals are those containing iron. Iron is still the most common constituent of metals used in farm machinery. Iron is produced by a process which starts with the removal of iron ore from the ground. The ore consists of iron oxides mixed with earthy impurities, and is put into a blast furnace, together with limestone and coke. During the process the limestone combines with the earthy impurities, whilst the coke reduces the iron oxides to iron and also provides heat in order that the process may take place. During the process, hot air is blown in through the base of the furnace.

The molten iron accumulates in the base of the furnace with the very much lighter portion, the slag, consisting of the earthy impurities in the ore and limestone, floating on top of the molten iron. The slag is removed from the surface of the molten metal and is often used for road making. The molten iron remaining is tapped from the bottom of the furnace and either transferred into the steel-producing furnace or cast into moulds, called 'sows' and 'pigs'. It is then known as *pig iron*.

Cast iron

Cast iron is produced by remelting pig iron with scrap iron, limestone and coke. The limestone is used for the same purpose as in the blast furnace, to combine with any impurities in the pig iron. The slag is removed before the molten metal is poured into moulds. To get a casting of the desired shape, moulds made of sand are used. The rate at which the molten metal cools affects the properties of the cast iron. If rapid cooling takes place, the casting produced will be hard but brittle, whereas those moulds cooled slowly will be softer and less brittle. Cast iron is easily drilled, machined, threaded, filed or sawn. Cast iron can withstand high compressive stress, but it will fracture under medium tensile or shock loads.

The wearing properties of cast iron can be improved by the addition of chromium or nickel, and its resistance to corrosion by the addition of copper, but this does not improve its ability to stand shock loads which cause it to crack. This practice of combining metals is known as *alloying*, the resultant material being an *alloy*. In agricultural machinery, cast iron is widely used for cylinder blocks of engines and transmission casings, and for the production of cheap components.

Cast iron is not easily repaired by welding or brazing, because it is liable to crack, unless special care is taken to see that the temperature rise and fall on cooling is even over the whole surface.

Chilled cast iron

This is obtained by chilling the surface of the casting quickly, when the molten metal is poured into the mould. This results in a hard thin skin on the surface of the casting, which will have greater wearing properties; hence chilled cast iron is used for ploughshares, under conditions where they will not be subject to shock loads. The areas of a casting that have been chilled cannot easily be machined because of their hardness.

Malleable iron

Malleable iron is produced by the same method as cast iron, but the molten metal is cooled very slowly under controlled conditions to remove the brittle nature of cast iron. Therefore, it can be used for parts that have to withstand shock loads. It is used widely for mowing-machine fingers and baler and binder needles. Because it is not brittle, bent fingers can be hammered straight with little risk of fracturing the finger.

Wrought iron

Wrought iron is produced from pig iron by removing most of the carbon content. It is very ductile and can also be hammer-welded in a forge. Its use has declined, owing to the cheapness of mild steel.

Steels of all types are widely used in the construction of farm machinery. Steel can be produced by various processes, the most common today being the Basic Bessemer Process, in which pig iron and scrap steel together with coke and limestone are made into a molten state in a cupola and then put into a Bessemer convertor. In the convertor, the iron is refined by blowing hot air through it, the impurities again joining with the limestone to form a slag, which is removed in the same manner as in the production of pig iron. This slag is widely used in agriculture as a phosphatic fertilizer, *basic slag*. Alloy steels are produced by adding metallic elements such as nickel, chromium, tungsten and molybdenum to the molten metal after its conversion from pig iron to steel. The quantity and number of these elements will affect the characteristics of the steel produced, as will its carbon content. The higher the carbon content, the harder the steel.

Mild steel

Mild steel has a low carbon content, between 0·15 and 0·25%, and is widely used in the construction of farm machinery because of its strength and low cost. Mild steel can easily be welded by gas or electricity, drilled, filed and generally machined. Like wrought iron, it has a low carbon content and therefore its wearing properties are not good and it is unsuitable for hardening by normal heat treatment. Whilst its tensile strength is less than the higher carbon steels, it is adequate for many purposes, such as sheet metal, angle iron, nuts and bolts. It has the disadvantage that it rusts easily unless adequately protected.

Medium carbon steel

Medium carbon steel has a higher proportion of carbon (0·25 to 0·5%), and is used mainly for the poorer grades of cutting tools, the best being made from the high carbon steels. Its high compressive and tensile strengths make it suitable for frameworks carrying heavy loads, such as plough beams or the lower links of a tractor. Because of the higher carbon content, it can be hardened and tempered.

High carbon steels

High carbon steel (0·5 to 1% carbon) is used where hardness is needed in tools used for cutting or drilling, the compressive strength being more important than the tensile strength. Again, it can be hardened or tempered easily by heat treatment. Unlike mild steel, it is difficult to weld satisfactorily.

Alloy steels

In addition to the carbon steels, there is a group called alloy steels. These are produced by the addition to high carbon steel of various other metals, each one being used for a specific purpose. Manganese and vanadium are often used in spanners to give them toughness and resistance to strain. Tungsten is added when making twist drills, as it improves hardness and maintains a cutting edge. Chromium is used in the production of stainless steel.

Identification of ferrous metals. Cast iron and steels can be identified by the sparks produced when they are put on a grindstone. Cast iron produces dark orange sparks; mild steels throw off spear-shaped sparks, some yellow, some orange; medium carbon steels throw off a few orange and a lot of yellow sparks, and high carbon steels all yellow sparks.

Heat treatment of steels. Heat treatment is used only on medium and high carbon steels.

Annealing

This process may be carried out for one or more of the following purposes.

1. To relieve internal stresses induced by some previous treatment, for example forging, rolling, uneven cooling.

2. To soften the steel, to make it less brittle.

Annealing is carried out on forgings and steel castings. There are three stages in the operation.

1. Heating the steel to a certain temperature.

2. Maintaining the temperature for a specific period.

3. Slowly cooling in the furnace.

Normalizing

The process called *normalizing* differs from annealing in that the metal is allowed to cool in air. This process is used to relieve stress produced through working the metal.

These treatments will increase the tensile strength of the metals treated and therefore reduce the risk of fracture from tensile loads.

Tempering

Tempering is carried out after the steel has been hardened. The steel is heated to a high temperature and then quenched, making it very hard and brittle. If reheated to a lower temperature and requenched, varying degrees of hardness and toughness can be obtained, dependent on the temperature to which it is reheated.

Case hardening

Case hardening of mild steel is a process commonly used during the manufacture of certain parts of farm machinery, such as gudgeon pins, valve tappets, shafts and transmission housings, in which only the surface of the metal is treated. Case hardening of the surface increases the wearing qualities of the steel, but it leaves the body of the steel tough and therefore less likely to crack under shock loads.

During the process, the carbon content of the entire layer which is to be case hardened is increased. The carbon is obtained by heating the metal with wood or bone charcoal, or by putting the metal into a bath of liquid sodium cyanide with soda ash. The temperature and length of treatment in both cases is controlled according to the depth of case hardening required.

Non-ferrous metals

Copper

Copper is used widely in electrical circuits because of its high conductivity and flexibility. Another common use is for low pressure fuel and oil pipes on tractors. It is now used frequently in water supplies, in preference to lead. It is very easily soldered, but it can only be brazed and not welded.

Brass

Brass is an alloy of copper, zinc and lead. It has better wearing properties than copper and it is therefore used in moving parts such as bushes and bearings. It is also a good conductor of electricity and is used in electrical fittings. It is resistant to corrosion and is used for thermostats, water pump fittings and sprayer nozzles.

Tin

Tin in agriculture is mainly used for coating steel to increase its resistance to corrosion, particularly with dairy equipment. It is also used in the production of soft solder.

Bronzes

Bronzes are alloys of copper, tin and zinc in various proportions. They are very hard wearing and are used for bearing materials. When phosphorus is added, an alloy called *phosphor bronze* is produced, and this has even harder wearing properties.

Lead

Lead is not used widely in agriculture, except in batteries where it is used for the plates. Due to its cost, it is no longer used for water pipes.

White metal

This is an alloy of tin, antimony and copper used in bearings of high-speed engines. Where part of the expensive tin is replaced by lead, the alloy is called *babbitt*.

Zinc

This has the valuable property of resisting atmospheric corrosion and is used as a protective coating for iron sheets. The resultant material is called *galvanized iron.*

Solder

This is an alloy of tin and lead. It is used for joining metals, particularly in plumbing and electrical equipment.

Other materials

Plastics

The use of plastics in the construction of farm machines and in pipes for conveying water or milk is increasing. Plastics are widely used in milking equipment, because they are light, easily moulded, resistant to acid attack and corrosion. Care must, however, be taken to see that plastics are not subjected to high temperatures, otherwise warping or melting may occur.

Rubber

Rubber is widely used in milking equipment and for tractor, trailer and implement tyres. There are two types of rubber—artificial and natural. These are often mixed to give the desired properties for a particular use. Some of the artificial rubbers are better than natural rubber in their resistance to milk fat, petrol, oils and grease. Artificial rubber is not as elastic as natural rubber and special care has to be taken with it. For example, one should not fit an undersize inner tube of artificial rubber and hope that the elasticity will make up for the discrepancy. Rubber is affected by sunlight and oil. The former causes perishing and the latter is absorbed and causes softening and swelling. All rubber components should be stored in dark, dry places.

5. Tools and Parts of Machines

Most implements and machines used in farming have some parts which wear gradually in the course of normal use. For ease of replacement, these parts are made detachable. Often they can be adjusted to compensate for wear, or to produce a setting which will allow the machine to work efficiently under variable conditions. Tools are used to adjust or replace parts of machines and a knowledge of the correct tool to select and use is essential for efficient and safe working. This chapter covers both the tools and the parts of machines on which they are used.

Nuts and bolts

The most common device to hold two parts of a machine together is the nut and bolt. The nut is square or hexagonal in shape and has threads inside. The bolt has a square or hexagonal *head* and a partially threaded *shank* with parallel sides (Fig. 13).

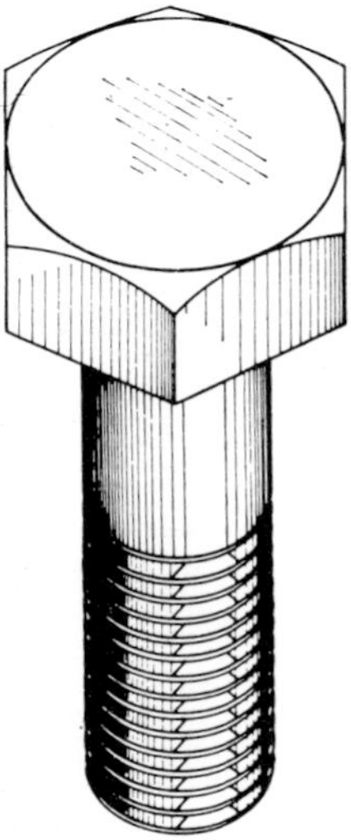

The nut and bolt is used to hold two pieces of material together and the bolt generally passes through holes slightly larger than its diameter. It should be noted that the threads go only part of the way up the shank. A plain steel washer should always be fitted under a nut, allowing it to be tightened without danger of damage to whatever lies underneath. This is especially important with soft materials, such as aluminium alloys and bronze.

Another type of bolt has threads to the head and this is called a *setscrew* (Fig. 14).

Fig. 13. Bolt

This is used for holding two pieces of material together, the bolt passing through a hole in one of the pieces of material and then being screwed into threads on the other piece. It is also used for adjustment in conjunction with a lock nut.

A third type of bolt has no head but has threads on both ends with an unthreaded portion in the middle. This is called a *stud* (Fig. 15).

One end of the stud is screwed into one of the

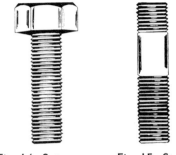

Fig. 14. Setscrew   Fig. 15. Stud

parts to be held together, then the other part is fitted over the stud and retained with a nut. Studs are usually used to hold the wheel of a tractor or car to the wheel hub.

Sizes and types of nuts and bolts

Nuts and bolts are made in many different lengths and thicknesses. They also have various forms and numbers of threads per inch, so it is important to know that a difference exists and to know something of the various sizes found on our tractors and implements.

Most manufacturers have agreed that wherever possible they will used a standard of thread called Unified series. It is a combination of British and American threads. There is *Unified coarse* (UNC) and *Unified fine* (UNF). The British threads from which these arose are called *British Standard Whitworth* (B.S.W.), a coarse thread, and *British Standard Fine* (B.S.F.), a fine thread. Metric (M) threads are of one series only.

The size of a bolt in the Unified Series, B.S.W. and B.S.F. is denoted by its length and diameter, for example: 3 in $\times$ $\frac{1}{2}$ in in U.N.C., 1 in $\times$ $\frac{5}{16}$ in B.S.F. In the Metric series the numbers refer to millimetres of diameter and length, for example, M6 $\times$ 25.

Wrenches or spanners

The tools that should be used for tightening or loosening nuts and bolts are known as wrenches or spanners. There are several different types of these available and the one chosen for use is often governed by the accessibility of the nut or bolt. Damage is easily caused to nuts and bolt heads by the wrong choice of wrenches. The size of a wrench is denoted by the distance across the flats (A/F) of the hexagon head in the case of those used on Metric and Unified nuts and bolts, and by the diameter of the bolt in the case of B.S.W. and B.S.F. sizes.

Socket wrenches (Fig. 16).

These consist of a socket with six or twelve grooves which fit the six flats of a nut or bolt in a variety of positions. The wrench fits into a square or hexagonal hole in the socket. There are various types available and by using them singly or in

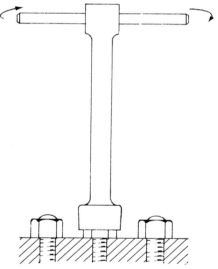

Fig. 16. T-bar socket wrench

combination, nuts and bolts can be reached in places which are not easily accessible. However, they cannot be used on a nut where the bolt protrudes too far, nor can they be used where there is insufficient space above the head of the bolt.

Ring wrenches (Fig. 17)

These have the two ends cranked to allow them to be used on flat surfaces. They have twelve grooves and can be used in twelve different positions, yet each side of the nut is given an

Fig. 17. Ring wrench

even twist. They can be used on protruding bolts. Their limitation is that they require space around the nut or bolt for movement. The smaller the nut or bolt, the shorter the wrench, so that with normal use the nut or bolt cannot be over-tightened.

Box or tubular wrenches (Fig. 18)

These are round tubes with hexagonal ends shaped to fit the nut or bolt. A tommy bar fitted through holes in the tube is used to turn the wrench. They are extremely useful for locating nuts in recesses or nuts with protruding bolt shanks. One of their main uses is for removal and replacement of sparking plugs.

Open end wrenches

These are probably the most popular type of wrench in use. The head consists of two open jaws set

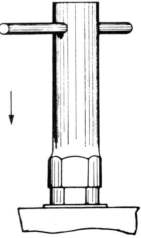

Fig. 18. Box wrench

at an angle to the shank (Fig. 19). One of the jaws is slightly
thicker than the other and if a large force is to be used, then
the wrench must be fitted so that the thicker jaw is in tension.

Fig. 19. Open end wrench

The angle of the jaws increases the versatility of the spanner,
allowing it to be used in different positions by turning it over,
except where a large force is necessary.

Adjustable wrenches

These can be obtained in a variety of lengths and each one
will cover a large range of nut sizes. They are very useful for odd
nut sizes, where it would be uneconomic to buy separate
wrenches. They have two limitations.

1. The head is rather large and sometimes cannot be fitted in
the available space.

2. If the wrench is not fitted correctly, or if it is not adjusted
correctly, either the nut or the wrench may be damaged. It is
good practice to use them only when absolutely necessary.

Screws

Several different types of screw are used in farm equipment.
The heads, which may be round or hexagonal, are slotted for
turning with a screwdriver.

Self-tapping screws

These are tapered throughout their length. The type used for
wood has threads only part way up the shank, but the type used
to join two pieces of metal together has threads running to the
head. Both types of screw may have a cross-shaped slot in the
head, and are then known as *Phillips' headed screws*. In this case
a special screwdriver with a cross-shaped blade is used.

Setscrew

This has been mentioned before, as having parallel threads up to the head. The head may be hexagonal, in which case one of the wrenches is used, or it may be slotted for a screwdriver.

Allen screws

These are special screws with a hexagonal recess in the head (Fig. 20). They are used when the top of the head must be flush

Fig. 20. Allen screw   Fig. 21. Allen key

with the surface and where clearance sufficient for a socket wrench is not possible. A hexagonal wrench or key is used to tighten or slacken them (Fig. 21).

Screwdrivers

These can be divided into two main groups.

1. Electrician's screwdrivers. These have an insulated handle and are often sold tested to withstand 6000 V. They are not as robust as screwdrivers for general work.

2. General-purpose screwdrivers for non-electrical work. A steel blade is fitted into a wooden handle and sometimes passes to the end of the handle, to prevent damage should the screwdriver be abused by being struck with a hammer. Where the blade enters the handle, it is often flattened or square so that a spanner can be used to obtain extra leverage on the screw.

Screwdrivers are sold according to the length of the blade. Generally, the larger the blade, the broader it is, but special-purpose screwdrivers can be obtained with various lengths and widths.

In selecting a screwdriver for a particular job, choose the largest one which fits to the bottom of the slot. Hold it absolutely in line with the screw, apply ample force and turn. Remember that if it slips out of the slot, due to lack of force directed towards the screw, it is very likely the sides of the slot will be damaged and removal of the screw made very difficult indeed. Where considerable force has to be applied to a screw, it is dangerous to hold the object in one hand and the screwdriver in the other, as a slip can cause an injury to the hand. It is far safer to hold the object in a vice.

Hammers

One of the most common hammers used in the farm work-shop is the *ball pane* or *pein* (Fig. 22). It consists of a wooden

shaft, fitted into a steel head. One end of the head is flat, the pane, and the other is rounded, the ball. They are sold according to their weight.

There are many occasions when a steel hammer would cause damage to threads or castings, so a softer hammer is used. This has two flat faces, one consisting of soft copper and the other rawhide. It is called

Fig. 22. Ball pane hammer

a *combination hammer* and the copper or rawhide can be re-placed as it wears out. Plastic headed hammers are also available.

Punches

These are used to remove rivets or split pins. They have either parallel or tapered shanks. The tapered type will only go so far into the hole before it jams on the sides, but it can be used on a varied range of holes, whereas a complete set of the parallel type must be bought to cover the same range adequately (Fig. 23).

A centre punch has one end ground to a point and is also used for making a mark on a piece of metal where a hole is to

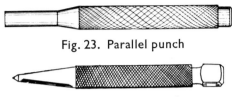

Fig. 23. Parallel punch

Fig. 24. Centre punch

be drilled (Fig. 24). The mark helps the drill penetrate by preventing it from sliding on the surface of the metal.

Chisels

The most common type used on farms is the cold chisel, which is designed to cut cold metal. It has a hexagonal shank, which gradually flattens out and is ground to an edge at an angle of about 60°, although this angle varies with the type of metal to be cut (Fig. 25). Only the cutting end is hardened but the

Fig. 25. Chisel edge

other end is tough enough to withstand hammer blows without chipping or splitting. It will, however, gradually mushroom over, and chips of metal may fly off unless the burred edges are ground to prevent this happening.

When sharpening a cold chisel, it must be pressed lightly against the carborundum wheel, or it becomes overheated locally and may lose its temper or develop fine hair cracks causing it to chip when next used.

Files

These are used to remove small amounts of excess metal from one piece when it is required to fit accurately into another. They have diagonal rows of teeth which point away from the handle and which cut only when being pushed away. The pointed end of the file is called the 'tang' and should always be fitted with a wooden handle. Some files are called *farmers' files* and have a metal handle, made in one piece.

Files are classified according to the number of teeth per unit length (this is likely to be 1 cm). Of those in common use, the coarsest is the *bastard file*, then the *second cut*, and the finest is the *smooth cut*. The files at each end of the range, the *rough cut* and the *dead smooth* are rarely used. They may be obtained with various cross-sections, square, rectangular, flat, round, rat tail, half-round, triangular. The rectangular type frequently has one 'safe' edge without teeth, so that one side of a corner can be filed without damaging the other. Files are also sold in varying lengths. The most useful files on a farm are 250 mm flat files in bastard, second and smooth cut.

Files are selected according to the metal on which they are to be used. Soft metals, such as aluminium and copper, would clog the teeth of a fine file, so a coarse one must be used. Finer files are needed for harder metals, such as wrought iron, mild or medium carbon steel. File teeth do not clog up as readily if the file is rubbed with chalk before use. The chalk prevents the metal filings getting right into the teeth and the filings can be removed by tapping the file on the bench. File cleaning brushes are also available and it is important to keep the file teeth clean, to prevent wasted effort.

The workpiece must be securely clamped or held in a vice. Select the correct file and hold it with the thumb on top and fingers underneath. The handle should rest in the palm of the hand. The other end should be held with the thumb on top pointing down towards the handle, as shown in Fig. 26.

Stand squarely to the work, with the left foot leading for a

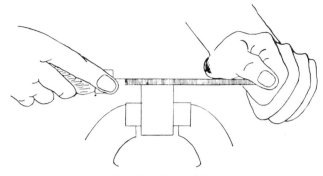

Fig. 26. Use of file

right-handed person, and with the weight taken equally on both feet. Press down on the forward stroke and lift on the return. Apply greater pressure on the front at the beginning of the stroke and more at the rear towards the end. This keeps the surface level and avoids causing a bump in the middle of the workpiece. Do not work too quickly, 50 to 60 strokes/min is fast enough. Apply sufficient pressure to feel the file bite but take care when starting new work that there is no hard skin of metal which could cause the file to slide and perhaps injure the operator.

Files should be stored in racks or wrapped in paper. Stored loose they are easily damaged. They have a limited life and should be discarded when worn out.

Hacksaws

The most common hacksaw found on the farm is the hand type, consisting of a frame taking a 250 mm or 300 mm blade; 250 mm blades are probably more suitable, as they are less likely to be broken. Blades are graded according to the distance between the points of the teeth measured in millimetres. As with files, the softer the metal the coarser the blade and the harder the metal the finer the blade. When cutting thin metal or tube, a fine blade should be used to allow three or four teeth to be cutting at the same time, so preventing the hacksaw from jamming. The blade should be fitted with the teeth pointing away from the handle; thus cutting will take place on the forward stroke. It should be tensioned so that it emits a high-pitched note when plucked. The workpiece must be securely clamped and the cut started with light forward pressure. The rate of stroke should be similar to filing, but the hacksaw should be drawn back *on* the work and not *raised*, or it may break if it is dropped and pushed forward at the same time. Should a worn blade break when half-way through the metal, start from the other side with the new blade, as it will cut a wider slot and will not pass down the original slot.

Drills

These are used for making accurate circular holes in nearly all types of metal found on farm machines. The modern drill has two cutting edges at the tip and two spiral grooves or flutes running up the shank. These flutes carry away the chips of metal or *swarf* as they are cut off.

The machine used to turn the drill may be powered by electricity and operates at high speeds or be turned by hand at relatively low speeds. The powered drilling machine produces much more heat and the drill must be able to stand this heat without losing its temper and becoming soft. Special drills are made for this purpose and whilst they look exactly similar to the carbon steel drills for hand machines, they are stamped on the shank with the letters H.S.S. (high-speed steel).

A centre punch is always used to make a mark to assist a drill on its initial penetration and to prevent wandering. The workpiece should always be clamped securely before commencing to drill. The speed of the drill varies with the diameter and the type of metal. The larger the drill the less the speed, and the softer the metal the greater the speed. Large fixed drilling machines use a gearbox or V-belt and pulleys to alter the speed, but small portable electric types slow down automatically, because of the increased load due to the larger drill.

When drilling cast iron, brass or other soft metals, no lubricant is necessary; but a lubricant is sometimes useful when drilling steel, although it should be used sparingly, as it is difficult to remove if the job is to be painted when finished.

A few hints on drilling may well prevent breakage. If the drill is sharp, it should produce even-sized chips or spirals from both cutting edges and it should not squeak as it penetrates. With a little practice, it is possible to 'feel' when the point is about to pass out the other side, and the pressure on the drill should be eased slightly, to prevent it seizing on the last thin pieces of swarf. It is quicker and easier, when drilling holes 10 mm or larger in diameter, to drill a small pilot hole first. Special drills should be used when drilling thin metal plate, but as these are not generally available, great care is needed to prevent the drill seizing as it pierces the hole.

Feeler gauges

Certain parts of internal combustion engines have to be adjusted very accurately. These include the valve clearance, the spark-plug gap and contact-breaker gap. Feeler gauges are used to do this. They are strips of metal carefully rolled to a given thickness. The size is marked on each one in millimetres (mm). A set consists of up to 15 feeler gauges, varying from 0·05 to 1·5 mm. They can be used in combination to make up a range of thicknesses. They must be kept quite clean and stored carefully, to avoid becoming rusty.

Rules

These are made from steel in varying lengths and 300 mm is a useful length to obtain. They are marked in divisions down to 1 mm. Like feeler gauges, these should be kept clean and slightly oily to prevent rusting. They should never be used for any purpose other than measuring.

Components

It is very important to know the correct names given to various components of farm machinery to understand instruction books and when ordering spare parts.

Locking devices

The nut and bolt is the most common device used to hold two parts together, but due to bumps, jolts and vibrations, mechanical precautions have to be taken to prevent them working loose. These precautions are grouped under the heading of *locking devices*. The type used by the manufacturer depends on the cost and whether or not the nut needs to be removed frequently in the course of the operation of the machine.

A *spring washer* may have one or two coils which are compressed as the nut is tightened and tend to hold it in position, preventing it from turning due to vibration. They are cheap and can be easily removed or replaced, but like plain washers have a limited use.

A *tab washer* is similar to a plain washer, except that it has two tabs protruding at opposite sides. One of the tabs is bent into a recess or over an edge. The nut is then screwed down and the other tab is bent up against one of the flats of the nut. The nut is then securely fastened unless it first bends the tabs. This is a very satisfactory method of locking nuts which do not require frequent removal. If they are removed, however, a new washer should always be used.

When there is sufficient clearance, two nuts may be used. The first is tightened, then the second or *lock nut* is tightened on to the first. It is necessary to hold the first while tightening the lock nut, to ensure they are really locked together, and often this means that slim spanners must be used. Where there is not a great deal of clearance, two very thin nuts, equal in thickness to a normal nut, are used. It is often necessary to adjust a nut to allow a certain amount of movement. This needs a device which will lock the nut to the bolt. A special nut called a *slotted* or a *castellated* nut is used (Fig. 27). A hole is drilled through the bolt and a split pin passed through the castellations of the nut and bolt to prevent turning. The nut, of course, can only be fixed in certain positions: where the castellations are in line with the hole. After the split pin has been put in, the ends are bent outwards holding the nut securely. A new split pin should be used every time a nut is fitted.

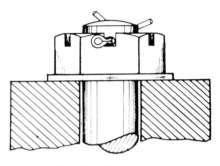

Fig. 27. Slotted nut

Nuts with a nylon or fibre band inside them are also used for locking. The nylon is compressed as the nut is tightened and it is held very securely indeed. They can be removed and replaced frequently without any detrimental effect, but they are expensive and only used where a cheaper device would be ineffective.

Bearings

Bearings are used to support and reduce friction caused by a revolving shaft. That part of the shaft in contact with the bearing is the *journal*. The simplest type of bearing is a plain tube, often made of brass, and is called a *bush*. The bush fits very tightly in a *housing* and the shaft turns in the bush. The shaft must be slightly smaller than the hole in the bush: the difference between the two is called the *clearance*. There is often a means of lubrication and a spiral oilway to carry the lubricant over the length of the bush. Some bushes are plain tubes with a shaft passing right through, whilst others are 'blind' and others are 'flanged' (Figs 28, 29).

Where bearing loads are very large, as in diesel engines, the bearing may be of the *shell* type (Fig. 30). This is made up from semicircular sections of a tube, with a very thin layer of

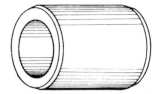

Fig. 28. Plain bush

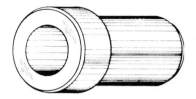

Fig. 29. Flanged bush

the bearing material on the surface. The shells fit into locating slots in the housing, which is then bolted together. This type is lubricated by oil at pressure and is used in all modern multi-cylinder engines, as it is cheaply replaced.

When large bearing loads have to be carried and there is no forced lubrication, ball, roller or needle bearings may be used.

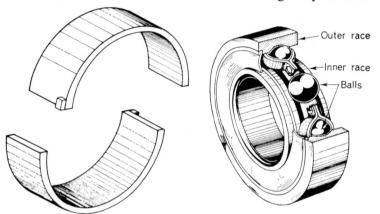

Fig. 30. Shell bearing   Fig. 31. Ball race

These have four parts: first, an *outer* race which fits tightly into the housing. Inside this run the *balls*, *rollers* or *needles*, according to the type. These are kept equally spaced by a *cage*. The last part is the *inner race*, which is a tight fit on the shaft (Fig. 31). As the shaft revolves, it takes the inner race with it. The balls, rollers or needles roll (not slide) around the inner and outer races with very little friction and therefore require the minimum of lubrication.

Gears

Gears are used to alter the torque in power transmission. They enable a tractor to develop high torque when in bottom

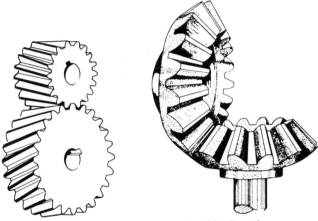

Fig. 32. Single helical cut gears   Fig. 33. Bevel gears

gear and pull heavy loads. They are used to reduce a high engine speed, e.g. 2000 rev/min, to a low rear-wheel speed, e.g. 15 rev/min. The torque is transmitted through the *teeth* of the gear. These teeth may be *straight cut* or cut at an angle—*helical* (Fig. 32) or *double helical.* Helical cut gears are much quieter in operation, due to a more gradual engagement and disengagement of the teeth.

Gears can be used to change the direction of a drive, as in the back axle of a tractor. There are several types, *bevel-* and *worm-gears* being common (Figs. 33, 34).

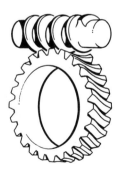

Fig. 34. Worm gear

Chains

These are used to transmit power as well as change the speed of a drive. A chain consists of rollers fitted over hardened steel pins, the ends of which are riveted to side plates. The ends of the chain are joined together by a connecting link and spring clip. The closed end of the clip should always point in the direction of travel.

Where the stresses in the chain are small and the speed low, a cheaper type of chain is used, known as a *malleable square link* or *pintle* chain. Each link has a curved tongue at one end, which wraps more than half-way round the plain bar end of the next link in the chain. It is therefore only possible to join these links by sliding the tongue in from the side with the two links lying close to each other. When the two links are straightened, the tongue fits inside the square frame of the next link and limits sideways movement. The chain may be made from malleable iron or pressed steel. In the latter case, the tongue of each link is more tightly closed and has to be sprung open when the side bar of the next link is pushed through it. When fitting the chain, the open side of each tongue should face away from the wheel on which it runs, and the tongue end of each link should face the direction of travel.

Chains run on *chain wheels* or *sprockets* (Fig. 35). These must be kept in line and the chain must be kept correctly tensioned. If the chains are too tight, they are subject to excessive wear; if too slack, they are liable to jump off the sprockets. When renewing a chain, always check the condition of the sprocket as it is false economy to put a new chain on a worn sprocket.

Shafts, splines and keys

Shafts are used to transmit power from one point to another. A good example of this is the p.t.o. shaft on a tractor, which transmits power from the gearbox to the implement being driven. In this case the p.t.o. shaft drives the implement by a series of external grooves known as *splines* which are located into

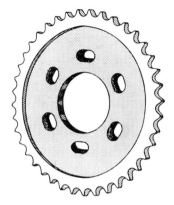

Fig. 35. Sprocket

a similar series of internal splines in the implement shaft (Fig. 36).

The p.t.o. shaft is often required to be able to operate out

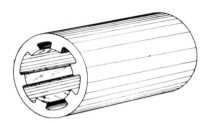

Fig. 36. Internal splined shaft

of line as on a trailed p.t.o.-driven implement turning a corner. Universal joints are used to permit this (Fig. 37). Two joints are used in such a manner that each absorbs half the total angle of the shaft. It is essential to connect the joints in the manner

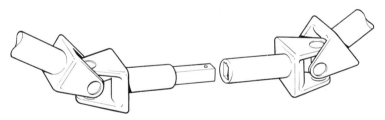

Fig. 37. Universal joint

shown in the diagram. There is a limit to the maximum angle at which the joints will operate. Above this angle severe vibration and damage will occur.

Shafts may be connected to wheels or gears by a *key*. This is a piece of metal which fits closely into a groove in the shaft and in the wheel or gear (Fig. 38). The groove is called a *keyway*. A special type of key is the *Woodruff* key, which is semi-circular

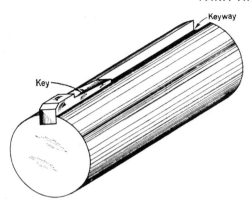

Fig. 38. Key and keyway

and fits closely into a similarly shaped slot in the shaft (Fig. 39).
It has the advantage that it is totally enclosed by the hub of
the pulley.

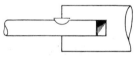

Fig. 39. Woodruff key

Belts and pulleys

A common method of power transmission is by means of belts and
pulleys. The belts can be *flat* or of
the V-type and are made from a bonding of rubber and canvas
(Figs 40, 41).

Flat belts run on slightly convex pulleys as this helps to keep
the belt on. Their ends are connected by a fastener. It is important when joining or repairing them to cut the belt at right
angles, so that the sides are straight and then it will run true
on the pulley. For efficient results, the pulleys must be pos-
itioned correctly. It should be possible to lay a straight edge
across both faces. The tension should be just sufficient to
prevent slip. Belt dressing can be used to increase the friction
between the belt and the pulley.

V-belts transmit their power by having the sides of the belt in
contact with the sides of the pulley. They are becoming in-

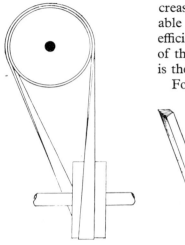

creasingly common as they are able to transmit power more efficiently, and there is no danger of their falling off the pulleys as is the case with flat belts.

For satisfactory performance,

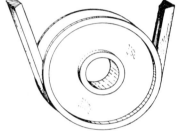

Fig. 40. Flat belt   Fig. 41. V-belt

there are several important points which must be noted. The angle of the sides of the V-belt must be exactly the same as those of the pulley. Oil and dirt must be kept away from the V-belt, and the face of the pulley must be clean. If the machine is to be out of use for some months, the belt should be slackened or removed, to prevent it deteriorating where it is in contact with the pulley.

A V-belt composed of removable links can be used where the pulleys cannot be moved for adjustment purposes.

Overload protection

It is often necessary to protect drive mechanisms and machines from damage due to overloading. Several devices are used.

Shear bolt. The drive is transmitted through a single bolt (Fig. 42) which is often stronger than a normal bolt of similar dimensions. If a sudden overload occurs on the drive shaft

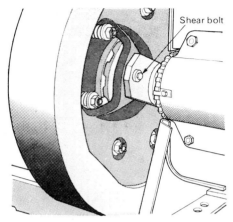

Fig. 42. Shear bolt

the torque causes the bolt to shear and breaks the transmission of power.

Slip or safety clutch. Where it is necessary to limit the torque transmitted by a shaft a slip clutch may be used. This may be a *dog-type* (Fig. 43) with an adjustable spring to keep the teeth of the two sections in contact. When an excessive torque occurs the teeth slide over each other compressing the spring. As the clutch slips a characteristic rattling sound is produced and hence it is commonly called a clatter clutch.

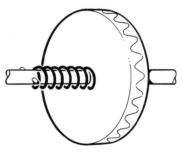

Fig. 43. Dog-type slip clutch

Alternatively a *friction*-type slip clutch transmits the torque through a *friction disc* held against two *metal* plates by a *spring*. The setting of the spring determines the maximum torque. When this is exceeded the metal plates will slip against the friction disc without making any sound, although an audible warning device may be fitted.

Adjustment of safety clutches. It is important that each clutch be set in a correct manner. The spring should be tightened gradually until the clutch *just* transmits the drive under *normal* operating conditions. The clutch will thus slip whenever the load increases above normal. When this occurs it is important to investigate the *cause* of the overload and correct it. The clutch should never be tightened excessively or damage will result to the components it is protecting.

6. The Internal Combustion Engine

The conventional tractor consists basically of two engine-driven wheels, usually at the rear, and two support wheels at the front. The type of engine used to power the tractor is an internal combustion engine. The engine is the heart of the tractor; it is here that the fuel, the chemical potential energy, is converted into the mechanical energy which causes the wheels to turn.

The difference between an internal and external combustion engine is simply that in an internal combustion engine, the conversion of potential energy into mechanical energy takes place wholly in the cylinder, whereas with external combustion the fuel is burnt outside the cylinder. A steam engine or a gas turbine is a good example of the latter.

How can liquid fuel be changed into rotational mechanical energy? This is achieved by accurately mixing the fuel with air and then burning it in controlled conditions. When this mixture burns, it expands and pressure builds up, forcing the piston to move down the cylinder in a straight line. It is said to have linear motion. This linear motion is converted into rotary motion by a connecting rod and crank arrangement joined to the piston.

To be able to use this energy effectively, the burning and combustion process and the force of expansion have to be controlled. To do this, the engine must have:

1. A tube or *cylinder* closed at one end, in which the mixture of fuel and air can be compressed and burnt.

2. A *piston*, which slides freely and yet fits closely in the cylinder, so that the expanding gases force it down the cylinder, and do not escape past it.

3. Two passages or ports in the cylinder. One for the mixture of fuel and air to enter the cylinder, the *inlet port*, and the other to allow the used gases to escape, the *exhaust port*.

4. Two valves, the *inlet valve* to control the movement of the

mixture to the cylinder, and the *exhaust valve* to control the escape of the used gases. By carefully timing the ignition of the mixture in relation to the opening and closing of the valves and the position of the piston, it is possible to make the piston move up and down the cylinder continuously.

The working of an internal combustion engine, once it is started, involves a sequence or cycle of operations in each cylinder. Two distinct cycles are recognized, the four-stroke, cycle and the two-stroke cycle. In the four-stroke cycle, the crankshaft completes two revolutions and the pistons four strokes, a stroke being the movement of the piston from one end of the cylinder to the other. In the two-stoke cycle, the crankshaft makes one revolution and the piston two strokes in each cycle.

The four-stroke cycle (a) spark ignition (Fig. 44)

Induction stroke

The cycle commences with the piston at the top of the cylinder. On the first downward stroke of the piston, the inlet valve is opened and the mixture of fuel and air is drawn into the cylinder from the carburettor, via the inlet manifold, due to a vacuum created by the piston as it moves down the cylinder.

Compression stroke

As the piston starts to rise on its second stroke, the inlet valve is closed and, as the stroke continues, the fuel/air mixture is compressed into the combustion chamber, formed by the cylinder and cylinder head.

Power stroke

When the piston almost reaches the top of its stroke, the fuel/air mixture is ignited by a spark, which jumps across the points of the spark plug in the cylinder head. The mixture burns and the resultant heat causes the gases to expand and the increased pressure forces the piston down.

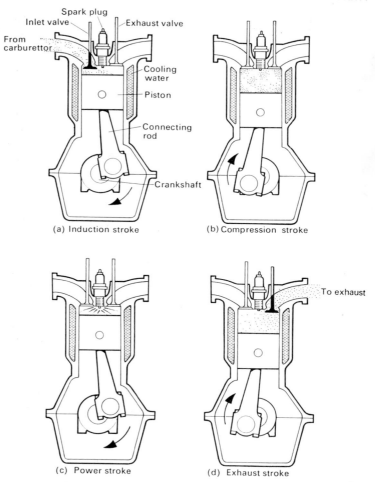

Fig. 44. Four-stroke cycle, spark ignition

Exhaust stroke

When the piston reaches the bottom of the cylinder, the exhaust valve is opened. Then, as the piston rises again, it pushes the burnt gases out of the cylinder, via the open exhaust valve into the exhaust manifold. When the piston reaches the top of the cylinder, the exhaust valve closes and the inlet valve opens as the piston descends to start the cycle again.

The four-stroke cycle (b) compression ignition

There is a slight difference in the cycle for a diesel engine, because air only is drawn into the cylinder on the induction stroke. The fuel is injected into the combustion chamber at about the same time as the spark occurs in the spark ignition engine, when the air has been compressed. The compression of the air raises its temperature to a point which is sufficient to ignite the fuel as it is injected.

During the cycle, it can be seen that only one in every four strokes is a working one, the piston receiving an impulse on the power stroke, which has to carry all the moving parts during the next three strokes. This tends to lead to erratic running in single-cylinder engines. To overcome this, a large flywheel is fitted to store energy, which provides the momentum to keep the piston and other parts moving during the other three strokes in the cycle. Another way of overcoming this erratic running, is to have more than one cylinder with each piston at a different point in the cycle, and a much lighter flywheel. For instance, in a four-cylinder engine, if each piston starts at a different place in the cycle, then one piston must always be on the power stroke and hence turns the crankshaft more evenly.

Compression ratio

The ratio of the initial volume of the fuel/air mixture, or air (in the case of the diesel engine), in the cylinder and combustion chamber, to the final volume is known as the *compression ratio*. Petrol and vaporizing oil (V.O.) engines have lower compression ratios than diesel engines, because there is an upper limit to which an explosive mixture, such as air and petrol or V.O., can be subjected. In a diesel engine, only air is being compressed, so a much higher compression ratio can be obtained. Spark ignition V.O. tractor engines do not usually have compression ratios above 5·5:1, whereas diesel-engined tractors have compression ratios around 18:1. It is this greater degree of compression in the diesel engine which causes the air temperature to rise sufficiently to ignite the fuel. The higher the compression ratio, the more efficient is the utilization of the fuel. The high compression ratio of the diesel engine creates a problem for starting the engine. A lot of power is needed to start turning the engine over and, for this reason, a compression release is sometimes fitted. This operates by holding the exhaust valves open and therefore no compression occurs. When the engine has gained momentum, the compression release is disengaged and the engine starts. It can also be used when turning a diesel engine by hand, to adjust the tappets.

The two-stroke cycle (spark ignition)

The two-stroke cycle varies from the four-stroke cycle in two ways.

1. For every complete revolution of the crankshaft, the whole cycle is completed.

2. The fuel/air mixture is first drawn into the gas-tight crankcase, before being drawn into the cylinder of the engine.

It was explained that, in an engine running on the four-stroke cycle, only one power stroke per cylinder was obtained for every two revolutions of the crankshaft, the other three idle strokes, the induction, compression and exhaust, being carried over by the momentum of the flywheel. With a power stroke for every revolution of the crankshaft, one would expect an engine running on the two-stroke principle to develop twice the power, size for size. This is not so, because of certain design features.

As can be seen from Fig. 45, valves are not fitted for the entrance and exit of the gases. The mixture is admitted via ports in the cylinder wall, which are covered and uncovered by the piston at the appropriate times. The crankcase acts as a store for the fuel/air mixture, until it is required in the cylinder. The mixture enters the crankcase via an inlet port and is passed into the cylinder via a transfer port. In the two-stroke cycle, the induction and compression take place on one stroke, power and exhaust on the other stroke.

The piston in Fig. 45(a) is moving up the cylinder to compress the fuel/air mixture. At first all the ports are covered. As the piston continues to travel upwards, it creates a partial

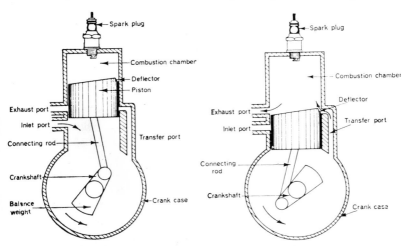

Fig. 45. (a) and (b). Two-stroke cycle, spark ignition

vacuum and uncovers the inlet port. The fuel/air mixture is then drawn into the vacuum.

In Fig. 45(b), the power stroke is almost complete. After a short distance of travel, the exhaust port is uncovered and the burnt gases escape. As the piston moves down, the mixture in the crankcase is compressed. Therefore, when the transfer port is opened, it rushes into the cylinder ready to be compressed on the next upward stroke of the piston.

Having a power stroke for each revolution of the crankshaft, there is no need for a heavy flywheel on a two-stroke engine.

This means that the two-stroke cycle is often adopted for smaller engines, where lightness is important. Engines running on the four-stroke cycle are more efficient, however, because they are able to scavenge the cylinder completely of exhaust gases before commencing the induction stroke.

The engine

The *cylinder block* is generally made of cast iron, because it is cheap and easy to manufacture. Replaceable sleeves or liners are fitted into the cylinder block, to form the cylinders. Below the cylinder block is the crankcase, usually cast as one in tractor engines. To the bottom of the crankcase is bolted the sump, which forms a reservoir for the engine oil. The sump is often made of pressed steel and is therefore unsuitable to use when jacking up the tractor. The cylinders are sealed at the top end by fitting the *cylinder head* to the cylinder block. In order to make a gas- and water-tight seal between the two, a gasket (copper/asbestos) is used. Most cylinder heads for tractor engines are made from cast iron. In the cylinder head, directly above each cylinder, is a depression where the actual combustion of the fuel/air mixture takes place. This is the combustion chamber.

The piston, usually made of aluminium for its lightness, is attached to the connecting rod by a pin, called the gudgeon pin, and fitted into the cylinder. The bearing formed between the pin and the connecting rod is commonly referred to as the *little end* bearing. To obtain a perfect seal between the piston and the cylinder wall, and so prevent gases 'blowing by' to the crankcase and oil leaking up into the cylinder head, cast iron rings are fitted to the piston. These are the *piston rings*. The rings fit into grooves cut in the side of the piston to locate them. Generally, there are two or three plain compression rings in the upper grooves, and one oil or scraper ring in the lower groove. Most diesel engines (see Fig. 46) have an additional scraper ring in the base of the skirt of the piston. These rings, together with a fine film of oil, form the seal required.

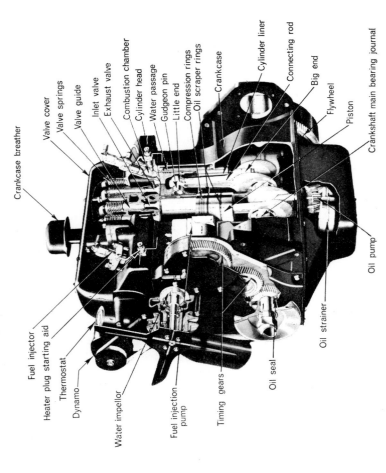

Crankcase breather

Valve cover

Valve springs

Valve guide

Inlet valve

Exhaust valve

Combustion chamber

Cylinder head

Water passage

Gudgeon pin

Little end

Compression rings

Oil scraper rings

Crankcase

Cylinder liner

Connecting rod

Big end

Flywheel

Piston

Crankshaft main bearing journal

Oil pump

Oil strainer

Oil seal

Timing gears

Fuel injection pump

Water impellor

Dynamo

Thermostat

Heater plug starting aid

Fuel injector

Fig. 46. Section of a diesel engine

The connecting rod has cylindrical ends, the smaller end being attached to the gudgeon pin in the piston and the larger end attached to the crankshaft. This *big end*, as it is commonly called, is split into two and clamped to the crankshaft. Between the big-end housing and the crankshaft is fitted a bearing (big-end bearing), which is again split, to facilitate fitting round the crankshaft.

As already mentioned, the crankshaft is responsible for converting the reciprocating linear motion of the piston into rotary motion. Each time the piston is forced down, the crankshaft has to withstand a considerable thrust, and to withstand this it is supported along its length by bearings. These are known as the *main bearings*. The specially hardened area to which the connecting rod big end is attached is called the *journal*. The movement of the *valves* must coincide with particular positions of the piston. The valves are opened and closed by *cams*, mounted on the camshaft. The camshaft is either gear- or chain-driven from the crankshaft, which ensures that the valves open and close relative to the position of the piston. Because each valve opens only once per cycle, the camshaft is driven at half the crankshaft speed.

The type of engine is often classified by the position of the valves in relation to the cylinder. Those engines with valves situated at the side of the cylinders are known as *side valve engines*. Those engines with the valve above the piston are known as *overhead valve engines*. The latter are more popular today, because they are more suitable for use in high-compression petrol and diesel engines. This type of engine is more efficient.

Two-stroke engines have no valve gear, but use the piston as a valve for uncovering inlet ports in the cylinder wall. Other than this feature, the construction of two- and four-stroke engines is very similar.

Timing of the engine

To ensure that the engine runs satisfactorily, it is necessary for everything connected with its cycle of operation to take place at exactly the correct time. This is referred to as the *timing of the engine*. The components of the engine involved are the valves and ignition on a spark ignition engine, and the valves and fuel injection system on a compression ignition engine.

Most tractor engines are three- or four-cylinder units, operating on the four-stroke cycle. The position of the cranks on the crankshaft is designed to produce an engine which will run as smoothly as possible. This is achieved by arranging the cranks of the crankshaft, and the order of firing in the cylinders, so that each power stroke occurs at an even distance in the rotation of the crankshaft.

In a three-cylinder engine, operating on the four-stroke cycle, the distance between each crank is one third of the rotation. In a four-cylinder engine, operating on the four-stroke cycle, the inner pair of cranks is in line, and the outer pair is also in line, opposite the inner pair. This means that the outer pair of pistons moves up and down together, and the inner pair moves up and down together. When the outer pair is at the top of the cylinder (top dead centre), the inner pair is at the bottom of the cylinder (bottom dead centre). From this, we can determine the possible firing orders of a four-cylinder engine. In order to identify the pistons, it is usual to number them from 1 upwards, with 1 at the radiator end of the engine.

Let us assume, in a four-cylinder engine, No. 1 is falling on the power stroke. Then No. 4 must be falling on the induction stroke. The centre pair of pistons will be rising on the compression and the exhaust strokes. The piston on the compression, and the piston on the exhaust stroke, will depend on the arrangement of the cams on the camshaft, which controls the operation of the valves. Thus we have two possible firing orders, either 1, 2, or 1, 3. The third cylinder to fire will be No. 4, as the outer pair of pistons will be rising again with No. 4 on compression. The other cylinder of the centre pair will fire last. This gives possible firing orders of 1, 2, 4, 3, or 1, 3, 4, 2. The firing order of a three-cylinder engine is 1, 2, 3. This timing is achieved by using the crankshaft as the common drive for the valve mechanism and the ignition or fuel system. The drive from the crankshaft may be by gears or chain. Once set correctly, it ensures that each mechanism is synchronized with the crankshaft. If, however, the gears are meshed incorrectly, the valves may open and close early or late. This would result in the engine not starting, or running very erratically. To avoid this, the gears are usually marked, making it easy to place them in the correct position.

7. Fuel Systems

A correctly adjusted fuel system is one which gives the engine the maximum opportunity to convert the chemical energy of the fuel, whether it is petrol, V.O. or diesel oil, into mechanical energy. How and where this conversion takes place is described in the previous chapter. It is important that the proportions of air and fuel drawn into the cylinders are correct, to ensure that maximum use is made of the fuel. The ratio of air to fuel varies for both types of engine and different operating conditions. For a petrol engine, 14·6 parts of air to 1 part of petrol, by weight, is considered to be chemically correct. Mixtures containing more than 1 part of petrol per 14·6 parts of air are termed *rich mixtures*; those containing less than 1 part of petrol per 14·6 parts of air are termed *weak mixtures*. Within narrow limits, a rich mixture gives maximum power and a weak mixture maximum economy.

The function of the fuel system is to store and supply the engine with clean fuel, in the correct ratio, over a wide range of engine speeds and loads. The fuel system on spark ignition engines differs from the diesel fuel systems of compression ignition engines, the important mechanism in the former being the *carburettor* and in the latter, the *fuel injection pump*.

Petrol and V.O. fuel systems

The carburettor has a dual function:

1. To maintain the correct air/fuel ratio, under all operating conditions.

2. To break the fuel droplets into a fine mist, to be carried into the cylinder in a stream of air.

To indicate how it does this, it is necessary to follow the path of the fuel and air into the cylinder.

The fuel is stored in the tank. It leaves via a fuel pipe situated in the base of the tank. The pipe usually protrudes 10 mm into the tank, so that any sediment present on the base of the tank does not get into the pipeline and the rest of the system. In the pipeline itself, there is usually at least one gauze filter and a glass sediment bowl.

The fuel in most engines reaches the carburettor from the tank by 'gravity flow', because the tank is situated above the carburettor. This saves the cost and complication of a fuel pump. The fuel enters the float chamber of the carburettor through the needle valve operated by the float (Fig. 47). The float is designed

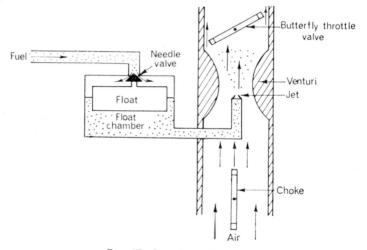

Fig. 47. Simple carburettor

to maintain the level of fuel in the float chamber at the level which the jets of the carburettor require. On some simple carburettors, fitted to stationary engines, a tickler knob is fitted in the top of the float chamber, which allows the fuel to rise to a higher level 'flooding' the carburettor, and giving a richer mixture for starting.

It is at the jet or jets of the carburettor that the paths of the air and fuel merge. The air is drawn in by the induction stroke of the engine. It is important that this air be free from contamination, such as dust or grit particles. To ensure this, the air is drawn through an air cleaner, which will be described later in the chapter. The flow of air is speeded up, as it passes along the induction tube, by a narrowing of the tube known as the Venturi. This increase in speed causes a drop in the air pressure in the region of the jets from the float chamber.

The fuel in the float chamber is at atmospheric pressure and is, therefore, drawn out through the jets by the decrease in pressure in the induction tube. The fuel leaves the jet in very fine droplets, which mix easily in the stream of air and are carried to the combustion chamber.

Engines have to work under varying conditions and loads. Therefore, it is necessary to be able to alter the strength and the volume of the mixture entering the combustion chamber. The *choke* or 'strangler' restricts the passage of air through the Venturi, which enriches the mixture for starting, the suction caused by the induction stroke drawing directly on the jet. The throttle valve controls the volume of the mixture entering the combustion chamber, hence the speed and power of the engine. The amount of fuel flowing from the main jet does not increase in strict proportion to the increase in the amount of air passing through the Venturi. It rises at a very much faster rate and, unless corrected, a very rich mixture would result. Therefore, the simple system illustrated in the diagram is only suitable for engines running at constant speed or load. A more complicated carburation system, with a multiple jet carburettor, is needed for an engine running at variable speeds.

These carburettors have at least three jets—an idling jet to provide richer mixtures at low speeds, a main jet for normal running, and a compensating jet to assist with the change from idling to normal speeds. In a motor car, the butterfly throttle valve is controlled directly from the accelerator. This is not so in a tractor, where it is often necessary to keep a constant engine speed, despite frequent variations in the load. In the tractor, the butterfly throttle valve is controlled by the *governor*, which in turn is set at a speed determined by the tractor driver, and is therefore known as a variable-speed governor. This saves the tractor driver having to make frequent throttle changes to meet the variable load placed on the engine.

Fuel vaporization

The finer the condition of the fuel and the more intimately it is mixed with the air, the more efficient is the combustion process in the combustion chamber. If the fuel can be vaporized before entering the cylinder, it mixes completely with the air. This is achieved, in petrol engines, by attaching part of the inlet manifold to the exhaust manifold, to create a 'hotspot' where petrol, being quite volatile, quickly vaporizes. V.O. is not as volatile, so special provision has to be made by fitting a vaporizer. In effect, this is a large section of the inlet manifold which is heated by the exhaust gases, to ensure that the V.O. becomes vaporized.

It is for this reason that tractors which run on V.O. start on petrol, until the vaporizer is sufficiently hot to vaporize the V.O. Care should be taken not to run the engine on V.O. at too low a temperature, since the fuel then passes into the engine as a liquid, which washes the oil film from the cylinder walls and piston rings, resulting in high rates of wear, together with dilution of the engine oil. Therefore, running an engine too cold can cause as much damage as running it too hot. An average operating temperature is about 82°C, but this varies with the make of tractor and reference should be made to the instruction book.

Diesel fuel system

It has been mentioned that, in the four-stroke cycle of the diesel engine, only air is drawn in on the induction stroke, and the fuel is injected when the air is compressed. To do this, a fuel injection pump and a series of injectors are used (Fig. 48). The standards of accuracy of feed and cleanliness of the fuel are more critical in a diesel engine. Therefore, the system is rather more complex.

The system is comprised of the main storage tank, from which the fuel may flow by gravity or a fuel pump. The fuel, on leaving the tank, may have a preliminary cleaning by passing

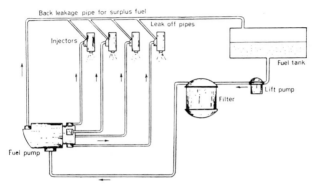

Fig. 48. Diesel fuel system

through a sediment bowl, or it may go straight into the fuel filter or filters. These vary in number and size, generally one large or two small ones are used. They are fitted to ensure that the fuel is absolutely clean before it passes into the injection pump. The filters must be serviced as and when recommended by the makers of the tractor. The intervals of attention vary widely with the type and number of filters fitted.

The fuel injection pump, like the carburettor, has two major functions.

1. To feed the correct quantity of fuel to the engine.

2. To raise the pressure of the fuel in the fuel line to the injector, in order that it will atomize and mix easily with the compressed air in the cylinder.

The fuel injector (Fig. 49), which acts as a valve and a distributor, is extremely important in the correct running of a diesel engine. When the pressure rises in the fuel line leading to the injector, the valve in the nozzle of the injector is forced open, and the fuel is injected into the compressed air in the cylinder. When the pressure falls in the fuel line, the valve closes and injection ceases. Injectors vary in design, some having a single hole whilst others have more than one hole, depending on the cylinder head and piston design of the particular engine.

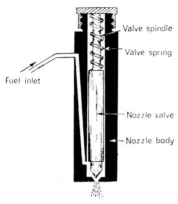

Fig. 49. Fuel injector

The high pressure part of the fuel system, the pump and injectors, does not need frequent servicing. When attention is necessary, it should be undertaken by a skilled mechanic, not by the tractor driver.

The air cleaner

The type of air cleaner most widely used is that incorporating an oil bath (Fig. 50). The dust-laden air is drawn into the top of the cleaner which is usually fitted with a filter, or pre-cleaner, which removes some of the larger dust particles. The remaining particles of dust are trapped either by the oil as the air turns round the bottom of the stack pipe, or on the oil-coated filter screen.

It is very important that the oil in the cleaner is changed regularly and kept at the correct level in the base of the cleaner. Underfilling leads to inefficient cleaning. Overfilling may cause the oil to be drawn into the cylinder, resulting in excessive carbon deposits and, possibly, fouling of the spark plugs.

A dirty air cleaner restricts the smooth flow of air into the engine and thus the power output from the tractor. Regular servicing is therefore important. The operator's manual gives specific details for each tractor.

Maintenance of the fuel system

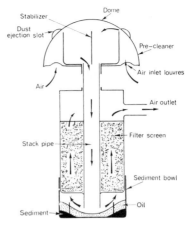

Fig. 50. Section through an air cleaner

1. The air cleaner should be checked weekly on most tractors, and in dusty conditions more frequently. Remove the base of the cleaner soon after the engine has been stopped, and check the level of oil and the amount of dirt in the bowl. If there is little dirt and no marked thickening of the oil, it is not necessary to clean the bowl or change the oil. If the oil level has risen, it indicates that the oil is contaminated and needs changing.

When changing the oil, the correct grade or viscosity should be used, as indicated in the instruction book. Often it will be the same as that used for the engine, but old engine oil is unsuitable for the air cleaner.

The filter mesh in the body of the air cleaner should be checked once per month and cleaned at least once per year. Diesel oil or V.O. should be used for this, allowing the surplus after washing to drain off the filter, before refitting it into the air cleaner.

2. The glass sediment bowl should receive regular attention to remove sediment and water which collects in it. Care should be taken to ensure that it is properly sealed on replacement, to avoid leaks.

3. With diesel tractors, the fuel filter has to be changed periodically, the normal interval of attention being 400–1000 h. The outside of the bowl should be carefully cleaned, before removing the filter. The bowl is cleaned in diesel oil and the sealing washers changed before fitting a fresh filter. All the air must

be removed from the fuel system by 'bleeding', as detailed in the instruction manual. Where two fuel filters are fitted, it is normal to service only the first or primary filter, the second filter being serviced at major engine overhauls. The engine should be run for a few minutes whilst a careful check is made for fuel leaks.

Fuel storage on the farm

Most fuels are delivered in bulk by road tankers and stored in bulk on the farm. Bulk buying and storage has the advantage of reduced cost per gallon. It makes it easier to keep out contaminants, such as water, sand and dust. There are special regulations governing petrol tanks, which mean they have to be placed underground. The following comments apply primarily to V.O. and diesel oil storage tanks.

The tank should be sited to allow easy access for the road tanker and for tractors to be filled. Undue variations in temperature can cause condensation in the tank. Siting out of direct sunlight is an advantage. The risk of fire should also be considered. The tank should slope towards the rear, where a sludge cock can be fitted, to drain off any water or sludge which collects. This avoids any contaminant getting into the tractor fuel tank from the main cock at the front. Internally galvanized tanks are unsuitable for diesel oil as the zinc is attacked by the diesel oil.

Fault finding

See Chapter 11, pp. 120–124.

8. The Electrical System

Ignition system

The function of the ignition system is to provide the spark in the combustion chamber, to ignite the fuel/air mixture at the correct time. The system used on petrol/V.O. tractors may be either *coil* or *magneto* ignition. Coil ignition has superseded magneto ignition on all modern tractors but magneto ignition is still widely used on single-cylinder stationary engines.

Coil ignition

This system normally consists of a battery, induction coil, distributor and spark plugs (Fig. 51).

The function of the *coil* is to produce the high voltage impulse required to make the spark at the plugs. It consists of two coils

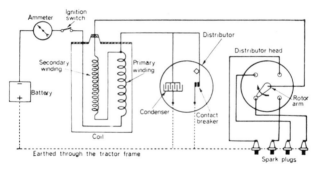

Fig. 51. Coil ignition system

of wire, the *primary* and *secondary* windings. The primary coil consists of a few turns of thick wire, the secondary a large number of turns of fine wire. The primary coil is wound round the secondary coil, though it is not connected to it electrically.

The *distributor* consists of a central shaft (usually driven by the camshaft of the engine), round which a casing is mounted to hold the parts of the distributor that do not rotate with the engine. Near the top end of the shaft is a lobed cam. The number of lobes is determined by the number of cylinders in the engine, there being one per cylinder. As the cam rotates, it opens the *points* of the *contact breaker* against a spring which closes them as the cam moves round. One of the contact breaker points is earthed to the frame of the tractor. Mounted on the top of the shaft, there is a rotating arm, known as the *rotor arm*. Surrounding and over the rotor arm is an insulated cap, the *distributor head*. This contains a spring-loaded carbon brush contact in the centre and one contact for each cable, leading to a sparking plug, spaced round the inside of the distributor head. The *spark plug* consists of an insulated shell carrying the central electrode, surrounded by a metal body which is screwed into the combustion chamber (Fig. 52). At the bottom of the plug body, there is a small lip or side electrode set so that there is a small gap between it and the central electrode, across which the spark is able to jump.

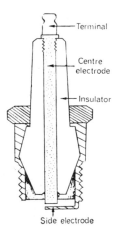

Fig. 52. Section of a spark plug

Terminal

Centre electrode

Insulator

Side electrode

There are two separate electrical circuits in the ignition system, the *primary* or *low tension* (L.T.) and the *secondary* or *high tension* (H.T.) circuits. The primary circuit is supplied with current stored in the battery when the ignition switch is turned on and the points are closed. Current flows from one terminal of the battery via the ignition switch through the primary coil, to the distributor where it passes across the closed contact-breaker points and is conducted back to the other terminal of the battery via the frame of the tractor. When using the frame of the tractor in this way, the circuit is said to have an earth return. A *condenser* or *capacitor* is fitted in the primary circuit to prevent arcing and burning of the contact-breaker points. The current flow in the primary circuit is intermittent when the engine is turning, because the lobed cam in the distributor rotates, causing the contact-breaker points to open and break the circuit. This causes a collapse of the magnetic field surrounding the primary coil, which induces a high tension current at 10 000 V or more to flow in the secondary circuit. The high tension current flows in the heavily insulated leads from the secondary coil to the top of the distributor, and from there to the rotor arm via the carbon brush. As the arm rotates, it passes close to each plug-lead-contact in the distributor head, and allows the high tension current to flow along the high tension leads from the distributor to the central electrode of each plug, in turn. The secondary circuit is completed when the spark jumps from the central electrode to the side electrode of the plug, which is screwed into the cylinder head and therefore earthed.

It is essential that the spark reaches each spark plug at the correct time. This is achieved by setting the distributor so that the contact-breaker points open as each piston reaches the end of its compression stroke. The rotor arm is then opposite the plug lead contact to this cylinder. The leads from the distributor head are connected to the spark plugs, in a sequence dependent on the firing order mentioned in Chapter 6.

Checking the coil ignition system should be done systematically, starting at the battery. Trace all leads through the coil ignition system and check that the insulation is not cracked or the terminals loose. To check the primary circuit, remove the lead to the contact breaker at the distributor. When the ignition is switched on a small spark is produced when the lead is struck against an earthed part of the engine. A faulty condenser usually produces excessive burning of the contact breaker points. The high-tension circuit can be checked by removing the lead at the centre of the distributor, holding it close to the cylinder block and opening the points with an insulated screwdriver. A bright blue/white spark should be produced. A red or yellow spark is of poor quality. The lead should be replaced together with the distributor cap, and the plug leads held one at a time close to the cylinder block. As the engine is turned, sparks should jump from the lead to the block. If this does not happen check the distributor and rotor arm for cracks.

Magneto ignition

The principles involved in magneto ignition are similar to those in coil ignition, the main difference being that the current for the primary coil is generated by a rotating permanent magnet. The magneto is usually coupled to and driven from the camshaft, though it may be attached to the flywheel (flywheel magneto) on some small two-stroke engines. A magneto produces a relatively weak spark at low speeds and therefore an *impulse starter coupling* is usually fitted to both intensify and retard the spark. This consists of a spring connecting the magneto rotor to the drive. When the engine is cranked, the magneto rotor is held back by the spring, whilst the crankshaft continues to turn. The spring is released automatically, when it has become wound, which results in the magneto rotor turning quickly, producing a strong spark, later than in normal running. The characteristic click when this spring is released is probably a familiar sound. When the engine starts, the impulse starter mechanism is automatically kept out of engagement. The ignition switch in this system, when in the OFF position, either bypasses or short-circuits the current flowing in the primary circuit to earth, before it reaches the contact-breaker, and prevents a build-up of current in the secondary coil; or, alternatively, earths the high tension current before it reaches the spark plug. In order to comply with the farm safety regulations, it must be capable of being set in the OFF position.

Magneto ignition systems are more popular on small single-cylinder engines, because of low cost and simplicity, a battery and battery-charging system not being required. On tractors fitted with self-starters, a battery and battery-charging system are necessary and therefore coil ignition can be used. This has the advantage over magneto ignition of producing a strong spark at low speed.

The battery

The battery is a device capable of converting electrical energy into chemical energy and storing it until it is wanted again as electrical energy, for use by the starter motor, lights or the coil ignition system (Fig. 53).

The batteries used on tractors are of the lead/acid type. They consist of a series of box-like cells, inside which is a series of lead plates, each separated from the next by insulating material.

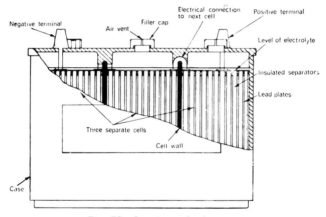

Fig. 53. Section of a battery

All the negative plates are joined together at the negative terminal; all the positive plates are joined together at the positive terminal. A single cell of a lead/acid battery has a voltage of approximately 2 V, six cells connected in series being needed for a 12-V battery. The plates and separators are surrounded and just covered by dilute sulphuric acid. This solution is called the *electrolyte*. The capacity of a battery depends on the surface area and volume of the plates, and it is expressed in ampere hours (Ah). For example, a tractor battery, rated 100 Ah, is capable of supplying 5 A for 20 h.

The battery charging system

During the operation of the engine the battery is kept charged by the dynamo driven from a V-belt from the engine (Fig. 54). The *regulator* controls the amount of current generated according to the requirement of the battery, reducing it to a trickle as the battery becomes fully charged. A *cut-out* on the regulator acts as an automatic switch and disconnects the dynamo from

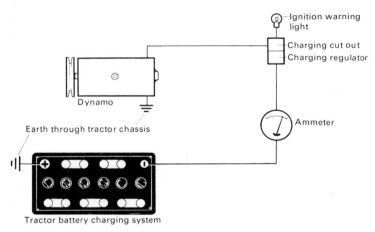

Tractor battery charging system

Fig. 54. Tractor battery charging system

the battery whenever the engine is turning slowly and the dynamo voltage is reduced to less than that of the battery. This cut-out switch is often connected to a red *ignition warning* light which is lit whenever the system ceases to charge. The light goes out as the dynamo speed increases. An ammeter may be fitted to indicate the rate of charge from the dynamo.

The dynamo and regulator need little maintenance. The fan belt must be kept adequately, but not excessively, tensioned and the plain bearings on some dynamos require periodic lubrication. All electrical contacts require to be kept clean and tight and it is important never to interfere or adjust any component other than those previously mentioned, or there is a great risk of severe damage occurring.

Some tractors are now fitted with *alternators* instead of dynamos because of their greater efficiency at lower speeds. These generate alternating current which is converted to direct current by a *rectifier* to enable it to be stored in the battery.

The starter motor

Starter motors for spark ignition tractors are of lighter design than those used for diesels, because of the lower compression ratios of the former. The starter motor drives a pinion-gear, which engages with the starter ring gear of the flywheel, and so turns the engine. When the engine starts, the speed of the fly-wheel exceeds the speed of the motor and causes the pinion-gear of the starter to come out of mesh with the ring gear.

Fuses

Fuses are incorporated to protect the wiring of the electrical system. When faults occur in the electrical equipment, heavier currents may flow in the wires than they are able to take. Unless a fuse were present, the wire would overheat and there would be a risk of fire.

On tractors, fuses are normally incorporated in the lighting system. These fuses are of the cartridge type, with the fuse wire contained in a glass cartridge. The rating of the fuse is usually indicated on a slip of paper inside the glass. It is essential always to use a fuse of the correct rating and to eliminate any fault before replacement.

Maintenance of the electrical system

1. *The battery*. To function properly, a battery must be maintained in good condition. This involves:

(a) Checking the level of the electrolyte in the cells. It should just cover the plates and, if low, be topped up with distilled water only.

(b) Keeping the casing and terminals including the earthing strip clean and dry. If terminals become corroded, cleaning with hot water and smearing with petroleum jelly helps to prevent corrosion recurring.

(c) Keeping the ventilating holes in each filler plug free from blockage.

(d) Ensuring the battery is always firmly secured, to prevent shocks and vibration.

(e) Giving the battery a monthly booster charge, when it is not regularly in use, to prevent it remaining in a discharged condition.

2. All leads must be kept firmly attached to terminals and free of oil, water and corrosion products.

3. Cracked and frayed wires should be replaced, to ensure good insulation, particularly on the high tension circuit.

4. The contact-breaker gap must be adjusted to that specified in the instruction manual.

5. The spark plugs require regular cleaning. Some types of plug can be dismantled for cleaning, but care is needed to prevent damage to the insulation. The spark plug gap must be kept at the correct distance. This adjustment must always be made by bending the outer, and never the central, electrode.

The battery charger

A situation may occur where a greater amount of energy is removed from a battery than is replaced, causing the battery to become discharged and unable to start the engine. Frequent starting and stopping during a period of cold weather could cause this by not allowing sufficient re-charging of the battery. When this occurs it is necessary to use a mains-operated *battery charger* (Fig. 55) to replace the energy in the battery. The battery charger transforms mains voltage (240 V a.c.) to either 6 V or 12 V and rectifies or converts it from alternating to direct current. A *selector* switch controls the output voltage whilst an

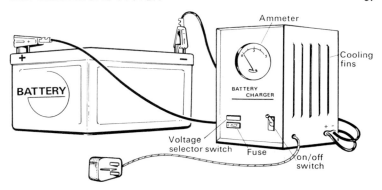

Fig. 55. Mains battery charger

ammeter indicates the current flowing to the battery. Some chargers may have a control to regulate the current, but all will normally have a fuse to protect against overload.

To operate the charger the clips should be firmly connected to the battery terminals, the positive clip being connected to the positive terminal. If the terminal is not clearly marked remember that the positive terminal is larger than the negative. If *two* 6-V batteries are to be charged they should be connected together in *series* and treated as *one* 12-V battery.

The battery filler caps should be loosened to permit gas being evolved to escape easily. The selector switch should be moved according to the voltage required and the charger switched on. The ammeter should then indicate the charge and the charger may give off a slight humming sound. If no charge is shown check firstly that the battery charger clips are making electrical contact with the terminals. Corrosion frequently prevents a good contact from being made. The next step is to check the fuse on the charger and the fuse on the mains plug.

The length of time needed to charge a battery will depend on its capacity, state of charge and the capacity of the charger. Most medium powered tractors have batteries of about 100 Ah and if they were completely discharged would require about

25 h charging at 4 A to return them to a fully charged state. They would, however, be able to start the engine after about 4 to 6 h charging.

Discharge tester

A battery reaches the end of its useful working life whenever *one* of the cells ceases to function. It is important to be able to distinguish between a battery discharged due to normal use, but capable of holding charge and a battery being discharged and incapable of holding further charge. In order to test a battery's ability to hold charge a *discharge tester* is used. This comprises two *contacts* which are placed on the terminals across each cell. A heavy current flows through the resistance wire between the contacts and the voltage maintained is recorded on the voltmeter. If the cell is able to maintain a specified voltage for 10 s, then the cell is sound. It is necessary to fully charge the battery before testing to ensure that its state of charge is not due to normal use.

Fault finding

See Chapter 11, pp. 120–124.

9. Lubricating Systems

The satisfactory operation of tractors and in fact all types of machinery relies on efficient lubrication. To provide this, the right lubricant should be chosen, applied at the correct intervals and kept clean in storage and in use. Failure to maintain an adequate standard of lubrication can lead to costly and unnecessary repairs and delays, often during peak periods of work on the farm.

Principles of lubrication

A lubricant often has to perform many duties in any one situation, in addition to its fundamental job of reducing friction and wear. These duties may include acting as a rust preventative, a coolant, a sealing agent, a hydraulic fluid and a flushing agent to remove dust and metallic particles.

If two metal surfaces were examined under a powerful microscope, each surface would have projections on it rather like sand-paper. If these rub together, they would cut into each other's surface and cause wear. By the use of a suitable lubricant, this wear can be reduced to a minimum, for the aim of lubrication is to reduce metal-to-metal contact, by maintaining a film of oil between the two surfaces.

Friction is the resistance to motion which results from two surfaces sliding over one another. Lubrication, by maintaining a film of oil between the two surfaces, reduces the friction and hence the force required to move one or both of the surfaces.

Engine lubrication

While the primary duty of engine oil is to reduce friction and wear between the working parts of an engine, it also carries away a considerable amount of heat from the pistons, the valve stems and the main and connecting rod bearings. In addition, the oil forms a seal between the piston rings and the cylinder wall, and washes the working surfaces free of chemical deposits to protect them from corrosion.

Lubrication systems

The simplest method of lubricating an engine is to mix the oil with the petrol, as is done in two-stroke engines. As the oil enters the crankcase with the petrol and air, droplets settle on the connecting rod and main bearings and also lubricate the walls of the cylinder. In four-stroke engines, the oil is not drawn into the crankcase, and therefore must be fed to the bearings in some other way.

Splash lubrication

Lubrication of the engine by splash is a simple method and is widely used where complicated pressure circulation of oil is not essential, e.g. on slow-running single-cylinder engines. These are still used to drive stationary machinery, such as elevators and milking machine pumps. Some of the earliest tractors, especially the petrol/V.O. models, also used this method of lubrication. It consists basically of an oil reservoir or sump, through which passes a scoop attached to the big end bearing. This throws the oil up into small reservoirs, situated above the main bearing and timing gears. These reservoirs have small channels which lead the oil on to the main bearings. The cylinder wall and gudgeon pin is lubricated also by the oil, which is thrown up by the scoop. The big end is lubricated by the oil as it passes through the sump. On returning to the sump, the oil often passes through a strainer to remove the larger particles of dirt and carbonaceous matter.

The splash system of lubrication only works successfully if the oil in the sump is maintained at the correct level, neither too high nor too low, and the engine is kept horizontal. It is only suitable for side valve engines.

Pressure or forced lubrication (Fig. 56)

This system is used in practically all engines apart from those mentioned above, and is characterized by the oil being fed under pressure from a pump to the various bearings. The oil pump is situated in the sump of the engine and draws

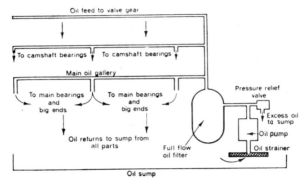

Oil feed to valve gear

To camshaft bearings   To camshaft bearings

Main oil gallery

To main bearings   To main bearings   Pressure relief
and   and   valve
big ends   big ends
Excess oil
to sump
Oil pump
Oil returns to sump from
all parts   Full flow   Oil strainer
oil filter

Oil sump

Fig. 56. Pressure lubrication

the oil through a fairly coarse mesh filter before delivering it under pressure through a finer filter to the various bearings. The oil is carried through drillings to the main bearings, the crank pins and occasionally through the connecting rod to the gudgeon pins. Alternatively, the gudgeon pin is lubricated by excess oil scraped from the cylinder wall by the oil scraper rings.

The camshaft on an overhead valve engine is lubricated by a subsidiary oil feed from the main gallery. Similarly, the timing chain, sprockets or gears are lubricated by a continuous small jet of oil. The cylinder walls are lubricated from the oil mist which is present in the crankcase when the engine is running and also from the oil that is dripping on to them on its return to the sump. In many tractor engines, the cylinder walls are also lubricated by a jet of oil from the upper surface of the big end bearing housing. This is directed on to the thrust side of the cylinder wall.

An oil seal is fitted to the front and rear main bearings to prevent oil leakage from the crankcase.

Oil pumps are designed to circulate more oil than is necessary for lubrication. The excess acts as a coolant and flushing fluid, as well as a lubricant. When the oil is cold, it is thick (its viscosity is high) and there is considerable resistance to its passage through the oilways. To prevent excessively high pressures, a spring-loaded pressure relief valve is fitted into the circuit taken by the oil. It may sometimes be fitted in the oil pump itself. The valve opens whenever the pressure in the circuit exceeds the desired pressure, which may be from 2 to 4 bar, allowing the excess oil to return to the sump. All tractors have either an oil pressure gauge or an oil warning light to indicate whether or not the oil pressure is satisfactory.

With the generous supply of oil in modern oil systems, this often results in the valve being at least partly off its seating, even when the oil is hot. The spring pressure on the valve actually controls the pressure within the system. This point should be borne in mind when checking for possible causes of low oil pressure.

With modern detergent oils which remove carbon, gums and abrasive materials from the working surfaces over which they flow, it becomes necessary to filter the oil to remove these deposits from the circulating oil.

The filter that surrounds the pump inlet is a primary strainer of rather coarse mesh, to prevent damage to the pump from the larger pieces of abrasive material in the oil. It would be undesirable to have a finer filter for fear of starving the whole lubrication system, should this filter become choked.

The main filter (Fig. 57) is fitted on the pressure side of the pump, usually in an accessible position on the outside of the crankcase or cylinder block. This filter may be a full-flow type, which allows all the oil through before it goes to the bearings, or it may be a by-pass type, filtering only a limited amount of the oil round the engine on each circuit. At normal running speeds, the oil passes round the engine in under two minutes. For a full-flow type, the filtering medium must necessarily be coarser or larger than one used for a by-pass system, in order not to cause a back pressure.

The filter element is mostly made from impregnated paper and must be discarded after use. Some filters, such as fine brass

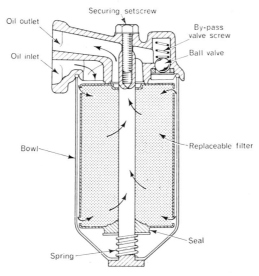

Fig. 57. Full-flow oil-filter

wire, are designed to be cleaned. The filter is usually spring-mounted. If it becomes clogged, the oil can by-pass automatically, as excessive pressure builds up.

Oil is likely to be contaminated and diluted by condensed fuel and exhaust gases, which leak past the piston into the crankcase. Both regular draining of the oil and changing of the filter, as described later, avoid the risk of trouble.

The engine crankcase is always fitted with some kind of breather, which connects the space above the oil to the atmosphere.

The functions of the breather are:

1. To prevent the build-up of pressure in the crankcase. During operation of an engine, the oil and the air in the crankcase get warm and expand, and would increase in pressure if unable to escape out of the breather.

2. To prevent water vapour and exhaust gases building up in the crankcase.

3. To allow air to be drawn into the crankcase when the engine cools.

The crankcase breather is located either on the side of the crankcase or, on overhead valve engines, it is often fitted to the top of the valve cover.

To prevent dirt and dust contaminating the oil when air is drawn in through the crankcase breather, the air is filtered through a gauze filter, on its way to the crankcase. To enable the breather to fulfil its other functions of letting gases out, it is essential to maintain this filter in a clean condition.

Classification of oils

It is important always to use the type of oil recommended by the manufacturer for a particular purpose. This difference in oils is indicated by various letters and numbers. The viscosity is denoted by its S.A.E. number (Society of Automotive Engineers). S.A.E. 10 is a thin (mobile) oil, whereas S.A.E. 40 is a thicker (viscous) oil. Oils suitable for being subjected to extreme pressure, such as those in transmission systems, often have the letters E.P. after the S.A.E. number.

Ordinary straight mineral oils will thin considerably on heating, and thicken on cooling. These considerable changes in viscosity can have a detrimental effect on engine performance and wear, for heavy oil makes starting more difficult, putting a bigger strain on the electrical system. Thin oil, when the engine is hot, may not provide adequate lubrication. To combat this problem, multigrade oils have been introduced. These have the characteristic of being fairly light for starting, but thick enough to give adequate protection when the engine is hot. The viscosity of these oils is denoted by the S.A.E. numbers and written 20/50. The first number relates to its viscosity at low temperatures, the second at high temperatures.

A further development from multigrade oils are oils which are multi-purpose or universal. A number of tractor manufacturers have approved the use of these for summer and winter use in all types of engines (diesel, V.O. and petrol), as well as in hydraulic and transmission systems.

Modern engine oils, both of normal and multigrade type, have a moderately detergent action, whilst the heavy duty oils (H.D.) intended for use in diesel engines have a marked detergency. The action of a detergent additive is to hold and retain solid particles of carbon and other contaminants in suspension in the oil, thus preventing the formation of carbon and lacquer deposits on the working surfaces of the engine.

Deterioration of oils

The two most important reasons for the deterioration of oil are contamination and internal breakdown.

The main sources of contamination are as follows.

1. Airborne matter. Some dust and grit reaches the oil in the sump, via the air cleaner and the crankcase breather.

2. Products of combustion. These substances include water, acids and carbon.

3. Products of corrosion. Corrosive attacks on metal parts by the acids of combustion may cause rust deposits to enter the oil.

4. Unburnt fuel, due to incomplete combustion.

5. Metallic particles, as a result of engine wear.

The internal breakdown of oil is often due to thin films of oil being exposed to very high temperatures, particularly large quantities of hot air, resulting in oxidation of the oil.

Deterioration of oil due to contamination results in increased engine wear, owing to the presence of metal particles, corrosion owing to the presence of acids, and the formation of harmful sludge. Deterioration owing to internal breakdown has little harmful effect, providing the oil is changed within its normal service life.

Maintenance of lubricating systems

Daily. Check engine oil level. With engine stationary and standing on level ground, clean area round dipstick holder and withdraw dipstick. Remove oil from the bottom with a clean non-fluffy rag. Replace fully into its holder and withdraw again, holding it almost horizontal to read the level. Fill to full mark on dipstick, if necessary.

Periodic. 1. Change engine oil. Refer to manufacturers' instruction book for exact interval between changes. This is generally about 60–100 working hours for V.O. and 120–300 for diesels. The oil should be drained from the engine, when it has reached its working temperature. With engine stationary, clean area round the drain plug and then remove it. After refilling, check carefully for leaks.

2. Change engine oil filter. This is done at every oil change on diesel tractors and every other oil change on V.O. tractors. Refer to manufacturers' instruction book. Drain the engine oil and clean thoroughly the outside of the filter and surrounds, using diesel oil or V.O., and brush. Remove the filter body carefully and discard the filter element. Clean inside of filter body and replace new element. Remove the oil sealing ring from inside groove in filter head, clean with a non-fluffy rag and replace with a new oil sealing ring. Replace filter body on to head, taking care to locate the filter body squarely on to the oil sealing ring. Clean outside of filter thoroughly. Tighten bolt or bolts carefully, following directions as laid down in manufacturers' instruction book. Some manufacturers recommend putting some oil into the filter body before replacing it. Refill sump to correct level, with correct grade and type of oil, and run engine, carefully checking for any oil leaks, especially round the oil sealing ring.

3. Clean crankcase breather. Refer to instruction book. Remove carefully and clean gauze in V.O. or diesel oil. Dry gauze and brush with engine oil, and replace.

Fault finding

See Chapter 11, pp. 120–124.

10. The Cooling System

The burning of the fuel/air mixture in the combustion chamber subjects the surrounding parts of the engine, the cylinders, pistons and valves, to high temperatures. Unless the heat is dissipated by the cooling system, the engine will be damaged, as overheating causes the bearing material to melt and the pistons to expand until they seize in the cylinders. The cooling system not only reduces temperature it also controls the temperature as excessive cooling is undesirable. This means that the running temperature of an engine is controlled between certain limits, to produce the best results. These limits vary for different engines.

An engine may be either air- or water-cooled, the latter being more popular. Most small single-cylinder engines have air cooling because air cooling is efficient on this type of engine, and it keeps the construction of the engine lighter.

Air- and water-cooled engines

Air-cooled engines. An air-cooled engine is one in which the heat is conducted direct from the working parts of the engine to the air stream. The engine is given cooling fins, the heat from the combustion chamber being conducted through the fins to the air. With motor cycle engines, the rush of air past the fins is sufficient to keep the engine cool, but with air-cooled stationary and tractor engines, a fan attached to the outside of the flywheel and housed in a cowling directs cold air over the cylinder cooling fins. The temperature of the engine can be controlled by shutters which regulate the amount of air delivered by the fan. These shutters may be under the control of a thermostat, to maintain a reasonably constant engine temperature.

Water-cooled engines. A water-cooled engine is one in which water is used to convey the heat from the working parts to a radiator and hence to the air (Fig. 58). Whilst air is used to remove the heat from the radiator, the water is the main carrier of the heat from the engine. The water in the cooling system forms a continuous jacket round the cylinders and combustion chambers, the channels in the cylinder block coinciding with those in the cylinder head and water leakage being prevented by

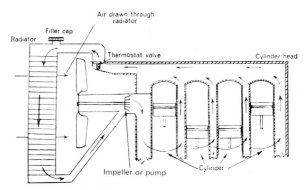

Fig. 58. Pressurized cooling system

the gasket between them. This water jacket is connected to the radiator by two hoses, one from the cylinder head to the radiator tank, and the other from the base of the cylinder block to the base of the radiator. The radiator consists of a series of fine tubes with fins, which present a large surface area to the air. The water is confined in the tubes in a thin film, which allows it to cool rapidly under the influence of an air flow drawn through the radiator by a fan.

There are two kinds of water cooling system:

1. The simple convection or thermo-syphon system.

2. The fully pressurized system.

The thermo-syphon system is based on the principle that hot water, being less dense than cold, rises above the latter. This results in the water rising to the top of the engine as it gets warmer and hence to the radiator. Being cooled in the radiator, it passes down through it to the base of the engine again. This system is found only on single-cylinder stationary engines. The fully pressurized system operates on the principle that the boiling point of a liquid varies with the pressure exerted on it. The greater the pressure, the higher the boiling point. This system incorporates an impeller, or water pump, fitted to the rear of the fan shaft and a spring-loaded cap on the radiator. As the engine warms up the cooling water expands and a slight pressure of 0·2 to 0·6 bar is developed in the air trapped in the header tank of the radiator. The circulation of the water is controlled mainly by the impeller, but convection also plays a part. The water temperature is able to rise above 100°C without boiling, which allows more efficient heat transference to the cooling air, because of the greater temperature difference. Thus the size of the radiator and the quantity of cooling water can be reduced. This in turn leads to a more rapid warming up of the engine on starting and an increase in the life of the engine.

Regulating cooling temperature

The optimum running temperature, whilst varying with different engines, is usually in the range of 75°C to 85°C. It is important to follow the manufacturers' advice on the correct operation of the cooling system. Running an engine too cool results in excessive carbon formation in the combustion chamber, increased cylinder wear due to unburnt fuel removing the film of oil from the cylinders, and subsequent engine oil dilution, in addition to a reduced power output. Running an engine too hot may cause local boiling at critical spots, round exhaust valve seats and plug bases, more rapid deterioration of the engine oil, hence increased engine wear.

The temperature of the water is controlled within certain limits by a device known as a thermostat. This thermostat, which is sensitive to the temperature of the water, operates a valve, which in turn controls the flow of water. When an engine is 'warming up', the valve is closed and prevents water circulating through the radiator. Therefore the engine warms up quickly.

Once working temperature is reached, the valve partially opens and regulates the flow of water through the radiator, to maintain the engine at the correct running temperature. Sometimes a radiator blind is fitted to control the flow of air passing through the radiator.

Precautions against frost

An obvious drawback to the use of water for cooling is the risk of freezing in winter. When the water freezes, it expands. Being in a confined space, this can cause damage to the engine, but it can be overcome by draining the water from the engine and radiator. It is important to ensure that all the water is removed and frequently a drain cock, on the lowest point of the cylinder block, has to be opened in addition to the drain cock on the radiator. However, this is not a very satisfactory way of protecting tractors from frost, because it is possible for the radiator to freeze when the system is refilled and the engine running, causing serious overheating. The wisest precaution is to use an anti-freezing compound in the cooling water during the winter months. This lowers its freezing point. Before putting the anti-freeze solution in the radiator, always flush the system, using a proprietary flushing compound. It is important to add the right amount of anti-freeze solution for the quantity of water in the cooling system, and the required amount of frost protection. With farm tractors, it is advisable to fill the cooling system to 25% of its capacity with anti-freeze, that is one part anti-freeze to three parts water, to ensure adequate frost protection. Anti-freeze solutions quickly find out any leaks in the cooling system and it is worth checking for these.

Maintenance of the cooling system

1. Check the level of water in the radiator daily. Top up preferably with soft water to prevent chemical deposits.

2. Clean chaff and dirt from the radiator and grill when necessary.

3. Keep a frequent check on:
 (a) the tension and condition of the fan belt;
 (b) the hose and radiator, for leaks.
4. Lubricate the water pump bearings, as recommended in the instruction book.
5. Flush radiator and water jacket at least once per year.
6. With an air-cooled engine keep the cooling fins free from oil and dirt.

Fault finding

See Chapter 11, pp. 120–124.

11. The Farm Tractor

Types of tractor

The first farm tractor replaced the horse, simply as a vehicle to pull implements. Developments in tractor design, which have taken place since then, have enabled the tractor not only to pull an implement, but also to operate an implement attached to the three-point linkage, in such a manner that it can be considered as being part of the tractor and not a separate item. The modern tractor can also supply power to operate a machine through the p.t.o., by hydraulic means, or by belt.

In Great Britain, the most popular type of tractor is the *general purpose* tractor (see Fig. 59). This, as its name implies, is designed to perform a wide range of tasks. Details of design differ with make and size, but most have:

1. An engine capable of producing between 25 and 60 kW.

2. A transmission system with up to eight or twelve forward speeds and up to four reverse speeds.

3. Four rubber-tyred wheels, with wheel width adjustments within the range of 1·2 m to 2 m.

4. A drawbar conforming to a specification to allow attachment of p.t.o.-driven implements as well as trailed implements.

5. A p.t.o. shaft for driving implements.

6. A three-point linkage for mounted implements.

7. A hydraulic system to control the movement of the link arms and containing several 'tappings' to supply external hydraulic power for such tasks as tipping trailers.

8. A robust front axle and engine chassis with mounting pads at the front, mid and rear for attaching implements such as loaders and hedging or ditching equipment.

9. A low centre of gravity, to give stability and reduce the risk of overturning. This low ground clearance creates a problem in designing, fitting and using mid-mounted equipment.

Row-crop tractors

Whilst self-propelled toolbars for row-crop work are made in Great Britain, specialist row-crop tractors are not produced. However, general purpose tractors can do this work, due to their adjustable wheel widths, particularly if fitted with narrow tyres. Specialist forms of general purpose tractors are made with high ground clearance to straddle row-crops and allow easy attachment and vision for row-crop work.

Tracklayer tractors

The main difference between the general purpose tractor and the tracklayer is the replacement of the four wheels by two endless tracks. These tracks transmit the power and the weight of the tractor to the soil and it is therefore able to pull or push very heavy loads. The weight of the crawler is distributed over a large track area and this keeps damage to a wet soil to a minimum, and allows a tracklayer to operate under conditions unsuitable for wheeled tractors. It is steered by controlling the speed of one track relative to the other. Hydraulic power is available for the operation of external equipment and three-point linkage may be fitted.

The tracklayer is expensive to buy and to operate, due principally to the high rate of track wear at speeds above 8 km/h. Also, the work it can perform on the farm is obviously limited and therefore tracklayers tend to be used as farm tractors only on heavy land arable farms, where they can work in conditions unsuitable for wheeled tractors. They are used primarily by contractors for heavy tasks such as mole drainage and earth moving. Farm tracklayers usually have engines in the range of 25 to 75 kW, but larger and more powerful tractors are used for earth moving.

Transmission system

The purpose of the transmission system of a tractor is to transmit the power produced by the engine to the rear wheels. It

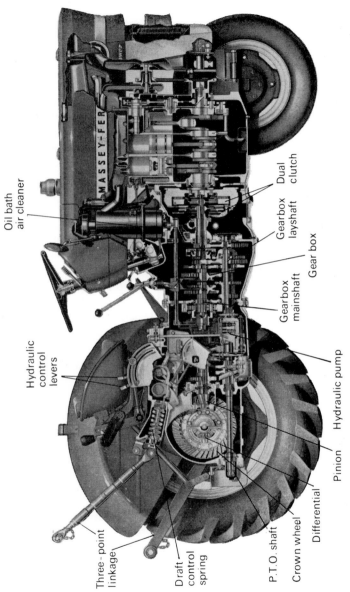

Oil bath
air cleaner

Hydraulic
control
levels

Three-point
linkage

Draft
control
spring

P.T.O. shaft

Crown wheel

Differential

Pinion

Hydraulic pump

Gear box

Gearbox
mainshaft

Gearbox
layshaft

Dual
clutch

Fig. 59. Section of a tractor

must also provide varying speeds for the tractor, according to the operation being undertaken.

The transmission system consists of a *clutch, gearbox, differential* and *final drive.*

Clutch

This is attached to the engine flywheel and provides a means of gradual engagement of the engine power to the tractor rear wheels (Fig. 60). It consists of a friction plate (fibre) fitted into the flywheel between two metal plates, one of which is the face

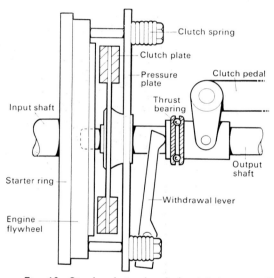

Fig. 60. Single plate clutch (pedal depressed)

of the flywheel. The friction plate is splined in its centre and fitted round an output shaft. The metal plate revolves with the flywheel and the friction plate with the output shaft which forms the mainshaft of the gearbox. Both plates are held together by a series of coil springs arranged in a circle. The clutch is connected by a linkage to the clutch pedal. When the pedal is depressed, the spring pressure on the plates is reduced. They cease transmitting the drive from the engine to the output shaft. Conversely, when the pedal is slowly released, the drive is gradually taken up as the metal plates engage the friction plate. It is most important that the clutch pedal should have some free play before the spring pressure can be felt, as lack of free play can prevent the springs exerting their full pressure against the plates, and cause clutch 'slip', when under power.

On the first tractors incorporating a hydraulic system and a p.t.o., both were controlled by the same clutch as the transmission. Therefore, when the clutch pedal was depressed, the tractor came to a halt and the hydraulic system and the p.t.o. ceased to function. On more recent tractors, two clutches are bolted together, one to take up the drive to the transmission and the other to take up the drive to the p.t.o. These two clutches are operated by two pressures on the clutch pedal, the initial pressure disengaging the drive to the transmission, and on full depression of the pedal, the drive to the p.t.o. A tractor fitted with this dual clutch is said to have a live p.t.o. system. The hydraulic system on most tractors is also controlled by this second stage of the clutch. Some tractors have a hand lever to control the p.t.o. and this allows the p.t.o. to be engaged or disengaged while the tractor is in motion. This is known as independent p.t.o.

Gearbox

The gearbox consists of a *mainshaft*, carrying the friction clutch plate at one end, and a short *layshaft* parallel with the mainshaft. The mainshaft is usually in two sections: the *input* and *output* shafts. A series of gears of different sizes connects the layshaft with both parts of the mainshaft. The drive enters from the clutch on the input shaft, passes to the layshaft and then back to the output shaft. The gears are moved in and out of mesh by selectors, which in turn are moved by the gear lever. This can only be done when the clutch pedal is depressed and no power is transmitted. Top gear is engaged when the input and output shafts are connected together and thus it becomes a 'straight through' shaft.

On most tractors it is necessary to stop in order to change from one gear to another. Some tractors, however, are designed to enable changes to be made while the tractor is on the move. This type of gearbox is called a *synchromesh* gearbox, and its use is most suited for transport operations where the rolling resistance of the tractor and its load is low. Where high-draft operations, such as ploughing, are being carried out, the tractor would stop on depressing the clutch, due to the high resistance to motion, before the new gear could be engaged. In order to be able to change gear without interrupting the flow of power some models of tractor have gearboxes of a design which enables gear changes to be made without using the clutch. By being able to do this it is possible to utilize the power of the tractor to a greater degree.

Despite the increasing numbers of gears being fitted to tractors and the ease with which they can be changed there is still a series of steps in speed between each gear and the tractor may not be able to provide a suitable combination of forward speed and power required for a particular task. Stepless transmissions have been developed with the power being transmitted by oil at high pressures. These hydrostatic transmissions enable maximum power to be transmitted at all times while the tractor speed is altered by varying the rate of flow of the oil. A single lever controls the speed in both forward and reverse and no clutch is necessary. They require considerable skill to obtain maximum performance from the tractor and are at present costly.

Differential

The drive from the output shaft must be taken through a right angle before passing to the rear wheels. This is done by the *crown wheel* and *pinion* (Fig. 61). The pinion is a small bevel gear on the output end of the gearbox and it drives the larger crown wheel. As well as turning the drive through a right angle, the crown wheel and pinion also reduce the speed.

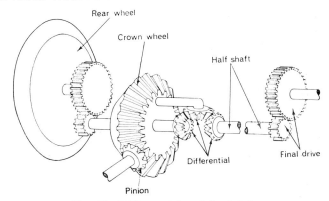

Fig. 61. Differential and final drive

The crown wheel and pinion are generally bolted to the *differential*. This is a mechanism which allows the rear wheels to turn at different speeds, while still delivering power to both. The differential causes an equal turning force to be applied to each wheel, but it suffers from the disadvantage that if one wheel is on a greasy surface and spins, and therefore requires only a small turning force, it transmits the same small turning force to the wheel which is resting on a good surface. The tractor may well come to a standstill through wheelslip. Modern tractors overcome this problem by fitting a *differential lock*. This cuts out the action of the differential. It can be used only while travelling in a straight line and must be disengaged for cornering.

The drive from the differential comes out on either side by half shafts. On most tractors, the half shafts rotate too quickly to be connected directly to the rear wheels, so they drive through two *final drive gears* to each wheel.

Maintenance of the transmission system

1. The oil should be kept at the correct level in the gearbox, transmission housing, back axle or final drive, depending on the construction of the tractor.

2. The oil should be changed at intervals of 750 to 1000 h according to the make of the tractor. Where magnetic drain plugs or gauze filters are fitted, they should be cleaned carefully at each oil change.

3. The clutch should always have some free play at the pedal, but where a dual clutch is fitted, the procedure for setting both stages varies with the make of tractor.

Brakes

One of two main types of brakes is fitted to a modern tractor. They are *drum* and *disc* type. They are usually fitted on the half-shaft coming from the differential and being thus mounted high up on the transmission system are less likely to be affected by mud and water. The function of any brake is to slow the vehicle, by converting kinetic energy into another form of energy: heat.

Drum brakes consist of two semicircular shoes fitting in a drum which rotates with the half shaft (Fig. 62). A strip of friction material, the *brake lining*, is riveted to the periphery of the shoes. The shoes are attached to the chassis by pivots and a cam, rotated by the brake pedal and its linkage, forces the shoes against the drum. Springs withdraw the shoes from the drum.

Disc brakes are fitted on the latest models of tractor and consist of two circular friction discs rotating with the half shaft (Fig. 63). On applying the brake, the friction discs are forced against a smooth pad machined on the chassis and another on the brake housing. These brakes require less adjustment than drum brakes, and will withstand more continuous application without overheating.

To enable the tractor to make sharp turns, the brake on each wheel is capable of *independent* operation. For normal braking, the two independent brakes are latched together and should always be kept this way, except when being used *independently*. If one brake has been used more than another, it may become excessively worn and when the driver attempts to stop the tractor with the brakes coupled, he finds that the unworn brake

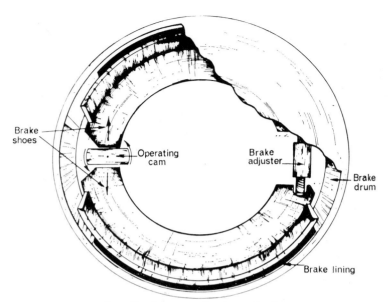

Fig. 62. Section of a drum brake

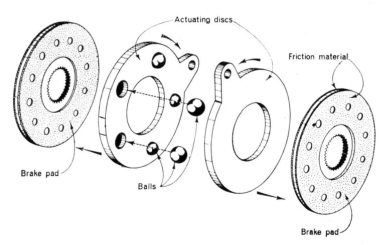

Fig. 63. Exploded view of disc brake

operates first, and the tractor veers to that side. This can result in a serious accident, if the brake is applied sharply at speed.

Maintenance

This consists of two operations:
1. To take up wear on the brakes.
2. To balance the brakes.

The exact method of brake adjustment and balancing depends on the make of tractor. Basically, it consists of reducing the free play on the pedal and then braking the wheels, whilst travelling, and noting which wheel locks first. This brake is then slackened slightly and the operation repeated until both act together, pulling the tractor up in a straight line.

Tyres and wheels

The size of a tyre is indicated by two numbers on the tyre wall. The first number refers to the width of the rim and the second to the diameter of the rim on which it fits. A range of tyres can be obtained for both front and rear wheels of all tractors, to suit particular types of work.

Rear tyres

The broader the rear tyres, the greater the drawbar pull the tractor can generally exert. Narrow rear tyres are used for row-crop work, to avoid damage to the plants. The thickness and strength of the casing is denoted by the terms 4-ply or 6-ply, which indicate the number of layers of material in the tyre. The 4-ply is for normal use. The 6-ply would be selected for flinty soil conditions. The bars or lugs on the tyre are designed to give maximum grip, and they are also self-cleaning, as they allow mud and soil to fall out as the wheel turns. The tyres are fitted so that the point of the V enters the ground first.

Front tyres

The selection of a front tyre also depends on the work that the tractor will undertake. For jobs involving heavy loading on the front of the tractor, e.g. fore-end loader, a broader and stronger front tyre may be fitted. For row-crop work, or work involving driving along a mark, many drivers prefer narrow tyres, to allow more accurate driving. Again, there is a choice of 4-ply or 6-ply. Obviously, the larger the tyre or the thicker the tread, the more expensive it is.

The widths between the wheels of a tractor are capable of adjustment, and are always measured from the centre of each tyre. The front wheel widths are adjusted by sliding the section which forms the front axle, and re-bolting.

The rear wheel rims are attached by a reversible dished plate to the axle. Offset lugs are welded to the rim and bolted to the dished plate. Wheel width adjustment is effected by a combination of the position of the offset lug, relative to the dish, and also the position of the dish. The range is normally 1·2 to 2 m, in 100 mm steps, i.e. 50 mm on each wheel. In order to keep the tread pointing in the right direction, it is necessary for certain settings to change the wheels from one side to the other.

Maintenance

Tractor tyres are very costly items, and can easily be ruined through lack of care and attention. The following should be carefully carried out.

1. Keep tyres at the correct pressures.

   Rear tyres 0·7 to 0·8 bar: field work

   0·8 to 1·2 bar: road work.

   Front tyres 1·6 to 2·0 bar.

2. Keep tyres free of all oil and grease.

3. Avoid driving too quickly over large stones or other objects.

Aids to traction

As already mentioned, both a differential lock and larger-than-standard rear tyres increase the pulling ability of a tractor. There are several other aids, which can be used for the same purpose.

1. *Ballasting* is the cheapest of these, and consists of filling the

tyre with water and calcium chloride (to prevent freezing) in a
ratio of 1 kg/12 litres water, for protection down to −7°C.
A special valve must be fitted as the chemical attacks ordinary
valve seals. The tyre is filled with the valve in the highest position, by gravity or with a pump. A special coupling is necessary
to allow the air to escape as it is replaced by water. When filled
level with the valve, it is 75% ballasted. The remaining space is
kept at normal air pressure, care being taken to move the valve
to its highest position before measuring the pressure and to use
a pressure gauge, made specially for ballasted tyres, as the
calcium chloride destroys the seals on a conventional gauge.
The tyre can be ballasted to 100% with special equipment and
then, of course, there is no need to check the pressure. The
disadvantage of ballasting becomes apparent when tyres punc-
ture and when wheels have to be changed.

2. *Wheel weights* can be bolted to the dish of the wheel and are
generally made in units of 45 kg. They make the overall width of
the tractor greater, but can easily be removed when not required.

3. *Twin wheels* are expensive but most suitable for travelling
on very wet land, as they prevent the tractor from sinking. They
are favoured by contractors who spread lime and slag as they
allow work to be carried on under difficult soil conditions and
make the tractor more stable on sloping ground. Tractors fitted
with twin wheels are unsuitable for use with mounted ploughs
as the wheels will not fit into the bottom of the furrows.

4. *Retractable strakes* are bolted to the wheel dish and can be
pushed out or withdrawn as needed. One set can be used when
ploughing, fitted on the land side of the tractor. They must, of
course, be withdrawn for road work.

Hydraulic systems

The first tractor hydraulic systems could only raise and lower
an implement. They have now become extremely complex and
can perform some, or all, of the following:

1. Raising and lowering implements.
2. Controlling the depth of soil-engaging implements.

3. Lowering and holding an implement to a pre-determined position.

4. Operating external hydraulic equipment, such as tipping trailers and loaders.

The system consists basically of a gear or piston pump, driven from the engine or transmission system, which pumps oil into a ram cylinder containing a piston. The piston is connected via a rocker shaft to the three-point linkage. Relief valves are fitted at the pump and in the cylinder. The levers operated by the tractor driver control the flow of oil by a series of valves. Maximum operating pressure is around 200 bar.

Draft control

This is a hydraulic method of depth control suitable for soil-engaging implements without depth wheels. The implement is suspended from the tractor three-point linkage, and its weight is added to that on the rear wheels of the tractor, thus enabling them to obtain more grip. The implement is lowered into work, until the top link and the spring to which it is connected are compressed to a pre-determined level. The hydraulic system then maintains the implement at this depth. Should the land become heavier or lighter, the draft and hence the compression of the top link alters. The mechanism of the hydraulic system automatically alters the depth of the implement, to bring the *draft* back to the pre-determined level. A change in the draft also occurs when the tractor front wheels move up or down. The hydraulic system then operates to ensure that the implement follows the contours of the land. Additional refinements on the latest tractors enable the rate of response of the hydraulic system to a change of draft to be controlled. This gives less variation in depth and a more constant weight addition to the rear wheels.

Position control

This is used for above-the-ground implements, such as mowers or transport boxes and occasionally for soil-engaging implements on level field conditions. The position of the control lever in the quadrant controls the height of the lower links. The pump goes into neutral and will only operate if the links drop due to a leakage from the ram cylinder.

The manufacturers' instructions must be carefully followed regarding the operation of the control levers, as it may be possible to select the wrong positions, so that the relief valve blows off continuously. This results in wasted power and can cause damage.

External application

The normal control levers may be used to operate external equipment and there may be a valve to isolate the flow to the ram cylinder and divert it to the external equipment. Some tractors may have extra valves fitted enabling more than one external cylinder to be operated independently. Most external cylinders, such as those used on trailers, are *single acting*; they are extended by the tractor's hydraulic system but retract under the influence of the weight of the trailer.

Double-acting cylinders are both extended and retracted under pressure. These require suitable control valves to be fitted to the tractor and are used in situations where the cylinder would not retract due to gravity and where greater speed and control of operation is required.

Three-point linkage. This comprises two lower draft arms and the top link. Ball ends are fitted on either end of the three mounting points, the outer set threading over pins on the implement. Three sizes of pin are used, *Category I* for the lightest implements and smallest tractors, *Category II* for medium sized implements and tractors, whilst *Category III* is used for the heaviest implements and largest tractors, particularly track-laying types. Some implements have *Category I* and *II* hitch pins and some tractors can convert by changing the ball ends or reversing the draft arms. *Category III* tractors are normally only used with implements of the same category.

Check chains are normally fitted to limit the side movem⌐

on an implement when raised or lowered and to prevent it contacting the tractor wheels and possibly causing damage. They may be adjustable and should be set according to the application required. Soil-engaging implements should be able to swing freely when lowered but less freely or not at all when raised. Above-the-ground implements normally require no side movement when either raised or lowered. It may be possible to control this using the check chains or it may be necessary to fit one or two *stabilizing bars*. Each make of tractor varies in the method of limiting side movement and it is important to consult the manufacturers' instruction book and carry out their recommendation. If an incorrect arrangement is used severe damage to the linkage or tractor may result.

Routine tractor maintenance

Modern tractors are fitted with a *proofmeter* which records the number of hours the engine operates. These hours are used as a basis for determining when certain attention is necessary. The average tractor operates less than 1000 h/year and its life is often about 10 000 h. The figures given below are a range of intervals for diesel tractors. The precise intervals for any particular model will be found by reference to the instruction manual.

Daily maintenance
   1. Check and replenish fuel, engine oil and water.
   2. Grease steering joints, king pins and axle trunnion and three-point linkage.
   3. Check air cleaner in dusty conditions.

Weekly maintenance
   1. Check and replenish transmission/gearbox and final-drive oil.
   2. Check tyre pressures.
   3. Check air cleaner.
   4. Check and replenish battery electrolyte.

Every 120–300 h
   1. Change engine oil and filter (60 h for V.O.).
   2. Check and adjust fan belt tension.

Every 400–1000 h
   1. Change transmission oil.
   2. Change fuel filters.
   3. Service injectors (Agent's task).

Periodic maintenance, to be carried out whenever necessary.
   1. Cleaning radiator and grill.
   2. Adjusting clutch.
   3. Adjusting and balancing of brakes.
   4. Removal of water from sediment bowl.
   5. Maintenance of batteries, other than adding distilled water.
   6. Adjusting valve clearances.
   7. Checking the tension of nuts and bolts generally.
   8. Cleaning crankcase breather.

Tractor engine fault finding

A correctly maintained tractor operating under *normal* farm conditions is a very reliable piece of equipment. However, certain faults may develop due to either wear of components, extreme operating conditions or inadequate maintenance.

It is necessary to be able to both recognize and correct these faults and also to be aware when the attention of a Service Engineer is required. To avoid serious and costly damage it is wise to limit the fault finding to the areas of maintenance recommended in the operator's instruction manual.

The type of fault which may be corrected by the operator may show itself either on *starting* or during *operation* of the tractor. In order to locate quickly and correct the fault, a systematic approach should be made. The operator should, during his daily work, note the performance characteristics of his tractor in order that he is alerted when one of these changes. The characteristics he should note include the:

1. time and speed the engine is turned by the starter motor before starting;
2. interval, after starting, before the oil-pressure warning light goes out, or a reading is observed on the pressure gauge;
3. ammeter reading or dynamo warning light going out;
4. sound made by the exhaust;
5. smoke, if any, produced by the exhaust;
6. ease of gear engagement;
7. performance of the brakes;
8. engine response when put under load.

The observant driver will be aware immediately should any *changes* in these characteristics occur. It is important to realize that extreme operating conditions may aggravate faults and result in tractor failure.

All the faults outlined are shown by *symptoms* which are produced by *causes* and which may be remedied by *action*.

Starting faults

Before attempting to start a tractor the operator should know the manufacturers' recommended starting procedure for different conditions.

The common faults which might arise when attempting to start an engine and the action which may be taken are most easily described in diagrammatic form:

Symptom	Cause	Action
Engine does not turn	Incorrect starting procedure	Use correct procedure
	Loose or dirty battery terminals	Clean and tighten
	Flat battery	Charge
	Poor earth connection	Clean connection
Engine turns slowly	Poor terminal connections	Clean and tighten terminals
	Flat battery	Charge
	Cold weather	Protect at night

Symptom	Cause	Action
Engine turns quickly, but fails to start (diesel)	Incorrect starting procedure	Use correct procedure
	Faulty fuel supply	Bleed fuel system
	Faulty air supply	Check air cleaner
Engine turns quickly, but does not start (petrol engine)	Incorrect starting procedure	Use correct procedure
	Faulty fuel supply	Check fuel supply to carburettor
	Faulty ignition system	Check security of ignition wiring Check clearance and operation of plugs and points
	Faulty air supply	Check air cleaner

Operating faults

The operator of a tractor should normally notice whenever an engine fault appears whilst the engine is running. Some faults gradually occur over a period of months or years, others may appear suddenly on an otherwise normal tractor. These faults may result either in loss of power or even cause the engine to stop altogether.

Symptom	Cause	Action
Low power (black smoke)	Dirty air cleaner or faulty injectors	Service Replace
Blue smoke	Wear	Contact Service Engineer
Erratic running (diesel engines)	Faulty injectors	Replace
	Fuel blockage	Change filter and bleed
Stops suddenly (diesel engines)	No fuel	Re-fill and bleed system
	Fuel blockage	Check fuel flow to filters
Erratic running (petrol engines)	Fuel blockage	Clean carburettor
	Faulty carburettor	Clean and re-adjust
Stops suddenly (petrol engine)	No fuel	Re-fill
	Fuel blockage	Check flow to carburettor

Symptom	Cause	Action
IGNITION SYSTEM (petrol engines)		
Erratic running	Poor terminal connections	Clean and tighten
	Broken leads	Replace
	Faulty contact-breaker points	Clean and re-set
	Dirty components	Clean
Stops suddenly	Faulty ignition system	Check, clean and re-set
	Poor terminal connections	Check and tighten terminals
COOLING SYSTEM		
Engine overheating	Low water level	Top up
	Fan belt slack	Tighten
	Radiator cap loose or worn	Tighten or replace
	Radiator fins blocked	Clean
LUBRICATING SYSTEM		
Engine oil pressure low	Oil change overdue	Change oil and filter
	Low oil level	Top up
Fluctuating pressure	Low oil level	Top up
ELECTRICAL SYSTEM		
Charging system not working	Fan belt slack	Tighten
	Loose connections	Clean and tighten

The most common and simple faults have been described. Many other causes will produce similar symptoms, but the action to correct them generally requires the attention of the Service Engineer.

It should be emphasized that the majority of faults occurring in tractors during normal operation are a result of inadequate maintenance. Whenever a tractor is operating under extreme conditions it is necessary to understand what faults can be caused and what action may be necessary. It is often necessary to provide extra maintenance to take account of extreme conditions.

Hot conditions

Special attention is needed to the cooling system, particularly radiator fins and fan belt tension.

Cold conditions

Keep the battery fully charged by supplementary booster charging at night if necessary. Keep terminals clean and fan belt correctly tensioned. Use correct cold weather starting procedure.

Dusty conditions

More frequent attention to the air cleaner and radiator fins is necessary.

Running faults

It is generally true to state that ignition faults produce *regular* misfiring or a sudden halt and fuel system faults produce irregular misfiring. However, exceptions occur. For regular misfiring, remove each of the plug leads in turn and listen to the sound of the exhaust. The faulty lead or plug is that which causes no change in the exhaust note. Irregular misfiring is generally due to some fault in the fuel system. If the engine will not 'tick-over', check the pilot jet. If the engine misses on wide throttle openings, check the main jet and the system for any restrictions.

This is a brief survey of some of the more simple faults a competent operator should be able to trace and diagnose.

Tractor safety regulations (U.K. only)

1. Power take-off.
   (a) Whenever the engine is in motion, the p.t.o. must be covered by either a shield or a cap.
   (b) Whenever a p.t.o.-driven machine is being used, the p.t.o. shaft must be guarded on all sides from the tractor to the first fixed bearing on the machine.
   (c) No one under 16 years of age may remove or adjust a p.t.o. guard.
   (d) Workers must report damaged guards to their employers.

2. Tractor operation. It is not permissible to:
   (a) Set a tractor in motion, unless in the driving seat.
   (b) Get on or off a tractor whilst it is in motion.
   (c) Ride on the drawbar or linkage of any machine, whilst it is being towed or carried.

3. Safety cabs.
   (a) New tractors may only be used when fitted with an approved safety cab except where it is not practicable such as in an orchard, hop garden or building.
   (b) All workers must report to their employer if the cab or its fittings become damaged or defective or if the tractor overturns. This includes the windscreen wiper becoming defective.
   (c) From 1st September, 1975 all new tractors fitted with safety cabs will have to be within a maximum noise level or decibel rating of 90 dBA.

4. General.
   (a) Children under 13 years of age must not drive or ride on tractors.
   (b) Children under 13 years of age must not ride in trailers with moving floors or trailers where the load is higher than the side.
   (c) When drawing a trailed implement, the drawbar pin must be firmly secured in position.
   (d) All tractors must be maintained in a safe condition with regard to brakes, steering and tyres.

12. Ploughs and Ploughing

For centuries men have realized that to grow good crops successively on the same area of land, it is necessary to cultivate the soil between each crop. The earliest cultivations were done with a pointed piece of wood, drawn by men or oxen. It is from these primitive beginnings that the modern plough and techniques of ploughing have developed.

Ploughing is the first and possibly the most important cultivation in the process of creating a seedbed, for the extent and effectiveness of subsequent cultivation is often dependent on the quality of the initial ploughing. When ploughing a field, the aims are:

1. To loosen the surface layers of the soil, and so allow a free movement of air and water and stimulate bacterial activity. This creates a medium in which the crop roots are able to thrive.

2. To invert the top soil completely, to bring a fresh layer to the surface for weathering. It is important to avoid going too deep and exposing sterile subsoil. This complete inversion is also very effective in controlling annual weeds, for these will only germinate when near the surface and many rot when buried too deeply. With our rainfall, which exceeds evaporation and transpiration during the winter months, some of those plant foods and very fine soil particles that tend to be washed down through the soil, are also brought back to the surface.

3. To leave as level a surface as possible, to facilitate the movement and work of subsequent machines.

The plough

The modern plough is mounted directly behind the tractor, attached to the three-point linkage, being raised and lowered hydraulically. The function of each part of the plough must be understood, so that adjustments can be made accurately.

The typical mounted plough consists of a *frame*, which is attached to the tractor (Fig. 64). The main components in contact with the soil are the *coulter*, the *share*, the *mouldboard* and

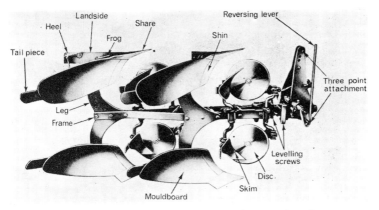

Fig. 64. Two-furrow reversible digger plough

the *landside*. The coulter is carried by the frame of the plough. The share, mouldboard and landside are all bolted to the *frog*, which in turn is bolted to the *leg* of the plough. The plough leg is carried by the frame.

The *share* is a triangular piece of steel or cast iron. Its job is to penetrate and then undercut the soil at the desired depth. When new, the share tip is slightly turned down to help it penetrate. This is called the *share pitch* or *share suction* (Fig. 65). The tip is also turned slightly to the left, when viewed from above and behind. This keeps the plough straight behind the tractor, and prevents it moving sideways or crabbing away from its work. It is appropriately known as the *lead to land* (Fig. 66). Under hard or stony conditions, ploughs with *bar point* shares may be more suitable. The wearing tip of the share consists of a square steel bar drawn to a chisel-shaped point. The point protrudes to provide the suction and lead. The remainder of the bar is held in position under the frog by a set pin. This type of

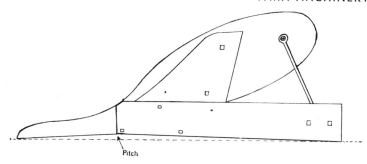

Fig. 65. Share pitch

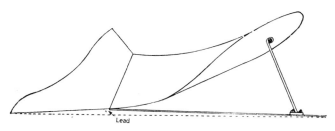

Fig. 66. Lead to land

share is able to withstand shock loads produced on striking stones, and as the tip wears the bar can be knocked through to restore the suction and lead. Shares wear according to the type and condition of the soil, and should be changed when the pitch and suction have been lost to such an extent that the work suffers.

The function of the coulter is to make a vertical cut and divide the soil being raised by the share from the unploughed land. The combination of the share and the coulter creates the furrow. The coulter consists of a disc mounted above the share, which cuts through the surface vegetation and the soil as it revolves. The setting of the coulter is quite critical. Properly set, it should leave a clean vertical face on the unploughed land, which is neither stepped nor ragged. The basic setting is one finger (15 mm) to the landside of the share point and two fingers (30 mm) above the share (Fig. 67 (a) and (b)). This has to be varied according to the depth of ploughing and conditions in the field. The vertical clearance has to be increased with deeper ploughing up to a distance equal to half the ploughing depth to prevent the bearing of the disc coulter fouling the ground. For straw or other surface trash, the coulter will have to be lowered

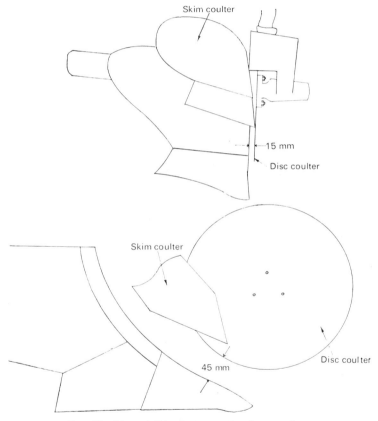

Fig. 67. (a) and (b). Setting of a disc coulter

slightly to ensure that it cuts cleanly. Hard or stony conditions will cause the disc to ride out of the ground, bringing the plough with it. The setting for these conditions is to raise the disc and move it back from the point of the share. In this way, the share will have more lead over the disc and will be less likely to rise. Under very stony or hard conditions, knife coulters may be used (Fig. 70). They are attached to the plough frame and although less affected by hard going, they require more

Fig. 68. Skim coulters at work

draft and will not cut surface trash very effectively. A *skim* (Figs. 64, 67) is often fitted to a disc coulter to move a small 'furrow' from the corner of the main furrow and place it under the latter (Fig. 68). This ensures all surface material is buried and prevents the top corner or crest of the furrow quickly growing green with weeds. The tip of the skim should be set over the centre of the disc and as close to it as possible. The skim should be angled to give a 5 mm clearance at the back. On some ploughs, the skims are attached to the frame and not the disc. This has the advantage of preventing blockage, in that the disc is able to swing away from the skim when the surface trash begins to accumulate, allowing the trash to pass. This type of skim is sometimes used without a coulter, the vertical cut being made partly by the skim and partly by the leading edge of the mouldboard.

The *mouldboard* is the part of the plough which turns the furrow over and consists of a long, curved piece of hard-wearing steel. The leading edge may be replaceable and is known as the *shin*. There are various types of mouldboard, designed to produce different finishes to the furrow and to produce the best work at particular depths, widths and speeds.

1. The *ley* body is long and narrow, and only ploughs to a maximum of 120 to 150 mm deep. This type of body, once famous in competition work, is now rarely used, as the furrow, being gradually turned, remains unbroken and requires considerable working to produce a seedbed.

2. The *general purpose* body is slightly shorter and broader and can plough to 200 mm deep. This also gives quite a continuous type of furrow.

3. The *semi-digger* body is shorter and deeper with a slightly concave surface. The furrows are turned over more rapidly, causing some breaking to occur which reduces the need for subsequent cultivation and creates a great surface area for weathering during the winter. This type of body will plough to a depth of 300 mm.

4. The full *digger* body is even shorter and capable of ploughing to a depth of 450 mm on suitable soils producing a very broken furrow slice.

As a plough turns a furrow, there is a force in the opposite direction which is resisted by the *landside* of the plough. This is a long piece of metal fitted on the side of the plough against the unploughed land (landside) which presses against the furrow wall. There is a landside on every body of a multi-furrow plough but that on the rear body is usually the longest. Some ploughs have a rolling landside which is a spring-loaded wheel running against the furrow wall. The rolling wheel produces less friction than the fixed landside, hence less draft is needed to pull the plough along.

Plough adjustments

Conventional ploughs. There are four major adjustments
which can be made to the plough (Fig. 69).

1. *Depth.* This may be controlled by a depth wheel fitted to
the plough, which can be raised or lowered by a handle within

Front furrow
width adjuster

Top link
(pitch control)

Levelling rod

Cranked cross
shaft

Fig. 69. Plough adjustments—conventional plough

reach of the tractor seat. In operation, the plough sinks until the
wheel contacts the ground and prevents it penetrating further.
The control lever on the hydraulic system is put to the drop
position and left there until the plough is to be raised.

Most modern ploughs are without depth wheels and are suspended from the tractor three-point linkage. The depth of work is controlled by the tractor's hydraulic system. As explained in Chapter 11, two types of depth control, draft control and position control, are found on modern tractors. Draft control is suitable for both undulating and flat conditions where the soil texture is fairly constant. Position control, where the lower links are held at a fixed height relative to the tractor, is only recommended for level field conditions, but it does maintain an even depth through changing soil texture.

Hydraulic depth control causes the weight of the plough and the soil on the mouldboards to be added to the tractor rear wheels. This reduces wheelspin and enables the tractor and plough to work under conditions where a tractor and plough with a depth wheel would come to a halt through wheelspin.

2. *Pitch*. This is controlled by altering the length of the top link between the tractor and the plough. It is set correctly when the frame of the plough is parallel with the ground and the end of the landside bears *lightly* on the furrow bottom. If the top link is too short, the plough rides on the shares causing excessive wear and a ragged finish to the ploughing. If the top link is too long, the plough does not penetrate to the correct depth and the landside makes a deep mark on the furrow bottom. The top link setting is very critical, one full turn can often make excessive pitch into lack of pitch.

3. *Lateral levelling*. When in normal work, the frame of a plough should be parallel with the ground, when viewed from the rear, and all furrows ploughing at an equal depth. For certain operations, it is necessary to make the front furrow deeper or shallower. This is done by using the adjustment on the right-hand tractor lift rod, which causes the front furrow of the plough to be raised or lowered.

4. *Front furrow width*. In normal work, the width of the front furrow is set in the same way as the others, but there are occasions when it has to be made slightly wider or narrower. While it is possible to make the front furrow narrower by driving the

tractor across to the right, it is difficult to keep the tractor straight and the furrrow width constant. The mounted plough is free to swing sideways on its linkage and this situation can be used to control the front furrow width. The plough is attached to the tractor lower links by a cranked cross-shaft. If this cross-shaft is rotated, the angle of the plough in relation to the tractor is altered and when the plough is lowered into work, it swings sideways until it is pointing in line with the tractor. The working rule is that when the cranks on the cross-shaft are vertical, the furrow widths should be equal and if the left-hand end of the cross-shaft is rotated *towards* the tractor, the furrow width is decreased, and vice versa. After an adjustment, the plough has to travel 3 or 4 m before the adjustment becomes effective.

Reversible ploughs

So far only ploughs which turn furrows to the right have been discussed. Ploughs which have two sets of bodies, one right-hand and one left-hand, are becoming increasingly common (Figs. 70). These are called *reversible* or 'one-way' ploughs, the

Fig. 70. Plough adjustments— reversible plough
(Note the knife coulters immediately in front of the plough shares)

right-hand body being used in one direction and the left-hand body in the opposite direction. Various mechanisms are used to turn the bodies over. These may be automatic on raising the plough from the ground, mechanical and hydraulic, both the latter being under the control of the tractor driver. The advantages of this type of plough will be mentioned later. It is important at this point to recognize how their adjustments compare with conventional ploughs (Fig. 70).

1. *Depth.* This can be controlled by the tractor's hydraulic system in a manner similar to that for the conventional plough. Wheels are also used to control depth, either by two wheels, one for each set of bodies, or by one wheel, which swings over and locks itself as the plough is turned.

2. *Pitch.* This is controlled by the top link, as with conventional ploughs.

3. *Lateral levelling.* Each pair of bodies has independent control on the plough and so each is adjusted separately.

4. *Front furrow width.* As with conventional ploughs, the reversible ploughs, when in work, will swing across until the thrust on the mouldboards is balanced by an equal and opposite thrust on the landside. The front furrow width is controlled by altering the angle of the plough relative to the cross-shaft on which it is carried. The plough will then swing until a new equilibrium position is reached.

Disc ploughs

In many countries where soils are dry and hard, or where there is a lot of surface trash or obstructions below the soil, a *disc* plough may be used. A mounted disc plough is similar to a mouldboard plough except that concave discs replace the share and mouldboard. These discs are about 0·7 m diameter and are mounted on tapered thrust bearings at an angle to the vertical and to the direction of travel (Fig. 71). Due to these angles they penetrate the ground to a depth of up to 0·3 m. The disc rotates by contact with the ground and as it does it carries soil up and partly inverts it before dropping it on the ground. It does not completely bury surface trash. *Scrapers* may be fitted to keep the disc clean in wet and sticky conditions.

Disc adjustment. On most ploughs provision is made for adjustment of the discs to suit varying conditions. The adjust-

Fig. 71. Disc plough

ments would normally be made when ground conditions become hard and have the effect of increasing penetration. The adjustments possible are:

Vertical adjustment. The more vertical the disc the greater its ability for penetration and the higher the draft the disc requires. It is normally set with the maximum tilt possible away from the vertical which just achieves the depth required. This will keep the draft required to a minimum.

Horizontal adjustment. This consists of altering the angle of the disc to the line of draft. As the angle increases so the depth increases and with it the draft.

The most suitable combination of adjustment can only be

found by experience but is that which provides adequate penetration with a minimum draft. Where adequate penetration cannot be obtained, even with each setting at its maximum, weights can be added. These may be designed to fit inside the tube of the main frame.

Sidethrust. Sidethrust is provided by discs in a similar manner to mouldboard ploughs and this sidethrust is resisted by a *thrust wheel* mounted at the rear of the plough. This should be set to absorb all the thrust and transmit none to the tractor. The thrust wheel is normally spring-loaded to avoid it carrying any weight from the discs. When set correctly the front furrow width is equal to the others and the tractor's check chains hang down slackly on both sides of the lower links.

The other main adjustments on the mounted disc ploughs are similar to mouldboard ploughs:

1. Depth—controlled by a depth wheel or the tractor's hydraulic system.
2. Pitch—controlled by altering the length of the top link the correct setting is when the frame of the plough isparallel with the surface of the groundw hen viewed from the side.
3. Lateral levelling—adjusted by the lift rod and is correct when the frame of the plough is level with the ground when viewed from the rear.
4. Front furrow width—the crank shaft is rotated in a similar manner to that on a mouldboard plough.

Ploughing

Before hitching the tractor to the plough, it is essential to check that the wheel settings of the tractor agree with those recommended in the plough instruction manual. Front and rear wheel settings are generally different as the *insides* of the front and rear tyres should be in line.

Ploughing in lands

This is the most common method of ploughing in the U.K. In this method, the tractor ploughs down one part of the field, lifts the plough out of work, travels 20 to 30 m along the head-land, then ploughs back up the field. When the tractor works round an unploughed piece of ground, it is called *casting*. When it works round a ploughed piece of land it is called *gathering* (see p. 148). Ploughing commences at a *ridge* where the furrows are turned towards each other and it ends at a *finish*, where they are turned away from each other.

Drawing a single shallow furrow. A single furrow 20 to 50 mm deep is used to make the headland mark and also in the first stage of a ridge. To set the plough to produce a shallow furrow, it is necessary first to drop the coulter on the rear body and adjust it, until it is lying against the side of the share with the tip of the disc level with the bottom of the share. This ensures that the furrow wall is cut cleanly. The front body (or bodies) is then

Fig. 72a. First run of a split opening

raised clear of the ground with the levelling lever. The depth
control mechanism is altered to allow the rear body to penetrate
20 to 50 mm. The plough will then draw a shallow clean-cut
furrow with the rear body (Fig. 72a).

Making the headland mark. The width of the headland depends on the length of the tractor and plough. It should be

Fig. 72b. Completion of a split using a rear body

sufficient to allow the tractor to turn on the headland without
reversing and to drive into work squarely. With a medium-sized
tractor and three-furrow plough, 7 to 9 m is adequate. It is always better and safer to have too large a headland, rather than
too small a one. Very little extra time is required to plough
an additional yard or two on the headland, compared with that

wasted by frequent reversing. Adequate headlands also reduce the danger of getting the tractor into the ditch or overturning by swinging round too quickly on a slope. Usually the furrow is turned into the field, by travelling in a clockwise direction. Under very hard conditions it may be an advantage to turn it towards the hedge, as the small furrow wall that is formed then helps the plough to penetrate when ploughing the lands.

Where the field has straight sides, marking sticks can be used for guidance. For curving sides, it is better to have an assistant, walking along the hedge holding a piece of rope the same length as the width of the headland, which has its other end attached to the tractor. The tractor driver drives so that the rope is just kept taut.

Making a ridge. The purpose of making a ridge is to ensure that all the soil in a field has been inverted or covered. This means that all the weeds and crop residues have been cut off from the roots and, being covered, quickly die. However, the ridge should be kept as flat as possible, to reduce subsequent cultivations. There are two types of ridge, the *double split* ridge and the *single split* ridge.

The double split ridge (Fig. 73) is used when ploughing arable land, particularly stubble, where there is likely to be annual weed seeds present, which must be buried. The sequence of making a double split ridge is:

First run: a shallow furrow is drawn the length of the field using the plough setting previously described.

Second run: the tractor travels in the opposite direction along the wheel marks of the previous run, with the plough set slightly deeper. This throws a furrow in the opposite direction from the first. The reason for going deeper is to provide a wall to absorb the side thrust of the plough and prevent it swinging. With some depth wheel controlled ploughs, the wheel runs in the bottom of the first furrow and it automatically causes the plough to penetrate a little deeper. Similarly, the same setting of a draft control will cause a deeper furrow to be produced on the second run.

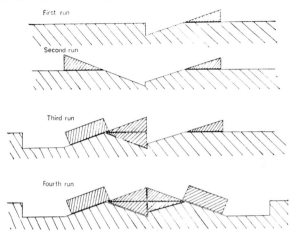

Fig. 73. Double split ridge with two-furrow plough

Third run: this is made in the same direction as the first. The aim is to turn the second furrow back and to cover it with another shallow furrow to give a 'sandwich' effect. This is done with the first body, while the second and third bodies plough deeper furrows. This means the setting of the plough must be altered in the following way. The front body is lowered into work with the levelling lever. Because it is only ploughing shallow the coulter should be lowered to get a clean cut. The depth of the rear body is increased and the coulter must be raised to its normal position. The right-hand tractor wheel is driven down the furrow bottom.

Fourth run: the plough setting is similar to the previous run and the remaining small furrow is turned in together with gradually larger furrows from the remaining bodies. The aim is to get this set of furrows to lie close to the previous set without a space, which would allow weeds to grow, or an overlap which would produce an uneven field.

The *single split ridge* (Fig. 74) is used when ploughing grassland and it is slightly quicker and easier than a double split ridge. With this type of ridge, not all the grass is cut by the share. It is possible that some may grow through, unless care is taken in making the ridge. The sequence is:

First run: similar to a double split, a shallow furrow with the rear body.

Second run: this is made with the front furrow set shallow and the remaining furrows slightly deeper. The front disc is

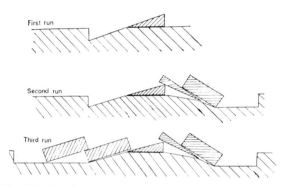

Fig. 74. Single split ridge with two-furrow plough

also lowered. The tractor is driven so that the front furrow half-covers the original shallow furrow.

Third run: this completes the ridge and is made with a similar plough setting to the second. The aim is to cover half the first furrow and to form a close seal against the front furrow of the second run, to cover the original scratch furrow completely.

An alternative and quicker method of making a single split ridge is to draw the shallow furrow with the front body of the plough, the remaining bodies working at a half to three-quarters the intended depth of ploughing. The second run is made with a similar plough setting but the front body working slightly deeper, the furrow from it completely covering that made by the front body on the previous run.

Ploughing the land. After completing the ridge, it is usual to plough round it two or three times, gradually increasing the depth each time and levelling the plough, until the desired depth is reached. The front furrow width is then set the same as the other furrows and the skim coulters just deep enough to do the work with the points just touching the disc.

The aim should be to have all the furrows identical, so that it is not possible to identify the number of bodies on the plough. Travelling at the same speed wherever possible will help to give this even finish. It is also desirable to keep the furrows as straight as possible. This saves time when making the 'finish'. Curves often develop at the beginning and end of a 'bout' and are generally due to not having the tractor 'squared up' before lowering into work, and turning the tractor before the plough is raised. Sometimes the furrows do not turn as they fall off the mouldboard when the plough is lifted. This is overcome by turning the tractor slightly to the left and then the plough will swing over to the right as it rises and pushes the furrow into place. If the hydraulic control lever is moved at the same place each time, when lifting or lowering the plough, it is possible to keep the headland an even width.

Making a finish (Fig. 75). As the area of unploughed land becomes less and less, it is necessary to prepare to make the 'finish'. The simple rules to observe are:

(a) the unploughed strip must be made absolutely parallel throughout its length;

(b) the width should be adjusted so that the final run is one furrow width *less* than the number of bodies on the plough;

(c) the last-but-one run should be made slightly shallower.

It is best to start measuring the land when it is still 10 or 12 m wide, so that adequate space is left to correct any errors. Pacing the land is sufficiently accurate and it should be done several times throughout the length of the field. Should one part be wider than another, it is possible, by altering the front furrow width, to plough a greater width at the wide part and less at the narrow part. Thus, after a series of bouts, the furrows can be made almost parallel. The final 'lining-up' is possible when the unploughed strip becomes so narrow that the

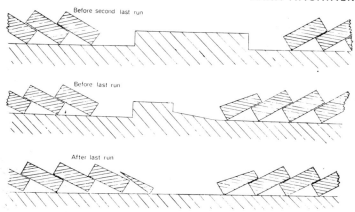

Fig. 75. Making a finish with a two-furrow plough

tractor can be driven close to the wheel marks made on the other side. By looking to the left and keeping the tractor wheels an equal distance from the wheel mark, a parallel unploughed strip will result.

The next task is to control the width so that one furrow less than the number on the plough will be left at the end (Fig. 75). The method of doing this depends on the size of the tractor and the number of furrows. Sometimes, when the tractor can just straddle the unploughed strip, it will leave the correct width. Useful advice on this is often given in the plough manufacturers' instruction book.

The last-but-one run should be more shallow. This is achieved by lowering the depth wheel and lightening *all* the furrows. The front furrow is lowered with the levelling lever, until it is at normal depth, giving a shallow rear furrow. The final run removes the remaining strip of land with the front bodies, while the rear body stabilizes the plough by turning the shallow earth furrow left from the previous run. For this final run, the plough is set with the rear coulter lowered, as for ploughing a shallow furrow, and the front furrow raised a little with the levelling lever. This means that the rear furrow is

Fig. 76. The final run

deep enough for the landside to prevent swinging (where a depth wheel is fitted, it will be running on ploughed land, so it may need considerable adjustment). The last run is made quite slowly (Fig. 76). If the plough tends to swing out of work, the rear body depth should be increased a little to stabilize it.

Ploughing the headlands. After the lands have been ploughed there remain the headlands. These should be ploughed alternately inwards, then outwards, to keep the field level.

To plough them outwards, drive round the field as close to the hedge as possible and for the first circuit set the front furrow shallow and lower the disc, to make a clean cut. It is safer to travel slowly, and so be able to stop should any roots or similar obstructions be met. Low branches and ditches or streams are other hazards which may be encountered. It is advisable to give the edges of ditches or streams a wide margin, as their sides may be undercut and collapse as soon as the tractor wheels touch them, causing the tractor to overturn.

When the first circuit is completed, the plough should be levelled before continuing. Gentle curves in the hedge can be followed, though it must be remembered that the plough follows the line of the front wheels of the tractor. When a corner of the field is reached, the tractor should be driven right up to the hedge before the plough is raised. It can then be reversed, lowered and ploughing continued along the next side.

One part of the headland may be narrower than the remainder To avoid ploughing the field over again, the plough is raised and driven round until an unploughed part is reached. The last circuit can be made shallower to avoid leaving a deep furrow round the field.

The next year the headlands should be ploughed inwards. Again, the front furrow is set shallow. This time, the tractor is driven round the original headland mark, even though this is sometimes rather difficult to find. After the first circuit, the plough is levelled and ploughing continued as close to the hedge as possible or as safety dictates.

Ploughing a field systematically in lands. Having described the various stages of ploughing in lands, it is necessary to indicate how each of these stages is approached, when ploughing a field, to avoid having too many ridges and finishes and also too much idle time travelling on the headlands.

The headland is marked out as already described. The same setting of the plough is used to mark out all the ridges. The distance apart of the ridges should be at least 11 m per furrow on the plough. Thus, for two- and three-furrow ploughs, ridges would be 22 and 33 m apart, respectively. In practice, the width of the land is adjusted to the overall width of the field, to give equal size lands. It is generally quicker to mark the ridges along the longest side of the field. If drainage has to be considered, the ridges should follow the slope. Marking poles are needed, to get absolutely straight furrows. At least two are necessary, although it is better to have one at each end and another 20 to 30 m away, so that when driving in either direction, the operator will always have at least two poles to use until he is 20 to 30 m from the hedge. A very long, or uneven, field may need additional poles.

The first ridge is set up $\frac{1}{4}$ land from the headland. The position of the first two poles is determined by pacing. The remainder are put in line with them. The tractor is driven square up to the first pole and then the pole is moved the width of a land across the field by pacing or by using a measured rope.

With the plough set to draw a small furrow, the tractor is driven in line with the poles. As each marking pole is reached, it is moved across the field, to be in place for the return journey. When the first ridge has been marked, the poles are in line for the second, and so on. Thus, the whole of the field can be marked out without wasting time.

It is not easy to draw a straight furrow and a few hints may be helpful.

1. Set the plough to run correctly, whilst marking the headlands, so that it will not be necessary to look behind when making the ridge, as this can easily lead to curves developing.

2. Sit quite centrally over the tractor, looking down the bonnet, holding the steering wheel loosely in the hands.

3. Do not travel too quickly or each correction of the steering is magnified.

4. Do not move the head to keep the tractor in line with the poles. Always use the steering wheel!

After marking out all the ridges, adjust the plough for the second run for the particular type of ridge which is being made. The second run is then made up and down all the ridges. The third and fourth runs are treated similarly. Thus, all the ridges are made with only one plough adjustment for each run.

The ploughing of the lands can then be started. Starting at the first ridge, gather round it until the headland is reached

(Fig. 77). Move to the next ridge and gather round it until
$\frac{1}{4}$ land on each side is ploughed. There will now be $\frac{1}{2}$ land unploughed between the first two ridges (Fig. 78). This should be
cast, to make a finish in the centre (Fig. 79). Repeat the same

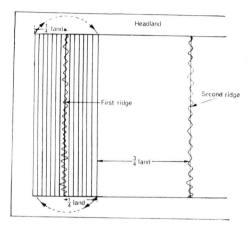

Fig. 77. Gathering round the first ridge

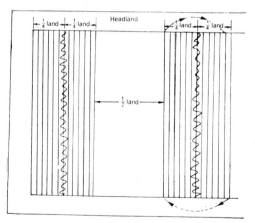

Fig. 78. Gathering round the second ridge

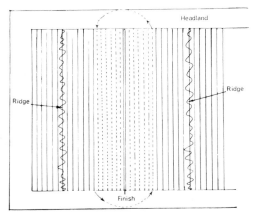

Fig. 79. Casting to a finish

process across the field and you will find that the tractor never has to travel more than $\frac{1}{2}$ land empty across the headland. This method is suitable for mounted ploughs, which can be turned and reversed easily.

To keep the surface of a field as level as possible, it is normal practice to make ridges in the finishes of the previous year. This means making the first ridge $\frac{3}{4}$ of a land from the headland. After gathering round this ridge for a $\frac{1}{4}$ land on either side, the $\frac{1}{2}$ land remaining unploughed toward the headland is cast to a finish. This finish will be along the first ridge of the previous year.

Ploughing round and round, or ploughing on the square

When using a mounted plough, it is quicker to plough a field round and round. It leaves the field in a more level condition than ploughing in lands. Also, when sowing winter wheat, it is possible for the drill to follow closely behind the plough. As with ploughing headlands, the field must be ploughed from the hedge to the centre one year, and the centre to the hedge the next year.

Ploughing the field from the hedge. The plough setting is similar to that used when ploughing the headland. A light front furrow is thrown into the hedge by driving the tractor as close to the hedge as possible. On the second circuit, the plough is levelled and the tractor driven to the hedge before raising the plough out of work. On subsequent circuits the plough is lifted when the front wheels of the tractor reach the furrow of the adjacent side. Then by turning sharply it is possible to avoid running on ploughed ground.

To finish the field, plough round and round, until the shortest side is about 25 m long. Then cast round the two sides which are nearer to being parallel. This produces a finish in the centre of the field and allows any curves in the other two sides to be ploughed in without difficulty.

Ploughing a field from the centre. It is first necessary to plough a miniature replica of the field in the centre. To do this, an assistant and a piece of rope some 25 m long are required. The assistant walks round the hedge and the tractor driver makes a small furrow 25 m out. The assistant then walks round the 25 m mark and a further furrow is drawn 25 m further into the field. This is repeated to the centre of the field, where the shape will be that of the field in miniature. A ridge is set up on the centre of this piece. Then it is ploughed along two sides only, until the innermost mark is reached. Ploughing is continued round and round. As the marks are reached, they serve as an indication of the accuracy of the ploughing.

Ploughing with a reversible plough

Despite the higher initial cost, reversible ploughs are increasing in popularity. They have several advantages.

1. Time is saved in ploughing, as there are no ridges or finishes to make.

2. The field is left level and therefore requires less working and gives a better surface for modern fast-moving and precision equipment.

3. There is much less travelling on the headlands. This

avoids the damage to soil structure which can result from conventional ploughing.

Having two sets of bodies, the ploughs are obviously heavier than normal ploughs. A tractor may require front wheel weights, to make it more stable when carrying the reversible plough. This weight can be used to improve wheel grip, when transferred through the tractor's hydraulic system to the tractor's rear wheels. It is important to ensure that the rear tyre pressures are correct and equal, to give wheel grip and even depth of ploughing.

Headland marks are usually made at the shortest ends of the fields. The ploughing follows the longest straight side. On the first run, the front furrow is set shallow, with the levelling lever on the tractor, which means the right-hand bodies are used. After the first run, the draft arms on the tractor are levelled. All subsequent levelling of the plough is achieved by the individual body adjustment on the plough. Also, after the first run, a check should be made to ensure that the furrows are of equal width, one adjustment generally controlling the front furrow width of both right- and left-hand bodies, and of equal depth. However carefully the width and depth are set, it is usually possible, with reversible ploughing, to pick out the work of the individual groups of bodies, because the furrows are smeared in opposite directions. Straight ploughing always gives a good appearance to the work, but the development of curves does not give the same problems as with conventional ploughing. The work is completed by ploughing the headlands in the opposite direction from that of the previous year.

Ploughing faults

A correctly set and maintained plough will operate in normal conditions with little adjustment or alteration. However, certain faults may develop due to wear, slackening of components, difficult operating conditions or inadequate maintenance. some of the more common faults, the factors which cause them and the way in which they might be overcome are as follows:

Symptom	*Cause*	*Action*
Poor penetration	Top link too long	Adjust to correct length
	Worn shares	Replace worn share(s)
	Coulters set too deep	Re-set coulters
	Hydraulic draft control incorrectly set	Check operation and setting
	Land unsuitable for ploughing	Wait until land fit to plough
Trash not buried	Disc coulters incorrectly set	Check and re-set
	Skim coulters absent or incorrectly adjusted	Fit or adjust skim coulters
	Furrow too deep for width	Reduce depth
	Unsuitable body	Change to suitable body
	Bodies not scouring	Remove adhering soil and polish mould-board
Broken furrow wall	Rear coulter set too close	Check and re-set
	Plough crabbing towards unploughed land	Check plough alignment
	Loose, recently-cultivated soil	Unavoidable
	Top link too short	Adjust to correct length
Stepped furrow wall Furrow slices standing on edge	Rear coulter too wide	Re-set coulter
	Unsuitable type of plough body	use a different plough
	Furrow too deep for width	Reduce depth
	Mouldboard too far out	Check mouldboard adjustment
	Skimmers or bodies not scouring	Scrape off adhering soil
	Top link too short	Adjust to correct length

Plough maintenance

Normal plough maintenance consists of replacement of shares and other soil contacting components when necessary and spraying bare surfaces with an anti-rust compound.

Before each season's work it is advisable to check that the plough has not been strained or distorted as may occur if it hit an obstruction when in work. This distortion may prevent the plough from producing even furrows despite all attempts at adjustment.

Most distortions occur in the leg of the plough in either or both of two directions. These are *vertical distortion,* where the leg and also the tip of the share are moved toward or away from the frame, and *horizontal (lateral) distortion,* where the point of the share moves laterally relative to its original position. Often distortion occurs in both these directions at the same time, but it is easiest to measure and correct each movement individually.

Vertical distortion. A measurement should be made from the underside of the tip of the share to the underside of the frame. It is essential that new shares are fitted, as unevenly worn shares could give a false picture. The correct distance may be given in the manufacturers' instruction manual, and all the bodies on a plough should conform to this. In some cases the angle of each body may be adjustable in relation to the beam and slight distortion may be corrected by this adjustment. In cases where this is not possible the leg should be straightened by a service agent as they are frequently heat-treated and skill is needed to avoid loss of strength. Where the correct distance is not given one assumes that any measurement different from the normal of the others is defective.

It is particularly important, with reversible ploughs, that the measurements of both sets of bodies are similar.

Horizontal distortion. With a two-furrow plough the usual method of checking horizontal distortion is to lay the plough on a level concrete floor, make a chalk mark using the landside

of each body as a straight edge. Remove the plough and extend
the chalk marks with a straight edge. The chalk marks should
be parallel and equal distances apart. The same approach can
be adopted with a multi-furrow plough but more often these
are checked by measuring the distance between similar points
on the mouldboard with a tape, in particular the distance
between the tops of the mouldboards at the front and at the
back. The distorted component should be returned to the service agent for straightening.

Field checking. A simple means of checking vertical and horizontal distortion in the field on a plough with three or more
furrows is to line up by eye the points of the shares when the
plough is in a raised position. The points should lie in a straight
line. If they are not it might be due to distortion or uneven
wear of the shares, and this should be borne in mind when
checking. Another method is to stretch a piece of string between a point on the top of the mouldboard of the rear furrow
and a similar point on the front furrow. All intermediate
mouldboards should touch the string at a similar place along
their length.

Frames. These may become distorted due to impact and to
check them a string should be stretched both along the length
and across the width at different points. Each frame member
should just touch the string. There must, of course, be at least
one section of frame between the outer two at the ends of the
string.

13. Cultivating Equipment

An important factor which influences the yield of crops is the arrangement of the physical structure or *tilth* of the soil in which the crops are grown. The tilth is produced as a result of a series of cultivating operations which may commence following the harvesting of the previous crop and proceed until the new crop is sown. Further operations may be carried out prior to its emergence and during its growth to the point of harvesting and these are often referred to as '*after cultivations*'. The type of operation carried out will depend on the crop being grown, the type of soil, the moisture content of the soil, and the time of year. The selection of the most suitable cultivating implements in the correct order is a skill which requires considerable experience. However, a knowledge of the effects of different cultivating implements on the soil is essential before attempting to produce a tilth. These effects may be broadly classified as follows:

1. A bursting and loosening of a compacted layer;
2. an inversion of a surface layer;
3. reduction of the size of clods;
4. the sorting of clod sizes;
5. soil smoothing or levelling of the surface layer;
6. consolidation.

Most implements have more than one effect on the soil, but their selection is normally made for their main effect. Not all cultivating implements are used for their effect on the soil and are primarily designed for other functions such as the control of weeds or the removal of the dead material from grassland.

Loosening

Soil gradually settles and compacts when a crop is growing and the first operation in preparation for a subsequent crop is to loosen this compacted layer. The loosening encourages weed seeds and any remaining seeds of the previous crop to germinate, and thus reduce their chances of causing competition to subsequent crops. In practice the mouldboard plough is often the first implement used to loosen the soil and in so doing it has the additional effect of burying the surface trash. However, the implement designed specifically for loosening is the *tine*. It consists of a bar up to 1 m in length and angled either vertically or up to $45°$ forward. At the tip of the tine there is a hardened steel *share*. The tine penetrates the ground due to its angle of approach and as it is drawn through the soil it produces a shattering effect with cracks occuring up to 0.5 m away from the tine throughout its length. Some soil may flow up the face of the tine to the surface if it is inclined forward. The optimum effect occurs when the soil is dry.

Many arrangements and sizes of tines are used on cultivating implements according to the type of loosening operation required. Where two or three long tines are used the operation is described as *sub-soiling*. The aim of this operation is to loosen the layer of soil immediately *below* the normal cultivating depth to encourage drainage and aeration. They are drawn through the soil about 1 m apart and require a high draft force.

A *chisel plough* (Fig. 80) has more tines and each is shorter. It operates to a depth of 0.3 m and is used to loosen the soil after a previous crop. The increased number of tines produces a rough surface to the ground and allows more weathering of exposed soil to take place. It is generally used more than once over a piece of ground and the subsequent operations are carried out at an angle to the original direction, to produce the maximum loosening effect. To reduce the risk of damage through striking obstructions, shear bolts may be fitted in the shank of the tine.

Where previously loosened soil has settled or where consolidation has occurred through other operations a *cultivator* may be used. This has more tines and each is shorter than those on a chisel plough. It operates at a depth which is less than that initially loosened. The soil immediately below the culti-

Fig. 80. Chisel plough

Fig. 81. Spring-tine cultivator

vator point may be consolidated depending on its moisture content. Two types of cultivator are made, *rigid* and *spring-tine* (Fig. 81). Both operate in a similar manner, but the spring-tine is less suitable for harder conditions as it tends to flex backwards and its angle of approach moves away from the optimum. This can be observed where cultivators are used on compacted soil for *stubble cleaning*. Stubble cleaning is an operation carried out immediately after harvesting a cereal crop. A rigid or spring-tine cultivator is drawn through the soil at a depth of 100 to 140 mm. The loosening effect creates conditions for germination of both lost grains and weed seeds. Having germinated they are more easily killed by either ploughing or subsequent cultivating operations.

Cultivators often have secondary effects on the soil in that they may allow some of the smaller soil particles to flow into the spaces between the larger particles and hence they have a sorting and consolidating effect. They may also break some clods into smaller particles depending on the strength and moisture content of the clods.

Inversion

This operation is carried out mainly to obtain control of weeds and to remove surface trash which could interfere with other crop-producing operations. The *mouldboard plough* is the implement used for complete inversion, but where partial inversion is required to combat wind or water erosion the *disc plough* may be used. The use of both have been fully discussed in Chapter 12.

Reduction of clod size

The purpose of these operations is to provide the most suitable conditions for the germination of seed. Several means are available to do this, and in general the selection of the particular equipment will depend on the crops to be grown, the soil type and its moisture content.

The exposed surface of the soil is normally easier to break

down due to the action of the weather on the furrows and operations are arranged to work from the surface downwards to the depth required for the particular crops. This avoids bringing unweathered material to the surface and produces the desired tilth with the fewest possible operations and at the lowest cost. Reduction in clod size can be achieved by various operations now described.

Crushing. Where clods are hard and dry the most suitable treatment is to crush them. This is carried out by using a *roll*. There are two types of these. The *plain* or *flat* roll consists of an iron cylinder or cylinders sometimes filled with concrete or water. Where it is divided into three or four lengths it allows a differential turning to occur when cornering. The *Cambridge* or *ring roll* consists of a series of ridged iron rings fitted on a shaft (Fig. 82). These rings leave a series of small grooves on the surface of the land.

Rolls are made in various widths and can be drawn singly or as a gang. Their crushing ability depends on the weight and to some extent the diameter in that the smaller-diameter roller of the same weight has the greater crushing effect. They are sold according to their weight per unit of length. The ring roll has a more even effect than the flat roll, as the rings are a loose fit on the shaft and can follow more closely the ground contours. Rolls affect only the clods lying on the surface. Due to their weight rolls have a *consolidating* effect on the soil surface and their use for this purpose is discussed later.

Cutting. Where the surface clods are not too hard they may be reduced in size by cutting. The *disc harrow* is normally used for this purpose (Fig. 83). It consists of a series of concave discs and spacers fitted on a shaft and supported by bearings at either end. Normally, four 'gangs' of discs make up a set. As the discs are drawn over the ground their weight and the knife-like edge to the disc cuts the clods into smaller particles. Their depth of penetration can be varied by altering their angle in relation to the depth of travel. The greater the angle the greater the penetration and the more draft needed to pull them.

Fig. 82. Cambridge roll

Fig. 83. Disc harrow

Their weight concentrated on the edges of the discs has a consolidating effect on the layers immediately below their working depth, and for this reason they are ideal to use on freshly ploughed grassland where it is essential not to expose freshly turned-in trash. When used in these conditions it is normal, in the first discing, to follow the direction of the furrows and have little angle on the gangs. After several passes of discs it is often necessary to carry out a loosening operation to overcome the consolidation effect of the discs and tractor wheels. The sidethrust on the bearings caused by the angle of the discs will produce rapid wear unless they are kept well greased.

Disintegration. With the advent of the I.C. engine, power-driven cultivating equipment has been produced. By having rapidly moving soil-contacting components it is possible to disintegrate clods by subjecting them to a sudden impact blow. Almost all the machines currently used for this purpose have the soil-contacting components attached to a horizontal shaft. The design of the contacting components varies between machines and is under constant development. One of the most common machines is the rotary cultivator. This machine,

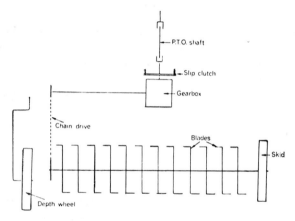

Fig. 84. Plan of rotary cultivator

which can be from 1 to 2·5 m wide and works to a depth of 0·2 m, consists of a series of L-shaped blades mounted on a shaft (Fig. 84). The shaft is driven from the tractor p.t.o. through a gearbox and slip clutch. The machine is generally mounted and the depth is limited by a landwheel. A skid may be fitted at the opposite side from the landwheel to prevent the rotor digging too deeply, should the wheels drop into a hollow.

The rotor is covered by a canopy with an adjustable shield at the rear. It is driven in the same direction as the tractor wheels, and the blades chop the soil out in lumps and throw them against the canopy and shield where they break along their natural joints of least resistance. The result produced will depend on the soil type and its moisture content. If too wet the structure may be damaged and this will diminish crop yields, whilst if too dry the impact may be inadequate to do more than produce pea-sized clods. The effect can be varied by controlling the forward and rotor speed together with the position of the canopy. The fewer chops per metre and the higher the shield, the coarser the resulting tilth.

As the rotary cultivator can operate to a depth of 0·2 m it produces a deep tilth of small soil particles unlike the previous implements discussed which tend to reduce clods on the surface only. It is frequently used immediately prior to planting potatoes where a good depth of loose soil is needed to cover them and form ridges.

Over the years machines with the soil-contacting components attached to a vertical shaft have been used, and it is likely that with modifications in design they could again become more widely used. These machines have a stirring action very similar to that of a domestic food mixer.

Sorting clods

When producing a seedbed it is often necessary to sort out clods of varying sizes and to leave those which are difficult to reduce in size on the surface. A tined implement is normally used for this operation as its action when flowing through the soil causes the smaller particles to filter downwards thus leaving the larger on the surface. The depth of the tilth required will determine the type of tined implement selected. Some implements previously described for loosening operations are used but they may have more tines fitted and operate at a reduced depth.

The smallest type of rigid-tine cultivator is called a *spike harrow*. It has a series of short vertical tines about 150 mm in length. The tines are usually drawn to a point, and they do not have a separate share. One end of the tine is threaded and a nut fastens it to the frame (Fig. 85). Owing to their low weight harrows are used in loose soil and they have a dual effect of both sorting and levelling. They may also be used behind

Fig. 85. Spike-toothed harrow

grain drills to ensure that all the seeds are covered by soil or, in the spring, on autumn-sown cereals to break up the surface cap and create a tilth.

Mounted versions are particularly suitable for raking together rhizomatous weeds, which may have been brought to the surface by previous operations, and depositing them in windrows.

A recent introduction is the *reciprocating* harrow. This harrow is driven from the p.t.o. and consists of two or four bars of tines which are oscillated laterally by the p.t.o. shaft (Fig. 86). These provide a more vigorous action but will only break clods which are weak. They are very effective in compacting loose soil, but should only be used in relatively dry conditions or they will greatly reduce the permeability of the soil to air and water.

Fig. 86. Reciprocating harrow

Smoothing

Where precision seeding equipment is used it is essential to
have a smooth surface to the soil to ensure that each seeding
unit operates efficiently. Similarly with the development of
faster moving arable and grassland machinery, smoothing
is becoming an increasingly important operation in most seedbed preparations. The achievement of this smooth surface is
contributed to by nearly all operations after ploughing in that
any wide implement with components running below the soil
surface tends to push soil from the high places to the low places.
The implements having this effect are disc harrows, spike
harrows and cultivators.

However, some implements are designed with the specific
purpose of smoothing and levelling the surface. The *dutch
harrow* is the most common example of this. It consists of a
heavy rectangular frame, one side of which has a series of short
tines. In operation the tines loosen some soil and the wooden

frame pushes soil from the high places, depositing it in the low places.

Consolidation

The implement used primarily for consolidation is the *roll*, which has been previously described. Its consolidating effect depends on its weight per unit length and it is applied to the surface layers.

To obtain the optimum effect it is essential that it is used correctly and some examples of its application will illustrate this.

The most common use of the roll is to produce a firm tilth either just before or just after sowing. It is particularly useful on light land which has been made fluffy by previous operations. The rolling reduces the rate of evaporation from the soil and encourages more rapid germination. It should only be used when the soil is reasonably dry and never when the soil sticks to it.

Newly ploughed land, particularly when dry, requires consolidation to prevent buried trash from being exposed by subsequent operations. This rolling should be carried out in the direction of the furrow to keep the draft requirement to a minimum. If attempting to roll across the furrow, the uneven draft created as the roll climbs the furrow slices will cause tractor wheelslip which may expose the trash.

Spring rolling of autumn-sown cereals is necessary to break the surface cap and consolidate the soil where it has become soft as a result of frost action. It is essential that the tractor is not overloaded or the resulting wheelslip will cause permanent damage to the young plants. This is most likely to occur when driving up a hill, and so this should be avoided wherever possible. It is also important for the same reason to avoid sharp turns.

Fields which are intended to be cut for hay or silage are normally rolled with a flat roll in the spring to push any stones below the surface. This will prevent them causing damage to harvesting machinery.

It is important to realize that a consolidating effect is produced by the passage through the soil of some implements when being used for a different purpose. This effect is not always beneficial and is generally just below the working depth of the implement and it may require action to alleviate the cumulative effect of this consolidation over a period of years. For example a plough pan can develop if land is mouldboard ploughed to to the same depth each year. The formation of this pan is assisted by the action of the tractor wheels slipping in the furrow bottom. Soil drainage may be impaired and a subsoiling operation becomes necessary to break up the pan. Similarly the edge of a disc on a disc harrow has a consolidating effect on the layers immediately below the working depth. If several discings are required the layer of loose soil will become shallower, and it may be necessary to carry out a loosening operation to restore the working depth.

Row-crop equipment

Some farm crops are grown in rows. Special equipment is used to cultivate the soil between the rows without damage to the crop. For accurate work the implement must be set carefully and the driver be skilled (Fig. 87). Row-crop equipment may take various forms: cultivator tines, weeder tines, ridging bodies, hoes. It is usually mounted on a toolbar frame which is carried on the three-point linkage of the tractor. It might also be mid-mounted or front-mounted.

Tractor hoes. Weed control in row crops is frequently obtained by drawing a horizontal blade just below the surface of the soil. This blade penetrates by having a slight downward angle and it cuts the soil and those weeds with thick stalks and roots. Shallow-rooted seedling weeds have their root systems disturbed and will dry out and die before they can re-establish themselves.

Two different *hoe* blades are used:

1. 'A' hoe. This moves down the centre between the rows loosening the soil.

2. 'L' hoe. These follow the 'A' hoe and control the weeds between the rows of the crops and the centre of the row. The vertical ends of these blades can easily be seen and therefore driven down the row accurately.

When crop seedlings are very young they are susceptible to damage, as a result of covering with soil. To prevent this, *discs* are placed between the 'A' hoe and the 'L' hoe. The discs

Fig. 87. Steerage hoe

are set as close together on each side of the row as the soil conditions and skill of the operator permit, without damage to the crop. By angling the discs the seedlings can be left set up on a small ridge. This facilitates hand-hoeing. Discs are not normally used after the first hoeing.

Hoes may be rigidly attached to the toolbar or they may be spring-loaded. The latter method gives better results where a wide toolbar is used, or where the field is not level, as the springs compensate for the unevenness of the ground. If there are hard patches, the spring-loaded hoe tends to slide over the ground, whereas the rigid one would have more weight for penetration. Before satisfactory work can be done, it is vital that the toolbar and tractor should be 'set up' correctly. The following is a simple description of how this can be done.

The fundamental feature is that the rows hoed must synchronize with each bout of the seeder unit and they should be the same or half the number sown. Thus a six-row seeder will require a six-row hoe and a ten-row seeder will require a ten- or five-row hoe. The tractor wheels should travel along the centre between the rows and to do this the wheel width (measured from the centre of the tyres) is always a multiple of the row width, within the available setting of the tractor. For instance a crop being grown in 0·5 m rows requires the wheels to be set at 1·5 m. Three rows will then pass in between the wheels the centre row being directly under the centre line of the tractor (Fig. 88).

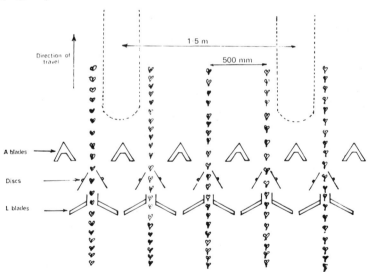

Fig. 88. Setting of tractor rear-mounted hoe

Having adjusted the tractor wheels the toolbar is connected to the tractor. The position of the row should be marked on the toolbar, working out from the centre. The hoe and discs should then be fitted also working from the centre. To take an example of the 0·5 m rows again, the first two 'A' hoes are fitted 0·25 m on either side of the centre line. Further 'A' hoes are fitted 0·5 m from these. The two 'A' hoes behind the tractor wheel should be set 20 to 30 mm deeper than the others to reduce the effect of compaction of the wheels. The discs are fitted up to 50 mm on either side of the row. Finally the 'L' hoes are attached, slightly wider and shallower than the discs. An 'A' blade is fitted on the outside of the extreme rows as indicated in Fig. 88.

Final adjustments are carried out in the field. These will include lateral and fore-and-aft levelling. Where depth is controlled by wheels they are set to run behind the tractor wheels.

Steerage hoes, which are rear-mounted, require an operator in addition to the tractor driver. The operator is able to guide the hoe within certain limits to avoid damage to the plants. Even so, careful driving is needed, with the tractor front wheels keeping in the centre of the space between the rows. Steerage is achieved either through the depth of wheels in contact with the ground, or by direct linkage with the tractor. In the former, there must be sufficient weight on the wheels to permit turning. This can be achieved by adjustment to the top link.

Front-mounted hoes and *mid-mounted* hoes have the advantage of only requiring the tractor driver as they are rigidly connected to the tractor. The rate of work is often lower than with steerage hoes. Front-mounted hoes are not popular, as the work is rather distant from the driver. Any movement of the steering wheel is magnified in the hoes. Mid-mounted hoes are becoming popular, as the driver is close to the work, and the effect in turning the steering wheel is reduced at the hoes, resulting in more accurate work. The hoe is lifted and put into work by a simple hydraulic cylinder, coupled to the tractor hydraulic system. The lack of ground clearance of many general purpose tractors can reduce the scope of mid-mounted hoes in the height of crop in which they can work without causing damage. High-clearance conversions to overcome this problem are available. Most tractors have a mounting pad to which a hoe can be fitted.

When hoeing the forward speed should be low and related to soil conditions, to avoid crop damage. It is advisable to watch only one row with an occasional glance at the other hoe blades, to ensure they are not fouled with trash. The discs on the row being watched can be set slightly closer than the others.

Use of cultivating equipment

As already mentioned, the selection and operation of equipment for working in the field is largely a matter of experience. A few general points in the use of equipment are worth remembering.

1. Care should be taken to level mounted equipment both laterally and fore and aft when it is at its normal working position.

2. The correct use of the tractor's hydraulic system, particularly with respect to the response control where fitted, will give an increased rate of working.

3. All mounted implements should be raised when turning sharp corners. Even with trailed equipment sharp turns should be avoided as this puts unnecessary strain on the implement and indeed, with harrows, there is the danger of a serious accident if the draw chain is caught on the rear wheel, lifting the harrow on to the operator.

4. Where adequate power and traction is available the use of implements in tandem will increase the rate of working and reduce the risk of light soil drying out.

5. Avoid working any deeper than required for the crops being grown and take care not to raise unnecessary clods to the surface. This can be achieved by working from the top downwards with the first working being shallow. On some of the heavier soils, particularly after a mild winter, rolling in the direction of the furrow has much to

commend it as this prevents clods forming from the crests of the furrows.

6. Land should not be cultivated when it is too wet or serious damage will be caused to the soil structure. This is particularly important after heavy showers of rain.

7. The speed of the operation has a considerable effect on the finished result.

14. Fertilizer Distributors and Seeding Equipment

Fertilizer distributors

For successful crop production, the crop plants must have adequate plant foods available. These plant foods are often applied to the soil, and hence the crop, in the form of fertilizers by *fertilizer distributors*. A fertilizer distributor should be capable of:

1. a wide range in the rate of application, from as low as 40 kg up to 4000 kg/ha;

2. applying different types of material accurately and evenly, fine powders, crystals, granules;

3. easy alteration of the application rate;

4. easy dismantling and cleaning, as metal parts are quickly corroded by fertilizers.

While various types and makes of fertilizer distributor exist, certain parts are common to all: a hopper to hold the fertilizer (usually between 200 and 2000 kg), an agitator to keep the fertilizer flowing, and finally a distributing mechanism. Fertilizer distributors are classified by the type of distributing mechanism employed. The most common of these mechanisms merit study in some detail.

Plate and flicker (Fig. 89a). This consists of a series of slowly revolving cast iron dishes or plates, which carry a layer of fertilizer under an adjustable 'gate' from the inside of the hopper to the outside, where it is flicked from the plate by a series of fingers on a rapidly rotating shaft. The rate of application is varied by altering the speed of the plates through the gears at one end of the machine or by raising or lowering the gates, hence altering the depth of fertilizer on the plate. For spreading very fine powders and other free-flowing fertilizers, such

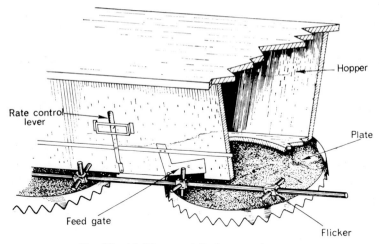

Fig. 89. (a) Plate and flicker mechanism.

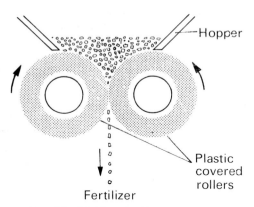

Fig. 89. (b) Twin roller mechanism

as basic slag, more even spreading can often be obtained by using a high plate speed and low gate opening. Poor-flowing fertilizers, lumpy or damp materials, are best spread with a low plate speed and a high gate opening.

The width of these machines is variable, the largest of them being wider than farm gateways. These are swivelled round on a two-wheeled bogey for transport, but in common with other plate and flicker mechanisms, they are driven from the land wheels. With narrow distributors, the mark left by the wheel of the distributor gives a guide to the tractor driver and prevents overlapping. On the larger machines, it is normal to drag a weight from the end of the hopper, particularly on arable land, to guide the tractor driver.

These distributors give very even spreading, although high speeds have to be avoided on bumpy ground as quantities tend to become dislodged from the plates and fall in concentrated patches, followed by unsown strips, until the plates are refilled. This attribute of even spreading makes them suitable for sowing grass seed, except when it is very windy, causing the seed to blow off the plates.

They can, on the whole, be completely dismantled without special tools, for cleaning. Owing to the many gear teeth on the plates, complete cleaning is quite a long task.

Twin roller (Fig. 89 (b)). This mechanism was developed in order to allow use of higher forward speeds without any loss in performance. It consists of two plastic-covered steel rollers running the full length of the hopper. The hopper and the rollers are usually divided into 1 m sections. The rollers turn toward each other and convey and distribute the fertilizer in a thin, even curtain along their length. The application rate is controlled by varying the speed of the rollers through a gearbox.

In addition to the plate and flicker and twin roller, there are other mechanisms used in machines which spread fertilizer along the full width of the machine. A current example is the *rotary agitator* (Fig. 90) which positively forces the fertilizer through adjustable feed gates in the bottom of the hopper and therefore spreads quite accurately at speed on bumpy ground.

Spinning disc (Fig. 91). This consists of a power-driven disc fitted with several radial fins or vanes. Fertilizer falls from the

Fig. 90. Rotary agitator

hopper to the centre of the disc through an adjustable gate, and is then accelerated down the vanes and thrown off the disc by centrifugal force. The driving shaft of the disc is often continued into the hopper, forming the agitator. There are other mechanisms which use centrifugal force to distribute the fertilizer. One

Fig. 91. Spinning disc distributor

of these consists of an oscillating tube or spout, the fertilizer being fed into the pivoted end and then thrown out in an arc, with the movement of the tube. Another employs a fan which blows air down a series of tubes which point out radially at the back. The fertilizer is fed into the fan and blown through these tubes.

These distributors are relatively cheap to purchase and because they have a wide spread are able to cover large areas in a day. The smaller ones are tractor mounted and carry 400 to 500 kg, while trailer versions can carry up to 2500 kg.

These machines have certain performance characteristics which it is necessary to understand in order to obtain the optimum results. The width of spread is controlled by the disc speed and it must be kept constant when operating. The rate of spread is controlled by both feed-gate opening and forward speed. The distribution of fertilizer falls off towards the edges of the width of spread and to obtain an even distribution across the field there should be a certain amount of overlap. The manufacturers' instructions must be followed very carefully particularly in relation to height of disc, levelling of disc, forward speed and disc speed. The manufacturers may give recommendations on spread width and overlap but the physical condition of the fertilizer may have a marked effect on both of these characteristics. It is good practice to check the recommendations with a new machine or whenever a change is made in application rate or fertilizer type.

An accurate method of doing this involves the use of a series of collecting trays each one being 1 m long by 300 mm wide, with sides 100 mm high. The trays are arranged transversely across the spreading width leaving a space for the tractor wheels. The machine is set according to recommendation and driven at normal operating speed across the trays and some distance beyond. The fertilizer is then collected from each tray and placed in a series of transparent tubes. The relative heights in the tubes shows whether the distribution is even on either side of the centre line and by estimating the overlap it is possible to see how even the total application rate will be. Having calculated the height of the average application rate the amount in one test-tube can be weighed and knowing the area of the tray the application rate can be calculated. This simple test will avoid the striping effect which so often occurs.

Star wheel (Fig. 92). This distributing mechanism is not used on machines solely for fertilizer distribution but is found

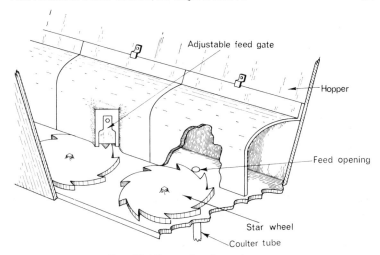

Fig. 92. Star wheel mechanism

on the fertilizer side of a combined grain and fertilizer drill. A series of star wheels rotate in the bottom of the hopper. The fertilizer is carried between and on the teeth of the wheels, under an adjustable gate from the hopper, then falls down a hole in the coulter tube, joining up with the grain run. The star wheels act as agitators and the teeth break up lumps. A small knocker drops on the teeth of the star wheel, to prevent fertilizer building up. To protect the remainder of the mechanism, should it seize up, it is driven via a shear pin.

Control of the application rate is by the height of the gate and the speed of the star wheel. There is also a separate adjustment on each gate to allow it to be raised and lowered independently of the others. This enables any wear in the raising mechanism to be counteracted. The mechanism can be dismantled quite easily for cleaning, but care must be taken to see that it is reassembled in the correct order.

Maintenance of fertilizer distributors. Before filling with fertilizer, the whole machine should be lubricated and the sowing rate set according to the manufacturers' recommendations. The machine is put in gear and pulled *by hand* or, if this is not possible, operated slowly under power to check that all parts are free and run correctly.

Due to the corrosive nature of chemical fertilizers, careful maintenance is necessary to prevent rapid deterioration of the machine and, consequently, a short life.

The first part of this maintenance is carried out during seasonal use of the machine, and consists of daily lubrication before work and after each day's work of emptying the hopper and storing the machine out of the rain.

The second part is carried out at the end of a season's use and consists of the following. First, dismantle the spreading mechanism altogether and remove all traces of fertilizer, either by high pressure steam, water or air or, if none of these is available, by thorough brushing with a wire brush or scrubbing with hot soda solution. Finally, coat all components with rust preventative and reassemble, noting carefully all parts that need replacement.

Seeding equipment

Having prepared a suitable tilth and ensured adequate plant foods will be available to the crop, the placing of the seeds in the soil at the correct rate, depth and distance apart is done by carefully designed seeding equipment. This equipment must be capable of:

1. accurate sowing of different sized seeds—small seeds such as turnips or kale, and large seeds such as beans;

2. a wide range of seeding rates from as low as 1·5 kg/ha for kale, up to 250 kg/ha for beans;

3. placing the seed at the required depth, from 10 to 100 mm and covering it with soil;

4. working at reasonable speeds, without damaging the seed.

These requirements demand a lot of any one machine and while machines are made which meet these requirements, it is often more satisfactory to use seeding equipment designed

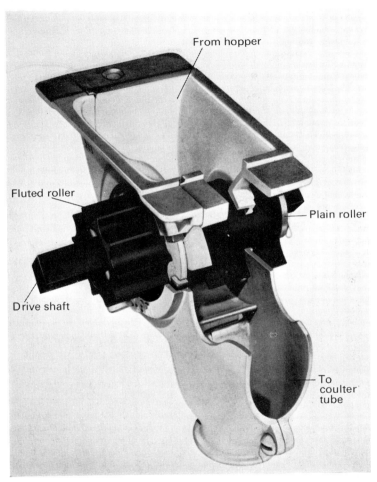

Fig. 93. External force feed

specifically for certain seed types where the acreage grown warrants it.

Grain drills

These are very versatile and can be used for a wide range of seeding work. In essence a grain drill consists of a hopper to hold the seed, a metering and feeding device beneath the hopper, connected to the coulter tubes, and planting and covering mechanism. The number of coulters varies with the size of the drill. The sowing width of a drill is the number of coulters multiplied by the distance between them.

A common metering device is the *external force feed* (Fig. 93). This consists of a roller, part of which is fluted, rotating in a housing below the hopper. Grain is carried from the hopper to the coulter tubes between the flutes of the roller. An adjustable flap may be fitted round part of the circumference of the roller, to permit different sizes of seed to be sown. The seeding rate is controlled by the amount of fluted roller exposed in the housing. The remainder of the space is occupied by the plain section of roller. If the maximum length of flute does not produce a sufficiently heavy sowing rate, the speed of the fluted roller can be increased by changing sprockets or gears in the drive.

The *internal force feed* mechanism consists of a series of flanged discs, each fitting in a housing carried below the hopper (Fig. 94). Each flange is fluted on the inside and one flange is broader than the other. A flap inside the hopper directs the grain into either the broader (*coarse*) or the narrower (*fine*) side of the disc. The disc is driven by a square shaft which passes through the housing and as it revolves some seed is carried round by the flutes and falls into the coulter tubes. The sowing rate may be altered either by using the coarse or fine side or by altering the speed of the discs. This is done by means of a *face gear*, a large flat gear with concentric circles of teeth. The driving gear is moved across these circles of teeth, each circle being a different gear.

A more modern metering mechanism is the *studded-wheel*

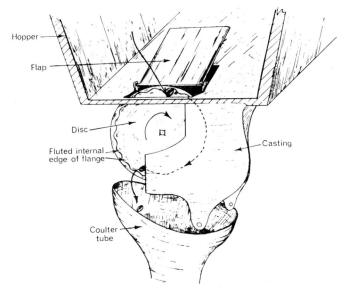

Hopper

Flap

Disc

Fluted internal edge of flange

Casting

Coulter tube

Fig. 94. Internal force feed

(Fig. 95). This consists of a shaft on which are arranged a series of studs. The seeds are carried round by the studs and eventually fall into the coulter tubes. The mechanism is suitable for high forward speeds. The seed rate is adjusted by varying the speed of the roller. Different seed sizes are accommodated by altering the clearance of the flap underneath the roller. This flap also enables the hopper to be emptied easily.

After the seed has been metered, it falls down the coulter tubes into a groove or furrow, formed by the coulters. These are usually discs, as they are suitable for most soil types and conditions. They are able to withstand blockage by surface trash or clods. On very stony ground the disc coulter is often replaced by a cast-iron shoe-shaped coulter known as a *Suffolk coulter*. The seeds are covered by soil falling back into place, after it has been disturbed. Each disc is attached by a lever

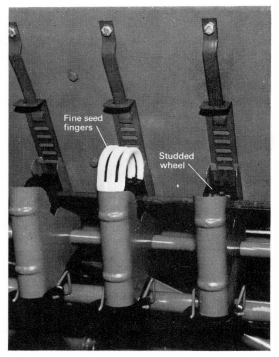

Fig. 95. Studded wheel

to the crossbar at the front of the drill and pressed into the ground by a spring. It is able to move independently of others, and rides over stones or other objects without damage. The depth of sowing is controlled by twisting the crossbar which alters the compression of the springs. The soil type and condition influences how far a particular spring pressure will cause the disc to penetrate. The discs are normally spaced 175 mm apart but on some external force feed types the spacing is reduced to 110 mm.

The drive to the feeding mechanism is taken from the wheels. In some drills each wheel drives through a ratchet to allow a differential effect when cornering to ensure that drive is taken from the faster of the two wheels. The clicking of the ratchets when cornering is probably a familiar sound. On other types, usually narrower models, each wheel drives half the mechanisms. The whole series of coulters may be either raised or lowered by a self-lift mechanism driven from the wheels or on the latest models by hydraulic linkage or hydraulic rams on each wheel, operated by the tractor's hydraulic system. As the coulters rise out of the ground the sowing mechanism is automatically disengaged.

Before drilling a field it is often advisable to check the sowing rate of the machine. This is called *calibration*. The wheels of the grain drill are jacked up and with a small quantity of seed in the hopper, the mechanism is put into gear and the wheels turned by hand equivalent to one-tenth of a hectare. The seed is then gathered up and weighed. The mechanism will, of course, have been carefully set beforehand according to the makers' instructions. The number of turns of the wheel is found from the following formula:

$$\text{number of turns for } \tfrac{1}{10} \text{ ha} = \frac{1000 \text{ m}^2}{\text{Sowing width in metres} \times \text{circumference of wheel in metres}}$$

Operation of a grain drill. It is most important to get correct matching of the bouts to avoid overlapping or double drilling and to prevent gaps between the bouts. On wide grain drills this is obtained by markers and these should be set so that when driving the front wheel of the tractor on the mark made by the marker on the previous bout the outside row of grain is the distance between the coulters from the adjoining bout (Fig. 96). The setting can be obtained by placing the marker away from the outside coulter a distance equal to the distance from the front wheel of the tractor to the outside coulter, plus one coulter spacing. Final adjustment will depend on the angle of the marker disc and the particular preference of the tractor

Fig. 96. Grain drill with markers

driver. This can be done as the drill is driven into the field and the wheel marks appear under the coulters.

Fields may be drilled in one of two ways, either 'round and round' or from one side to the other. Whichever method is used, it is important to remember that the machine has to move 2 to 3 m after the coulters have been dropped before the grain reaches the coulters and that drilling ceases immediately the trip rope is operated. Should the machine stop for any reason when in work, a gap will result as it moves off and the careful operator will always throw a handful of grain out to fill in the gap. Reversing with the coulters down must be avoided, as this will force the coulters into the ground and block the spouts.

Drilling from the centre is commonly used in conjunction with ploughing round and round, particularly for winter cereals, where it has the advantage that the land, which is likely to be getting progressively wetter, is cultivated and then drilled from the centre and thus the headlands receive less consolidating by tractors and implements turning. It is also a quick method. The area ploughed to form a miniature of the whole field is drilled first lengthways, before proceeding to drill round and round.

When drilling from one side of the field to the other, it has to be decided whether the headlands should be drilled first or last. It is easier and more common to drill them first but often in the autumn, when the weather is uncertain, it might be advisable to drill the field as it is cultivated and drill the headlands last. Where the headlands are drilled first, a start is made from one corner and the drill is driven as close to the hedge or fence as possible. The operator will have checked that the hectare meter is set at zero and that all spouts are running. The corners are taken without lifting the drill and the operator scattering grain into the extreme corner. The driver must keep the outside wheel of the drill on level ground and not let it climb up on to the hedgeside or the coulters will be lifted out of the ground and the corn will not be covered. On the second and subsequent circuits, the drill should be lifted on corners, then backed to make square corners. Five circuits should be made for the headland as this gives adequate room for turning the drill at the end of each bout.

Drilling is begun down the longest or straightest side of the field. Where the field has been ploughed recently and little working done to the furrows, the drilling should be across the furrows, to prevent the grain falling between the furrows and being covered too deeply. This is not as important where the furrow is completely inverted.

The operator on the drill should check each coulter at the beginning of each bout and see that the markers are turned at the end. The driver should make loop turns, the headland of five widths being enough for this to be done. Most grain drills will operate satisfactorily over a wide range of forward speeds. It is important to sow the grain as quickly as possible, so full tractor power should be used to get a forward speed of up to 9 km/h or, with some of the most modern drills, up to 16 km/h.

The operator should make an early check on the quantities of grain and fertilizer in the hopper and the area sown. It must be distributed evenly in the hopper, as some of the star wheel types of fertilizer distributor tend to push the fertilizer to one end of the hopper. When replenishing the hoppers, care should be taken that lumps of fertilizer are broken and that no pieces of string or labels from grain sacks are allowed to mix with the grain in the hopper, as they cause blockage. Checks should also be made, from time to time, on the rates of sowing, so that there will be sufficient to cover the field. It is always better to cut the rate down a little for the last few hectares, than to run out with half a hectare to sow.

Maintenance. At the end of each season's use, the hopper should be emptied and cleaned. If it is a combine drill, the fertilizer side should be treated in a manner similar to that described for fertilizer distributors. The coulter tubes should be removed and stored separately. If they are rubber, they should be kept out of strong daylight, and if metal they should be coated with rust preventative. Finally, the discs should be cleaned and coated, to prevent corrosion.

Precision seeders (Fig. 97)

In the production of many row crops, much time and money is spent removing unwanted plants. With the availability of seed of reliable germination arose the possibility of sowing crops at a lower seeding rate, so reducing the labour involved in thinning. Special drills have been designed to sow these low rates and to place seeds individually at predetermined spacings. These drills are known as precision or placement drills.

The machine consists of several units mounted on a toolbar. Each unit has a hopper, metering mechanism, sowing and covering mechanism and sows one row. The hopper holds the seed and often leads to a small seed chamber which keeps the seed at a constant pressure over the metering mechanism.

This metering mechanism may consist of a belt with a series of holes or a light alloy wheel with seed cells in its periphery the size of the seed to be sown. As the belt or the selector wheel rotates in the bottom of the seed chamber, a seed drops into each hole or cell. It is important that correctly graded seed should be used to avoid more than one seed dropping into the hole or cell, or projecting from them, resulting in seed damage.

A rubber-covered repeller wheel rotating against the metering mechanism prevents any seed not in a cell from being carried out of the chamber. The seeds are carried to the lower part of the machine and ejected down a small tube into a furrow in the

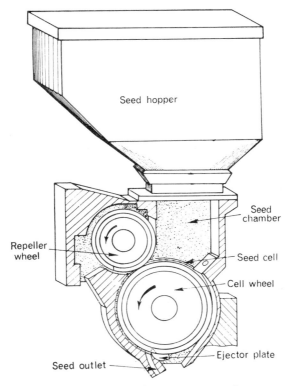

Fig. 97. Section of a precision seeder

ground. This furrow is made by a small shoe at the front of each unit. The seed is buried by a furrow coverer and is then compressed by a spring-loaded press wheel.

The whole mechanism is driven either by a belt from a land-wheel at the front of each unit, or from two large master wheels driving all the units. (Fig. 98). Landwheel drive units should not be operated above 3 km/h. as the drive wheels tend to slip and so reduce the speed of the metering mechanism and hence the seed rate. Master wheel units may operate up to 6 km/h but higher speeds prevent the cells from filling and so produce uneven spacing.

The seed spacing is modified by changing the cell wheel or belt or, in the master wheel drill, by altering the gear ratio on the drill. The depth of sowing is controlled by raising or lowering the shoe, relative to the two wheels, i.e. the furrow press and drive wheel.

Electrical indicators can be connected to the units and fitted to the dashboard of the tractor, to show the tractor driver when a unit is not working correctly.

Operation of a precision seeder. Before attaching the drill, check that the tractor wheels are correctly set. Both front and rear wheels should be set the same width. This width is determined by multiplying the row width by 2, 3 or 4, until the product lies in the range of wheel settings which is normally 1·2 to 2 m.

A typical example would be 5 units to sow rows 0·5 m apart for sugar beet.

2 × 0·5 m = 1 m—outside range of wheel settings.
3 × 0·5 m = 1·5 m—within range of wheel settings.

Where alternatives arise, the symmetry of the machine on the tractor should be considered. The units are clamped to the tool-bar at the required spacing commencing from one unit in the centre. The right-hand levelling lever should be set equal to the left, and the top link adjusted to make the toolbar pick-up frame vertical, when the frame is in the working position. Stabilizer bars should be fitted and markers set to make a mark for the tractor's front wheel to follow on the next bout (Fig. 98).

When using the machine in the field:

(a) check that the seed is being ejected by turning the drive wheel by hand before lowering;

Fig. 98. Master wheel drive precision seeder

(b) always keep moving while lowering or raising to prevent soil building up in the rear of the coulter;

(c) keep at the correct speed of 3 to 6 km/h for the type of unit;

(d) clean units daily to remove any large seeds which could clog the seed chamber, and possible excess seed dressing, particularly where farm dressed;

(e) keep the units dry and lubricated according to the manufacturer's instructions.

At the end of each season's work, remove the selector wheels and clean the inside of the machine of all traces of seed dressing. The selector wheels or belts should be stored separately.

Grass seeding equipment

Grass and clover seeds may either be drilled or broadcast. Many farmers use grain drills and fertilizer distributors, suitably adjusted, to sow grass and clover seeds. Special seeding equipment is available, with metering mechanisms particularly designed to deal with small differently shaped seeds. Equipment used for broadcasting is much wider and lighter in construction than for drilling.

One mechanism consists of a series of gears or sprockets carrying the seed between their teeth and forcing it through a hole in the bottom of the hopper. Seeding rate is controlled, either by varying the size of the hole, by means of a slide, or by altering the speed of the feeding shaft via the chain and sprocket drive.

A second mechanism consists of a series of small brushes mounted radially on a shaft. The seeds are flicked through a hole in the bottom of the hopper by the brushes. The seed rate is controlled by the size of the hole in the hopper, as with the previous feed mechanism.

Grass seeds are prone to bridging in a hopper, particularly where there is a high percentage of Italian ryegrass in the mixture and the brush-feed mechanism effectively prevents bridging by the flicking of the brushes.

Little maintenance is needed apart from keeping the hopper empty and dry when not in use.

15. Field Crop Sprayers

One of the most outstanding and rapid developments in crop production, over the last few years, has been the application of chemical sprays to control weeds, pests and diseases. More recently, it has been used as a substitute for mechanical cultivations in seedbed preparation and inter-row weed control. The purpose of the crop sprayer is to break up the spray liquid into very fine droplets and to distribute them evenly over the target.

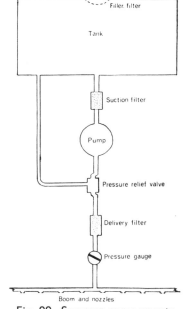

Fig. 99. Sprayer components

The sprayer

The principal components of the modern sprayer consist of the tank to hold the spray liquid, the pump and the spraybar or boom, carrying the nozzles. There are also filters, a pressure regulator and a control valve (Fig. 99).

The tank

This is generally mounted on the three-point linkage of the tractor and is made from coated steel or plastics. Its capacity varies from 150 to 500 litres, depending on the type of sprayer and the lifting capacity of the tractor hydraulic system. It may be locked in the raised position by a mechanical device, to prevent the weight being carried on the hydraulic system.

The pump

This is p.t.o.-driven and either mounted directly on the p.t.o. shaft or supported on a frame bolted to the tractor.

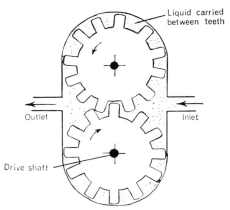

Fig. 100. Gear pump

Three types of pump are commonly used. *The gear pump* (Fig. 100) consists of two meshed gears rotating in a closely-

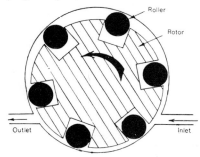

Fig. 101. Roller vane pump

fitting housing. One gear is driven by the p.t.o. shaft and the other by contact with the driven gear. The spray liquid is drawn in and trapped between the gear teeth and the housing, and is carried to the outlet by both gears. The second type of pump is a *roller vane pump* (Fig. 101). It consists of a slotted eccentrically-mounted rotor running in a housing. Nylon rollers are fitted in the slots and are thrown out against the housing by centrifugal force. Liquid enters through the inlet port and is trapped be-

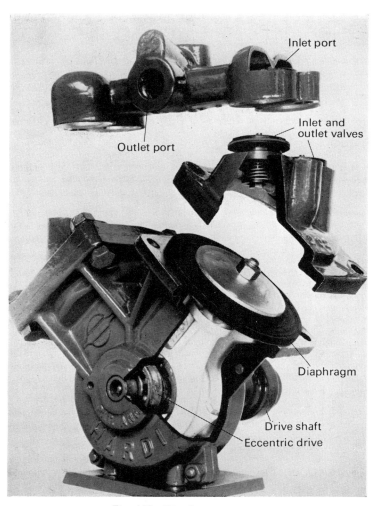

Fig. 102. Diaphragm pump

tween the rollers and carried round to the outlet port. As the space between rotor and housing decreases, due to the eccentric mounting, so the liquid trapped between the rollers is forced through the outlet port. The third type of pump is called a *diaphragm pump* (Fig. 102). It consists of a flexible diaphragm which flexes to and fro drawing liquid in through the inlet port and discharging it via the outlet port. In this type of pump the spray liquid is isolated from parts susceptible to corrosive or abrasive wear and thus maintenance is reduced.

Pressure regulator

A pressure regulator is fitted in the circuit from the outlet side of the pump to ensure that the pressure selected is maintained at the correct level during operation. It consists of a spring-loaded relief valve (Fig. 103), which is raised by the pressure of the liquid and allows the excess to by-pass to the inlet side of the pump or back to the tank. The pressure is controlled by varying the spring setting.

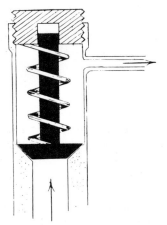

Fig. 103. Spring-loaded relief valve

Control valve

The outlet or pressure side of the pump is connected to the control valve. The purpose of this is to provide control of the liquid during the spraying operation. There are generally three positions on the control valve:

1. *Spray on*. The pump is then connected to the spraybar for work. Often a small bleed from the pressure side is led to the bottom of the tank to provide some hydraulic agitation in the tank, to keep the chemical evenly mixed in the water.

2. *'Suck back'*. This position connects the spraybar to the

inlet side of the pump. The liquid in the spraybar is thus sucked back into the tank, providing a sudden cut-off for the spray and preventing dripping of concentrated spray, which could cause crop damage.

3. *Neutral.* This recirculates the contents of the tank through the filters and back to the tank. It is used to ensure adequate mixing while travelling to the field.

For power filling an additional valve may be fitted. This connects the suction side of the pump to the filler hose and the discharge side to the tank thus enabling the pump to be used to fill the tank.

Spraybar

This consists of a metal or plastic tube, carried horizontally on either side of the tractor. The nozzles are fixed at intervals along this tube. In order to prevent damage, through striking obstructions with a wide spraybar, it is often hinged in two pieces and these 'break back' on contact. Spraybars are normally 6 to 10 m wide, but can be wider for exceptionally-level conditions.

Nozzles.

Their function is to break the liquid into fine droplets and distribute them evenly over the area to be sprayed. Two main types of nozzle are found. The *hollow cone* nozzle (Figs 104, 105) consists of a *swirl plate* with a series of sloping ports and a disc with a hole in the centre. There is a small space between the two. As the liquid is forced through the swirl plate, the sloping ports make it rotate at high speed. It then passes through the hole in the disc, while still rotating and is thrown outwards and broken into fine droplets. It gives a cone-shaped pattern on the ground, the centre of which contains few droplets. More recently a third type of nozzle has been introduced, the *Vibrajet*. This nozzle produces a fan spray and can be operated at low pressures resulting in larger droplets with less drift. The vibrating action of the nozzle is produced by a 12V electric motor in the nozzle powered by the tractor battery.

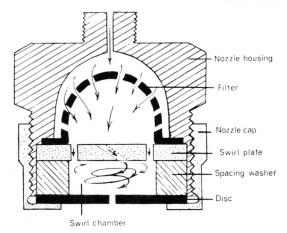

Nozzle housing

Filter

Nozzle cap

Swirl plate

Spacing washer

Disc

Swirl chamber

Fig. 104. Section through a cone nozzle

The second type of nozzle is the *fan* nozzle (Fig. 106). This consists of a nozzle holder and nozzle tip, the tip being manufactured from brass or a ceramic material. A longitudinal slot forms the orifice and the spray liquid emerges as a fan shape.

Filters

The number and location of these varies with the sprayer, but they may be found lining the filling hole of the tank, in the inlet pipe to the pump, in the pressure or outlet side of the pump and in the nozzles. Some sprayers have a sludge trap in each nozzle, which prevents large particles causing blockage.

Filters should always be cleaned before using the sprayer and it is important that the seals are carefully replaced to prevent leakage of air or fluid. Filters on the inlet side of the pump are coarser than those on the pressure side.

Spray chemicals and application rates

Most of the chemicals used for spraying are liquids, although some may be powders. They are added to water before appli-

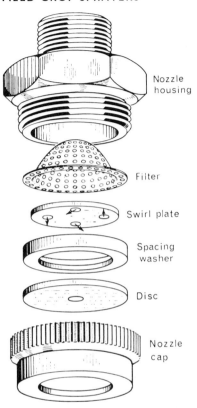

Nozzle housing

Filter

Swirl plate

Spacing washer

Disc

Nozzle cap

Fig. 105. Exploded view of cone nozzle

cation. If the chemical completely dissolves in water, the resulting mixture is called a *solution*. As the two components in a solution cannot become separated out once they are thoroughly

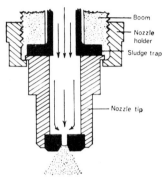

Boom

Nozzle holder

Sludge trap

Nozzle tip

Fig. 106. Fan nozzle

mixed, agitation in the tank is not required. If the chemical is a liquid and does not dissolve in water, yet when subjected to constant agitation mixes intimately, it is termed an *emulsion*. For example, milk is an emulsion of fat and water, where the two constituents separate out on standing. Agitation is therefore necessary with emulsions. This agitation may be hydraulic by re-circulating liquid or mechanical where paddles rotate inside the spray tank. If the chemical is a powder which is insoluble it can, by agitation, form a *suspension* in the water. In this case careful mixing and agitation is required to ensure the suspension maintains an even concentration and generally there is some wear of pumps and nozzles due to the abrasive action of the material.

The quantity of chemical required per hectare (ha) is extremely variable. Even when mixed with water the total volume of the mixture may range from as low as 50 to 1000 litres/ha. It is vitally important that the manufacturer's instructions should be read and adhered to when preparing chemicals for spraying. When 50 to 200 litres/ha are being applied, it is called *low-volume spraying*; 200 to 600 litres/ha is *medium-volume* and above 600 litres/ha is normally referred to as *high-volume*. Spraying machines are designed to apply a range of volumes, such as low, medium or high or a combination, low/medium, or even low/medium and high (universal). Obviously, the higher the volume being used, the larger and more expensive the sprayer. There also arises the problem of carrying large amounts of water with high volume machines. The most popular types are therefore low or low/medium sprayers applying up to 300 litres/ha.

Factors affecting the application rates

1. *Nozzle size.* This is the most suitable means of altering the application rate. Each manufacturer supplies a range of nozzle sizes. Large nozzles generally operate at lower pressures and so give coarse spray particles, reducing the possibility of spray drift.

2. *Forward speed.* Forward speed directly affects the application rate but in practice the forward speed selected is normally the maximum suitable for the ground conditions in relation to the nozzle being used and rarely exceeds 10 km/h if an acceptable standard of work is to be obtained. Having decided on a forward speed it is essential that it should be kept constant during operation.

3. *Nozzle pressure.* The optimum range of operating pressure is normally given by the manufacturer. It is important that the range is maintained. Pressures higher and lower than those recommended will affect both the droplet size

and its distribution and the output. As pressures are raised so a proportion of the droplets are reduced in size and become susceptible to drift. When it is lowered the resulting increase in size of drops causes an uneven pattern to form. The output of a nozzle is also altered by a change in its operating pressure. However, the output is only slightly affected by pressure—to double the output requires no less than four times an increase in pressure.

Preparing for work

Careful preparation of the sprayer will help to ensure good results. Before attaching the sprayer, the pump should be checked to ensure that it is free to rotate and that the pressure regulator adjusts easily. The pump and tank are attached to the tractor according to the manufacturer's instructions. The levelling lever and the top link are adjusted so that the tank is level in both directions. Pipe unions should be secure and kinks in the pipes avoided. All nozzles and filters should be removed and be cleaned by washing them under a tap or by using compressed air, not by blowing them with the mouth. The tank is filled with water and the pump operated to flush out the system before the nozzles are replaced. Then the nozzles are fitted, checking that all seating washers are present and that where fan nozzles are used, the slots are parallel with the spraybar. Finally, it is necessary to check that all nozzles are spraying and that there are no leaks in the system.

Testing the sprayer

Fill the sprayer with clean water and operate it at normal pressure. Examine the spray from each nozzle and if streaks can be seen in the spray pattern, remove and replace the nozzle. Next, compare the amount of spray from each nozzle. Suitable containers of the same size, such as jam jars, should be placed under each nozzle and the sprayer run for a set period of time until they are about three-quarters full. The water level in each container should be about the same. If this is not so, replace the

nozzle tips of those giving high or low output. Finally, spray
over a clean concrete or tarmac surface for a few yards and
note how the liquid dries out. If it dries in stripes the nozzles
are too low. Raise the booms and repeat the test until the liquid
dries out evenly. Check the height of the nozzles above the
ground as an indication to the height the nozzles should be set
above the target in the field.

Calibrating the sprayer

Calibrating the sprayer consists of setting the equipment and
checking that the correct volume of spray is applied per hectare.
It can be done simply and effectively by the following method:

1. Set the engine to give the standard p.t.o. speed. The
   engine should run at two-thirds to three-quarters maximum
   speed. Where the tractor is not fitted with a proof meter
   (tractometer) this should be checked by timing the distance covered and calculating its speed (6km/h = 25 m
   in 15 s)
2. Select a suitable gear to give the required forward speed.
3. Set the sprayer to run at the recommended pressure by
   adjusting the pressure regulator.
4. Check that the correct quantity of spray chemical is being
   applied. There are several methods of doing this. Knowing
   the effective width of spray and the forward speed, the
   time taken to cover a hectare or part of a hectare can be
   calculated:

$$\text{min/ha} = \frac{10\ 000\ \text{m}^2}{\text{effective width of spray (m)} \times \text{forward speed (m/min)}}.$$

With the tank full, the sprayer is operated for that length
of time and the quantity of water required to fill the tank
again is equal to the amount applied per hectare or part
of a hectare. An even simpler method of calculating the
application rate is by holding a calibrated measure under

a nozzle and noting the number of seconds required to fill it to a known mark:

$$\text{litres/ha} = \frac{\text{Time (min/ha)}}{\text{volume (litres)/min}}.$$

This method is only accurate when a number of nozzles are tested. A third method is to calculate from the boom-width how far the sprayer will need to travel to cover 0·1 ha:

$$\text{distance to be sprayed} = \frac{1000}{\text{effective width of spray (m)}}.$$

By spraying this distance and noting the amount of water required to fill the tank again the application rate per hectare can be calculated.

Having calibrated the machine, the tank should be half-filled with water before the chemical is added. This gives more thorough mixing when the remainder of the water is added. Some chemicals, particularly wettable powders, must be pre-mixed in a bucket and are best washed through the strainer in the top of the tank. The quantity of chemical added will depend on the amount of chemical required per hectare, the total application rate per hectare and the size of the tank. For example, if the tank is a 500 litre capacity and the sprayer is set for 100 litres/ha then each tankful covers 5 ha. If 5 litres of chemical are required for a hectare, then 25 litres of chemical have to be added to each tankful of water.

Spraying in the field

To obtain complete crop coverage, the boom should be set so that the spray pattern from adjacent nozzles just meets above the plants to be sprayed. This is best checked in the field with the tractor on the move, or the crop will be damaged by excess spray. As a guide, nozzles at 0·45 m spacing give a spray pattern which overlaps 0·45 m beneath the nozzle. The spray-bar can generally be adjusted, where it is attached to the tank.

It is best to spray two bouts round the headland first. Then begin spraying from the longest side of the field or, if there is any wind blowing, from the leeward side, causing any drift to blow over the field and not over the hedge. While turning at the ends, it is not usually necessary to turn off the spray. With most tractors and booms up to 7 m, it will be found that turning on full lock brings the tractor to the correct position for overlapping the bouts. Considerable skill is needed to arrange that the bouts just meet. It is often not possible to use the previous wheel marks as a reference and the drill rows of corn can only be used as a guide up to 50 or 75 mm high. The safest method, certainly for the inexperienced driver, is to use marker poles at each end of the field, switching the sprayer to 'suck back' while they are being moved. A recent development is the use of special nozzles at the end of the boom through which a marker foam is ejected.

Should a nozzle block, the valve should be put in the 'suck back' position and the operator replace it with a spare nozzle, cleaning the blocked one in water at the next refilling. Never put a nozzle near the mouth to blow it out, always use clean water or compressed air.

When the tank is nearly empty it can be noticed by a change in the sound of the spray, the valve should then be put to 'suck back'. This will ensure there is some liquid in the tank to lubricate the pump. Immediately this is done, the tractor should be turned towards the gate and on returning, with a new tankful, it is then easy to find the starting position.

Drift and scorch

Ideally, spraying should only be carried out when there is very little air movement. Obviously, this is not always possible. Precautions have therefore to be taken to reduce the incidence of spray drift and damage from it.

1. Keep the spray boom as near the plants to be sprayed as possible, while still getting good coverage. This can be helped by tilting the nozzle at 45° away from the vertical.
2. Spray when the wind is blowing off a susceptible crop or

leave an unsprayed strip when the wind is blowing towards a susceptible crop.

3. Fit larger nozzles and reduce the pressure. This increases
   the droplet size and therefore reduces drift.
4. Spray with the wind rather than upwind or with the wind
   abeam the tractor. Spraying with the wind can be dangerous when poisonous chemicals are being used and is
   unpleasant with any spray.
5. Shields can be fitted to the boom of some machines, which
   help to reduce drift.

Scorch can be caused by operating the sprayer while the
tractor is in neutral or more often with a live p.t.o.-driven tractor, by being sluggish when releasing the clutch. Tractor wheels
may cause slight scorch by running over crops immediately they
have been sprayed, but often this is unavoidable.

Band sprayers

The more recent development of selective herbicides for
use in row crops posed a number of new problems. The
chemicals used were often heavy insoluble powders, and it was
beyond the capability of a normal crop sprayer to distribute
these with the precision which was required, particularly where
they have to be evenly spread over the soil surface before the
crop germinates. Similarly many of the chemicals were expensive, and it was considered uneconomic to apply them over
all the ground when the area which was most difficult to keep
weed-free was a band of some 150 to 200 mm in which the
crop plants could grow. The unsprayed area between the
bands could be inter-row cultivated in the normal manner.

To overcome these two problems, spraying equipment was
developed which could be fitted to drills so that the operations
of spraying and drilling could be carried out at the same time.
Many of the principal components of this equipment are very
similar to that of a field crop sprayer. The tank may be mounted
on the front or side of the tractor, or the drill. The pumps used
are of similar design to those already illustrated and are driven

from the p.t.o. The pressure regulator is usually designed to permit a larger proportion of the output of the pump to return to the tank to make sure that the liquid in the tank is kept well agitated. Because low pressure application and extreme accuracy is required, a separate low-pressure regulator is usually fitted. The control valve is also similar, but there is a major difference in that the band sprayer has no spraybar. Instead a manifold divides the flow of liquid at the desired pressure into individual spray lines which carry it to the nozzles mounted on the drill units. The nozzles are usually of the hollow cone type and their careful manufacture and location in relation to the soil are necessary to enable very accurate work to be done. The whole system is prevented from blockages by the location of filters at strategic points.

Cleaning the tank

During its season of use, the spraying equipment should be rinsed out with water at the end of each day's work and then left full of water to prevent the chemical drying on the inside. This dried material might later cause blocked nozzles. When the chemical is to be changed, more elaborate washing is required, particularly if a different type of chemical is to be used or a crop susceptible to the previous spray is to be treated.

The tank, hoses and nozzles should be thoroughly washed out with cold water. Then the tank is refilled with water and a detergent, washing soda or soda ash (1 kg/500 litres water), added before scrubbing the inside of the tank. This solution is then passed through the whole system, followed by flushing out with clean water, especially when soda is used as it tends to be corrosive.

Storage

At the end of the season, this thorough washing procedure can be followed by putting a proprietary de-watering fluid through the system, which coats the internal surfaces against rust. The nozzles should be removed and stored separately, the pump emptied and stored, with the rubber pipes inside the tank.

Safety precautions

All chemicals sold are safe only as long as they are used according to the manufacturers' instructions. Any deviation from these instructions is likely to be dangerous to humans, animals and crops. The following is a list of general safety points.

1. Never allow the concentrated or diluted chemical to come into contact with skin, eyes or mouth.
2. Never smoke while spraying.
3. Dispose of old spray tins by burying, never use them for other purposes.
4. All washings from the tank should go on waste ground away from any drains.
5. Learn to recognize dangerous symptoms. They are headache, sore throat and nausea. Report to a doctor at once, taking the instructions or an empty tin with you.

The M.A.F.F. publication, 'Safe Use of Poisonous Chemicals on the Farm', (A.P.S.1—available free) should be read by all personnel handling spray chemicals.

Safety regulations

Certain chemicals are scheduled as being poisonous and for these, protective clothing *must* be worn. These chemicals are detailed in the M.A.F.F. annual publication on approved chemicals. The clothing may have to be worn only when mixing or for mixing and spraying. It consists of face mask, rubber gloves, rubber apron or mackintosh and wellington boots.

16. Harvesting Equipment

Hay and silage making machines

Mowing machines

The modern mowing machine is driven by the tractor p.t.o. and is either mid-mounted or rear-mounted on the tractor (see Fig. 107).

The important part of the machine is the *cutter bar*, which carries those parts concerned with the cutting action and lies on the ground whilst in work. It is raised and lowered by the

Fig. 107. Rear-mounted mower

hydraulic system. The *knife* is carried in the cutter bar and consists of a knife back to which triangular shaped *sections* are riveted. Each section has the two leading sides bevelled down to form a sharp edge. One end of the knife is reinforced and carries a coupling which moves it. This end is called the *knife head*.

The sections form one of the cutting edges. The other is provided by the *ledger plates* on the *fingers*. These fingers are bolted at 75 mm intervals to the cutter bar and are made from steel, with integral ledger plates, or from malleable iron with steel ledger plates riveted in. The sides of the ledger plates are very slightly bevelled back and provide the scissor-like action as the sections pass over them. The reaction to the knife in work is taken by adjustable *wear plates* bolted to the cutter bar and malleable *clips* prevent the sections rising away from the ledger plates.

The ends of the cutter bar are called *shoes*, there being an inner and an outer shoe. The *outer shoe* comprises an adjustable *skid* or *wheel* and a fixed ledger plate. Attached to the shoe are a *swath board* and *swath stick*, which clear a space for the tractor wheel and inner shoe when on the next bout. The *inner shoe* consists of a casting bolted to the cutter bar and carrying the *hinge pins*, which allow the cutter bar to articulate on uneven ground and to be folded for transport and storage. Also on the inner shoe, there is an adjustable *skid* or *wheel*, two large wear plates and a *grass stick*, which prevents the falling crop from getting caught in the knife head.

The knife is connected to a *pitman* or connecting rod, which is driven by a counterbalanced flywheel and crank. This in turn is driven by a V-belt and pulley from the tractor p.t.o.

The main frame of the machine is carried in a fixed position by the hydraulic system or other means, and a sub-frame comprising the cutter bar and *pull bar* is pivoted from a point near the flywheel. The majority of the weight of the cutter bar is taken by a long coil or *balance spring* from the main frame.

Mid-mounted mowers have the same components and adjust-

ments as the rear-mounted type. The drive from the tractor
p.t.o. is taken by belt and pulley to a shaft passing underneath
the tractor to drive the pitman and knife. The advantages of this
type of mower are, first, visibility from the driving seat while
mowing, and second there is no need to remove the mower from
the tractor when using other equipment on the drawbar and
hydraulic linkage. This gives the opportunity to condition the
grass as it is mown.

Preparing a mower for work. The mower is attached to the
tractor linkage and stabilizer bars fitted or check chains tightened. The main frame is levelled with the levelling lever and the
top link adjusted until the main frame is vertical. The operating
height of the main frame is indicated in the instruction book and
is generally measured from the mounting pins or the underside
of the frame to the ground. The frame is held in position by
hydraulic means (position control) or by an adjustable chain
from the frame to the tractor.

The knife back should be straight and all the sections of the
knife sharp and firmly riveted in place. A gentle tap on a hard
surface will soon verify this, as loose sections rattle. The sections
should neither be chipped nor bent out of line. Before fitting the
knife into the cutter bar, check that the corners of the ledger
plates are acute and not rounded. Sharpening can be done by
removing them and grinding, or by a revolving emery disc.
The ledger plates should all be in line with those on the inner
and outer shoes. This can be verified by laying a straight edge
along the cutter bar. The high fingers should be knocked down
and the low ones raised. The knife is carefully slid into the
cutter bar and the head attached to the pitman. The wear
plates are then adjusted, until all fore and aft movement has
just been removed, yet the knife can still move freely in the
cutter bar. The clips should clear the sections by about 1 mm
and all the sections should lie flush on the ledger plates (Fig.
108 (a) and (b).

The fingers are normally 75 mm apart and the stroke of the
knife is normally 75 mm. When the knife is correctly *registered*,

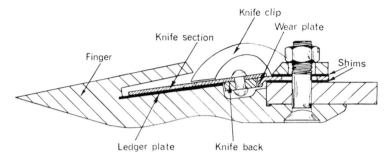

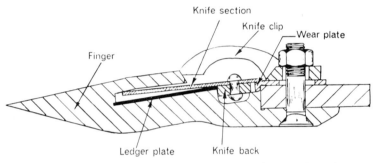

Fig. 108. (a) Section through cutter bar (correctly set).
(b) Section through cutter bar (wrongly set)

each section will travel from the centre of one finger to the centre
of the next (Fig. 109). This knife register should be checked and
if necessary adjusted, either by altering the *length* of the pitman
or by moving the whole cutter bar toward or away from the
crankshaft, depending on the design of the machine.

When the machine is in operation, the cutter bar should
float along the ground, so that it can follow undulations in the
ground easily. It is able to do this as the majority of the weight
is taken by the balance spring, which should be adjusted so
that the outer end of the cutter bar can be raised by two fingers.
It should be noted that on most machines the weight of the

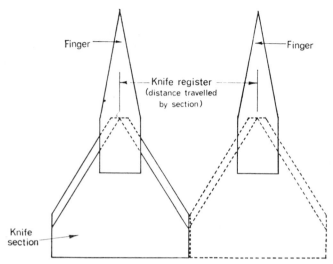

Finger

Finger

Knife register
(distance travelled
by section)

Knife
section

Fig. 109. Knife register

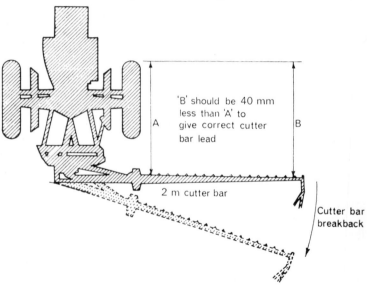

'B' should be 40 mm
less than 'A' to
give correct cutter
bar lead

A

B

2 m cutter bar

Cutter bar
breakback

Fig. 110. Cutter bar lead and break-back

cutter bar is taken on the linkage system when in the raised position, and the spring is relieved of carrying any weight. This linkage may require adjustment, but instruction manuals should be consulted on this point.

The cutter bar normally travels at right angles to the direction of travel. Due to the force of the grass, bending it slightly back, it is normal to have the cutter bar set so that the outer shoe is slightly in advance of the inner shoe when out of work. This is termed the *lead* (Fig. 110) and is measured by laying a straight edge on a line through the tractor back axle and then comparing the distance of both ends of the knife to this line. A cutter bar normally leads 20 mm/m of cut, e.g. on a 2 m cut machine the outer shoe should lead the inner shoe by 40 mm. Lead decreases as pins and bushes on the machine become worn. Should the hinge pins become worn, not only will the lead decrease but the pitman and knife are no longer in line and the resulting sidethrust causes rapid wear and knife breakage. Hinge-pin wear on some machines can be taken up by eccentric bushes.

Safety devices are fitted to prevent damage. Small obstructions, such as stones which jam between the sections and the fingers and prevent the knife moving, are catered for by either a spring-loaded dog clutch or by the V-belt drive which slips under excessive load. Large or fixed obstructions such as posts or stumps are prevented from damaging the machine by a break-back device (Fig. 110). The pull bar is held in position by a spring-loaded roller or pin and the force due to the obstruction overcomes the spring and the pull bar disengages. The whole cutter bar is then free to swing backwards from the flywheel. The tractor must be halted before the cutter bar reaches the limit of the break-back.

The height of cut of the machine is controlled by the setting of the skids on the inner and outer shoes, both of which must be set equal. The cutter bar can also be tilted on either side of the horizontal position. For rough or stony conditions, it would be tilted with the fingers pointing upwards to surmount the unevenness of stones, rather than be embedded or damaged by

them. Laid or tangled crops are best cut with the fingers pointing downwards to enable the knife to keep under the crop.

Lubrication of the machine is to be carried out as indicated
in the instruction manual. When the machine is being transported to and from the field, the points of the fingers must be
covered by a piece of wood or angle iron.

Operation of a mower. Start cutting in a clockwise direction,
driving the tractor close to the fence, but a safe distance from
any ditch sides. It is also worth removing any low tree branches
in the path of the tractor, as the driver may not notice them
while concentrating on the cutter bar. The swath board and
stick should be seen to be leaving a wide enough passage for
the wheels and the p.t.o. speed maintained at the standard
540 rev/min. The forward speed is adjusted according to the
condition of the crop.

When mowing, it is normal to make a reverse turn rather
than a loop turn, the cutter bar being raised and lowered in the
space cleared by the swath board (Figs 111 and 112). After two

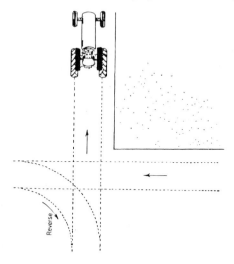

Fig. 111. Reverse turn

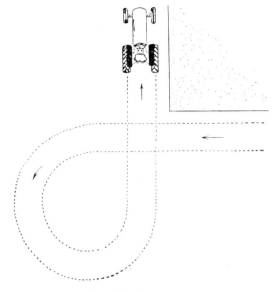

Fig. 112. Loop turn

or three rounds of the field, the knife head and other parts of the machine should be checked to ensure that they are not running hot.

Should the shape of the field produce a point, it will be found that laying the outer part of the cutting bar on a previously cut swath will cause the points to foul the swath. This can be over-come by cutting off the tip of the point, two or three times, and then cutting normally until the point re-forms, when the pro-cedure is repeated.

When blockages occur, the mower is backed out of work and the p.t.o. disengaged before clearing the knife. It is important to allow the knife to regain full working speed before re-entering the crop.

The frequency of changing the knife will depend on the con-dition of the field, the type of crop, the general condition of the mower and the skill of the operator. It is certainly worth keeping the knife cutting well and changing it at least every 4 h.

Opinions differ on when the outside or back swath should be cut. It takes a long time to dry and therefore should be cut fairly early. Against this is the possible damage to the knife and mower generally. Probably just before changing the first knife is a satisfactory time. Raking back the first swath mown prevents the inner shoe from becoming tangled.

Mowing machines are frequently used for topping pastures. This practice often causes a high wear and tear, due to overheating of the knife, as a result of the lack of sap in the grass. This wear and tear can be reduced by lowering the p.t.o. speed and removing the swath board. Other machines, to be mentioned later, should preferably be used for topping.

Storage. At the end of a season's work the knife should be removed, oiled and stored in a wooden case. The machine should be cleaned and the shiny parts coated with a rust preventative.

Rotating-disc mowing machines

These have been developed to provide a higher performance in difficult conditions than the reciprocating-knife type of machine. They also have a reduced maintenance requirement.

A typical machine is rear-mounted and in place of the cutter bar has a series of discs about 0·3 m in diameter (Fig. 113). Attached to each of these discs are small swinging blades. The discs are driven at high speed, 3000 rev/min, by a series of gears in the carrying frame. The discs may be protected from damage due to obstructions by shear pins fitted in the drive mechanism. The discs and their knives pass under the crop even when it is lodged and as it is cut it falls on the ground in a manner which exposes the stem and thus promotes quicker drying.

A balance spring and break-back mechanism are often fitted and perform in a similar manner to those on reciprocating knife machines.

It is essential that the top link is adjusted so that the knives cut horizontally. An incorrect setting will cause the crop to be

Fig. 113. Rotating disc mower (guard removed)

cut twice and will produce a mulch of chopped grass amongst the crop. It will also increase the power requirement for cutting.

The height of cut can, on some machines, be altered by changing the saucers under the knives or, if it is required to top pasture, by fitting two adjustable height-control castor wheels.

Hay conditioning machinery

Where weather conditions are changeable it is essential that the crop of grass is dried as rapidly as possible to prevent loss of feeding value. This can best be done by keeping the crop in a fluffed up condition and thus permitting the free passage of air through it.

The rotating-disc mowing machine tends to leave the swath loose while the reciprocating cutter bar type tends to leave the crop lying thickly on the ground.

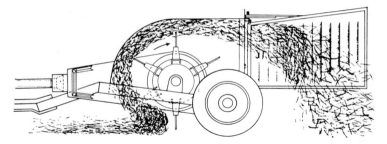

Fig. 114. (a) Section of a tedder

In order to loosen and aerate a cut crop a *tedder* may be used. This picks up the crop and throws it backwards where it falls gently on the ground. Deflectors at the rear may be used to move the crop sideways and fall on a fresh drier piece of ground (Fig 114b). Little inversion of the crop takes

Fig. 114. (b) Hay tedder in action

place with these machines. The tines might rotate in either a vertical (Fig. 114) or horizontal plane (Fig. 115).

Inversion or turning of the crop is done by *turners*, a widely used type consisting of a series of tined wheels trailed at an angle to the swath and in contact with the ground. These spider wheels, as they are known, rotate due to their ground contact angle and move the crop sideways thus inverting it. They tend to compress the crop, particularly if used more than once, so

Fig. 115. Hay tedder in action

optimum results are obtained by using them in conjunction with a tedder. Some machines combine the action of a tedder and turner.

As the crop moisture content decreases it is essential to reduce the vigour of the action or breakage of valuable leaf will occur and this will decrease the crop value.

Before baling the crop it is necessary to form a windrow by placing two rows into one or by taking the crop into a thick row. Many types of two row tedders can be used for this by setting the deflectors at the rear to guide the crop into a single thick row. The spider wheel type of turner and the horizontal rotating-tine machine can also be used for windrowing.

Balers

The ease with which bales of hay and straw can be harvested, transported, stacked and fed, has made baling almost universal in all but the wettest parts of the country. The most popular

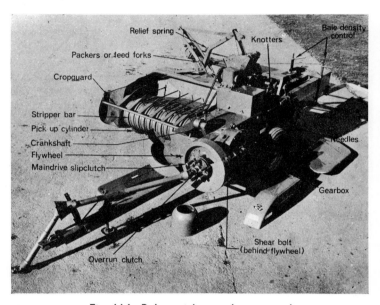

Fig. 116. Baler with guards removed

type of baler is that producing rectangular bales tied with twine, approximately 750 mm in length and a cross-section of 350 mm × 450 mm. Most of these machines are trailed, driven from the tractor p.t.o. and are capable of outputs of about 12 bales/min or 15 tonnes/h at a maximum.

The passage of the material through the baler is as follows (Fig. 116). The *pick-up* cylinder throws the crop under the *crop guard* and onto the feed platform. It is then moved towards the *feed opening* by an auger or similar mechanism. As the *plunger* or *ram* uncovers the feed opening, the *packers* push the material evenly across the *bale* chamber. The plunger descends and the *knife* on its side shears off the surplus material against the fixed *shear plate*. The material is compressed as it is forced down the chamber, which tapers towards the end. When the bale is the correct length, two *needles* carrying the twine come from under the baler through the chamber and into the *knotter*, where the strings are tied. The bale is then forced out of the chamber.

It is obvious that the baler is a complex machine and various mechanical drives are needed to operate it. The tractor p.t.o. operates at 540 rev/min and drives the flywheel, which acts as a reserve of energy should this be required by the plunger. Built into or against the flywheel are some or all of the following:

(a) an *overrun clutch*, which allows the drive to be transmitted one way only and is useful for tractors without live p.t.o., as it allows them to change gear without having to wait for the baler mechanism to become stationary;

(b) a *friction clutch*, which is tensioned to transmit a certain maximum torque and then to slip. This limits the maximum torque to the baler. It also limits the maximum torque the flywheel can transmit to the tractor, where no overrun clutch is fitted;

(c) a *shear bolt*, which couples the drive from the flywheel to the baler gearbox and breaks on sudden overload.

Inside the gearbox, the drive is reduced in speed and turned through a right angle to the crankshaft driving the plunger. This rotates at 60 to 90 rev/min, according to the make of baler. The plunger fits close in the chamber and runs on guides bolted to the top and bottom of the chamber, and may have roller bearings or wooden blocks in contact with the floor of the chamber. The knife, bolted to the plunger, works in conjunction with the shear plate bolted to the feed opening. The clearance is kept to about 1 mm by adjusting the slotted angle iron guide rails carrying the plunger. In order to keep the two cutting edges parallel, an adjustable wedge may be fitted to the side of the plunger. The face of the plunger may have small fibre blocks round the sides to prevent material escaping behind the face and causing seizure.

After the plunger has compressed a wad of material, *retainers* prevent it expanding. These are of two sorts, first spring-loaded retainers fitted to the top and bottom of the chamber which are forced out of the chamber, as the wad is compressed, and click back into position, holding the end of the wad firmly in place. The second type is really a series of wedges fixed to the top and sides of the chamber. Besides retaining the material, these provide resistance to the passage of the wad and hence increase its compression.

The drive to operate the packers and knotters comes from a *bevel gear* at the crankshaft. The packer crank and fingers are carefully timed in relation to the position of the plunger. Should a large wad of material be pushed into the chamber, the fingers may compress it. To prevent damage, the *packer relief* spring eases and limits the force on the fingers. Should the wad be excessively large, a shear bolt may break and allow the fingers to fly harmlessly out of the chamber.

The knotting mechanism is driven from the packers and consists of the *knotter shaft*, carrying the *two face gears* to operate the tying mechanism. A crank at the end of the shaft is connected to the needle pitman and needles. A starwheel penetrating the chamber is rotated by the passage of the bales and a connecting linkage to the knotter trips the knotter when sufficient material has been compressed to make a bale. The knotter drive is not engaged, however, until the plunger is in the correct position. The knotter shaft revolves once, drawing the needles into the chamber through slots in the plunger and into the tying mechanism. The knot is tied, the strings cut and the needles return to rest. A brake may be fitted to the knotter shaft to bring it to a more gradual halt and prevent it jumping back into the bale chamber.

Should the needles meet an obstruction in the chamber, the drive to them is disconnected either by a shear bolt or a spring-loaded safety device. This means the needles remain in the chamber. To prevent them being damaged by the next stroke of the plunger, a *plunger stop* or *safety latch* comes into operation from the bottom of the chamber. When the plunger strikes this stop, it breaks the main drive shear bolt which disconnects the power to the plunger.

The pick-up cylinder is driven by *sprocket and chain* from the crankshaft and consists of a series of spring tines, which pass through *stripper* bars and leave the crop on the feeding platform. The drive passes through a friction or ratchet clutch, which slips if the cylinder gets overloaded or if the cylinder strikes the ground.

The reason that so many safety devices are fitted to balers is that the inertia of the flywheel would cause the plunger, packer and needles to do considerable damage should obstruction occur. The baler mechanism cannot be stopped until this inertia is expended.

Operation of a baler. The baler must be correctly coupled to the tractor. The following are points to note.

(a) The baler drawbar should be adjusted to be parallel with the ground and the p.t.o. shaft be in as straight a line as possible.

(b) The coupling should consist of a clevis and an eye as two clevises would bend the drawbar pin when on undulating ground.

The machine should be lubricated and the tyres and oil level in the gearbox checked, as detailed in the instruction manual. The free movement of the plunger can be determined by turning the flywheel by hand. The knife and shear plate should be seen to be in good condition and the clearance between them measured with a gauge, when pressing the plunger away from the shear plate.

At the beginning of each season, it is advisable to check that the main drive friction clutch has not seized up, through corrosion, and that it will slip at the correct torque. This is done by fitting a rod (say, 1 m long) to the clutch. With the plunger locked against the plunger stop, slip the clutch by pulling on the rod with a spring balance. The torque will be the distance (1 m) multiplied by the balance reading (N), expressed in units of Nm.

The twine balls should be fitted the correct way up and connected together, a reef knot being used to couple the outside of the leading ball with the inside of the spare. Only recommended types of twine should be used. The twine is threaded through the *tensioner* and the various eyes to the needles, where it passes *over* the needle sheave. The twine tension is measured by attaching a spring balance to the twine, and pulling it through the needle, noting the reading when pulling steadily.

After the twines have been threaded through the needles, the ends should be drawn down the bale chamber and tied to some convenient object, such as the bale density control. Operate the baler at low p.t.o. speed and trip the knotting mechanism. The needles carry the strings into the knotter. The operator has to pull the two half-loops off this hook.

Set the pick-up cylinder to clear the ground by about 25 mm and with the p.t.o. at 540 rev/min, commence baling. The gear selected will depend on the size and evenness of the windrow, but it should produce a bale every ten to fifteen plunger strokes. The density control should be set when the chamber is full of material, to produce bales of the required weight. If the windrow is even and the correct forward speed selected, the majority of the bales will be straight but if 'banana'-shaped bales appear, it is probably due to faulty packing of the chamber. The packer arms ought to place the material evenly across the chamber, and adjustment is provided to increase, or decrease, the packing. The operator must also check that the bales are correctly tied, as rust on the knotter hooks at the beginning of a season can cause odd mis-tied bales.

Should the string break, the needles must be threaded in the way that has been described, except that the strings will have to be tied outside the bale chamber as it will be full of material.

Spare shear bolts should always be carried on the tractor. It should be noted that they are often heat-treated, to produce constant shear strength characteristics. This means that only the correct spare part should be used. In the event of shear bolt failure, the cause must be ascertained and the fault corrected before proceeding.

The slip clutch on the pick-up cylinder should be set so that it *just* transmits the drive under normal conditions, and will therefore slip immediately it becomes overloaded.

Whenever the baler is stopped, the flywheel should be turned by hand to bring the plunger away from the material. This allows it to gain momentum before compression.

When baling light and dry fluffy material, particularly straw, it may be found impossible to obtain sufficient compression of the material using normal density control. To overcome this problem, wedges can be fitted in the chamber, to provide an obstruction and so increase the weight of the bale.

Storage. At the end of a season's work, it is most important to empty the chamber and coat all bright surfaces, particularly the knotters, with rust preventative.

Roto-balers. Another type of baler rolls the crop between canvas belts and produces round bales. There is no knotting mechanism as the twine, much lighter than conventional baler twine, is wrapped round and round the bale before it is ejected. The main advantage of this machine is that the bales produced can lie in the field for several weeks without deterioration.

Forage harvesters

With the increasing emphasis on silage as a means of conservation, machines were needed to cut, lacerate and load the crop at a high output rate. The flail-type forage harvester met this demand.

The forage harvester consists of two basic parts (Fig. 117):

1. A carefully balanced rotor, carrying two, three or four rows of flails, driven by the p.t.o. from a gearbox and V-belt at 1200 to 1500 rev/min. The rotor turns against the direction

of travel. The flails shear off the crop due to speed. Skids are fitted at the ends of the rotor, to prevent it fouling the ground.

2. A chute, to collect and deliver the cut material. The material is propelled by the fan-like action of the flails. The top of the chute has a flap to control the delivery of the grass. It may also swivel to permit side-delivery.

Although mounted machines are available, most of those in use are trailed, the weight of the machine being carried by two

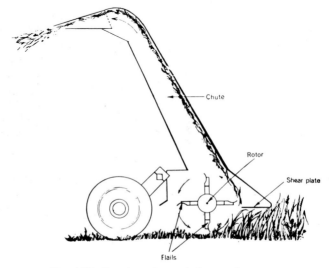

Fig. 117. Section through forage harvester

wheels. These wheels control the height of cut and often have lateral adjustment for use in row crops.

When choosing a forage harvester, the size of the machine must be related to the tractor power available. Generally, rotors 1 m wide are suitable for tractors of 25 to 30 kW, and 1·5 m rotors for tractors of 40 to 45 kW.

The crop is cut into lengths of 75 to 125 mm. This material tends to cling together in a heap, making mechanical handling difficult. It also requires considerable consolidation in a clamp or pit to expel the air which becomes trapped.

Machines have been developed which cut the crop and then chop it before blowing it into a trailer. These *double-chop* harvesters have a rotor with L-shaped blades which cut the crop and lift it to a cross auger (Fig. 118). This feeds the crop into a fly-

Fig. 118. Double-chop forage harvester

wheel chopper which is a fan with knives fitted on one side of the blades. These work in conjunction with a fixed shear plate, and chop the crop into shorter lengths 25 to 75 mm before blowing it into a trailer.

A further type of machine is available which cuts the crop into precise lengths of 12 to 25 mm. This material can fairly easily be handled mechanically and will settle in a pit or tower and expel the trapped air under the influence of its own weight and so does not require any mechanical consolidation. This type is called a *metered feed* (or precision chop) and is particularly suitable for picking up crops which have previously been cut and allowed to wilt (Fig. 119).

It consists of a pick-up cylinder which feeds the crop between a pair of rollers. These rollers positively meter the crop into a cutting cylinder. The cutting cylinder is similar to that of a

Fig. 119. Precision-chop forage harvester

lawnmower and has a series of blades running parallel to its axis. These blades operate in conjunction with a fixed shear plate and chop the crop into controlled lengths. The chop length is varied by adjusting the speed of the feed rolls supplying the cutting cylinder. A fan blows the chopped material into a trailer.

These machines have a high power requirement, and to obtain maximum output it is essential to keep the knives and shear plate sharp and correctly adjusted. They often have a knife sharpener built in to them for ease of operation. The shear plate should be as close to the knives as possible without actually touching.

Operation of a forage harvester. When using the machine in the field, the operator must set the flap, or swivelling head, carefully to avoid loss. He should adjust the height of cut or pick-up so that stones or soil do not contaminate the material as it is harvested. With simple flail-type machines the flap over the rotor should be raised so that sufficient air is allowed in to prevent the crop wrapping round the rotor.

A forward speed should be selected which allows the tractor to operate without loss of 'revs' and the driver should take particular care to avoid overloading where denser patches of crops are encountered. If the engine speed drops the reduced airflow up the chute causes a blockage which is time-consuming to rectify.

All cutting edges should be kept sharp and flail nuts and bolts tightened daily. If several flails break, all flails should be changed to keep the rotor balanced.

Buckrakes

They are used to carry grass which has previously been cut by a mower or forage harvester. They are capable of high rates of work when carrying over short distances. A series of long steel tines is mounted on the tractor hydraulic linkage. A trip mechanism near the top allows the tines to pivot round the lower hitch pins and so deposit the load. The linkage can be adjusted so that the tines pitch slightly towards the ground when lowered. The frame to which the tines are attached is to be set 50 to 75 mm from the ground, or just high enough to allow the toe to pass under.

A more recent development has been the *push-off buckrake*. This is similar to the previous type but, instead of tripping the tines to discharge the load, a series of boards operated by a hydraulic ram push the load off the tines. The accuracy of placing the load is improved by this method. Push-off types may also be fitted to fore-end loaders as this improves operator visibility (Fig. 120).

Combine harvesters

Ever since man started growing cereals for breadmaking, he has had the problem of isolating the edible kernel from the chaff and straw. The number of devices employing human,

Fig. 120. Push-off buckrake

animal and mechanical power, is legion. If they are carefully
studied, it will soon become obvious that from driving cattle
over corn laid on the floor, to the latest self-propelled combine
harvester, the principles of threshing and separation have not
changed from that day to this.

The corn is cut by a *cutter bar*, which differs from that of a
mower only in respect of the ledger plates on the fingers and the

knife sections, which may have serrated edges not requiring sharpening. The stroke of the knife is usually 75 mm.

The cutter bar is attached to the *table*, which carries a pick-up *reel* to lay the corn on the cutter bar (Fig. 121). There are several adjustments which can be made to the reel relative to the table: speed and position, both vertical and horizontal. After the crop is cut, it is raised by an *elevator* to the threshing mechanism on the main chassis of the combine. The weight of the table is counterbalanced by large springs. It is raised and lowered by hydraulic means.

The threshing mechanism consists of a large *cylinder* or *drum*, heavily constructed and carefully balanced. The drum itself consists of a series of longitudinal *rasp bars*. These bars have grooves cut in them at an angle to the axis. The cylinder varies in size according to the type of combine. The speed depends on the type and condition of the crop being harvested. The cylinder operates in conjunction with the *concave*. This is a series of curved wires in a frame, fitted below the cylinder. The gap between concave and cylinder is wider at the front than at the rear.

The *feeding drum* controls the flow of material from the elevator to the cylinder. A stone trap is fitted in front of the cylinder and this should be emptied twice a day. The rasp bars rub the grain out of the ears against the concave, in just the same manner as a head of corn is rubbed between the palms. The majority of the grain, chaff and broken heads or chobs fall through the concave, while the straw and some grain pass over. This completes the threshing operation. The remainder of the machine is devoted to separating the grain from the straw which passes over the concave, and the grain from chaff, chobs, pieces of straw and weed seeds which pass through the concave.

The passage of the straw will be considered first. Any tendency for the straw to wrap round the drum is avoided by the spring-loaded *stripper bar*, which is set as close as possible to the cylinder. A *stripper drum*, mounted just behind the stripper bar, deflects the straw and some grain on to the walkers. These are four long narrow open grids which have raised saw teeth on the edges to grip the straw. They are driven by a pair of crankshafts, one at each end. As one pair of walkers moves backward and up, so the other pair moves forward and down. The straw is thus thrown upwards and backwards. The trapped grain is shaken out through the grid. Canvas baffles may be hung over the straw to retard its progress and help remove all the grain. The agitation can be increased by adding risers to the walkers which throw the straw more violently. After passing over the walkers, the straw falls out of the rear of the combine.

The grain with chaff and other impurities is separated by a combination of air blast and sieving. The grain falls through a series of reciprocating sieves and is subject to a controlled air flow during this. The combination of sieves is called the *shaker* or dressing shoe.

The material which has passed through the concave and that from the straw walkers first moves over the *chaffer sieve*. The size of the openings in this sieve can be adjusted. Sieves of this type are called Peterson or frog-mouth sieves. A stream of air from the fan and controlled by deflectors blows through the sieve. The lighter elements are blown off and out of the combine. The small heavy pieces fall through and the large heavy pieces, such as broken pieces of straw, are carried along the sieve and out of the machine.

The second or *grain sieve* may be a fixed hole type, several being supplied with each combine, or a frog-mouth, adjustable to suit the grain being harvested. The grain and small weed seeds pass through this sieve and are collected by a *horizontal grain auger* which takes them to a *vertical elevator* and finally to the tank or bagging unit.

The debris which passes over the grain sieve consists of large weed heads, broken straws, some threshed grain and some chobs or broken grain heads. It travels by an auger and conveyor to the cylinder or shaker shoe, according to the setting of a valve. If the returns contain a large proportion of chobs, the

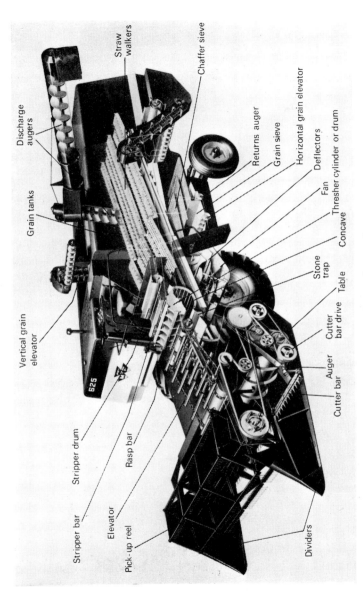

Fig. 121. Section of a combine

Straw walkers

Chaffer sieve

Discharge augers

Returns auger

Grain sieve

Horizontal grain elevator

Deflectors

Fan

Thresher cylinder or drum

Concave

Stone trap

Table

Grain tanks

Cutter bar drive

Auger

Cutter bar

Dividers

Vertical grain elevator

Stripper drum

Rasp bar

Stripper bar

Elevator

Pick-up reel

625

operator will set the valve to deflect them to the cylinder for
re-threshing. If loose grains only are present with the unwanted
material, the valve will be set to deflect them to the separating
mechanism. Some of the latest machines have a special re-
threshing mechanism for dealing with the returns. It consists of
a series of swinging flails which thresh the grain against an
adjustable concave and on to the centre of the shaker shoe.
The advantage of this is that any green material is not pulped
up and thus does not block the sieves. It also prevents the cylinder becoming overloaded by excessive returns.

All the mechanisms described are driven either by chains,
V-belts or rod links. Safety devices, in the form of slip clutches,
are fitted to many of them, to prevent damage should they be
overloaded. The general method of setting one of these is, first,
to slacken the clutch springs and then tighten gradually, until
they transmit the power necessary under normal conditions.

The engine which drives the threshing mechanism must
operate at a constant speed. The forward speed of the combine
must be alterable within wide limits, for various crop conditions.
The drive from the engine goes to a gearbox with two or three
forward and one reverse gears, then via two variable V-pulleys
through the differential to the driving wheels.

The V-pulley diameters are controlled hydraulically from
the driver's seat and therefore in any one gear an infinite number of forward speeds are possible at a constant engine speed.

Basic settings

Some of the basic settings of the machines are worth consideration.

Cutter bar height. This varies with the evenness of the surface of the ground, the height of the grass where the crop is
undersown, and height of the crop or the amount of straw that
is to be harvested.

Pick-up reel. When correctly set, this pushes the heads away,
cutting and feeding the butts first on to the auger. This method
ensures that the feed is even. If the heads were bent over first,

the crop would tend to be fed in bunches, as each tine bar on the pick-up came round. In laid crops, the pick-up is lowered and the rake of the tines set so that they raise the crop as they approach the cutter bar.

Cylinder speed and concave setting. The instruction manual will provide the basic cylinder speed and concave setting, according to the type of crop harvested. Typical examples for a 0·6 m diameter cylinder are:

crop	Cylinder speed rev/min	Concave clearance (mm) front	rear
clover	1098	3·0	1·5
barley	750	7·0	3·0
beans	400	7·0	4·5

The larger the seed, the slower the cylinder speed and the greater the concave clearance. These basic settings are altered according to the crop condition. The greater the moisture content of the crop, the more difficult it is to thresh, so a higher cylinder speed is used. Conversely, drier crops are prone to damage, so the cylinder speed is reduced. This operation may be carried out during the course of a day's combining as the grain dries out. The symptoms of overthreshing are broken grains and shattered straw. Underthreshing is shown by grains remaining in the heads. On combines where the cylinder is driven by chain and sprocket, it may be a tedious task to change sprockets when altering speed. The concave clearance is then adjusted to control the degree of threshing.

Straw walkers. The problem of separating grain from the straw on the walkers is the limiting factor to combine output, for the greater the volume of straw, the slower the forward speed of the combine.

Adjustable chaffer sieve. This should be set quite wide, so that it acts just as a grid to prevent large particles passing through.

Grain sieve. This must be changed for each type of crop.

Fan. The speed can be altered by changing the pulley sizes

and this is done for each crop. There are also shutters to vary
the intake of air throughout each speed range. Deflectors can
be adjusted to give an even blast of air over the whole length of
the sieves, so that the chaff is held off the sieves until it passes
out of the machine.

Grain losses from combines

The maximum acceptable loss is about 55 kg/ha but it can
easily be more than this. It is therefore important to be able to
find out which part of the machine is at fault.

Loss in standing grain. The loss can be assessed by walking
through the crop, before the combine, and counting the grains
in random samples, each of a square metre. Ten grains per
square metre represents 5·0 kg/ha.

Losses at the cutter bar. Halt the combine, switch off the
engine and estimate the grain on the ground underneath. Sub-
tract the grain which was there in the first place. This difference
will indicate how much is due to incorrect setting, or to operation of the cutter bar and reel. Whole heads may be found if the
cutter bar is too high, or has not been adjusted correctly for
laid patches of crop. It has to be remembered that certain diseases can cause random lodging in a field. Such heads, being too
low, will be left on the ground. Large amounts of grain on the
ground could have been knocked out of the ears by the pick-up
reel, from operating at too high a speed or too close to the crop.

Losses from the walkers. When the combine is operational,
hold a sheet over the end of the walkers and catch a sample of
straw. Take care to hold it high enough, to prevent material
being blown off the sieves onto it. Check the ears, to see if they
have been threshed out completely. If there are still some
grains unthreshed, check the concave clearance and increase
the cylinder speed. Shake the straw, to see if threshed grains
fall into the sheet. These would indicate lack of agitation over
the walkers. This can be caused by too great a forward speed,
with consequent overloading of the walkers. As previously
mentioned, risers can be fitted to increase agitation. Alterna-

tively, forward speed could be reduced or the cutter bar raised slightly to reduce the quantity of straw passing through the machine.

Shaker shoe losses. Collect a sample from the shaker shoe on the sheet and lift the straw fallen from the walkers, taking care that no grain in that straw falls through. Examine the sample remaining. Any grains present might have been carried over the adjustable sieve due to being opened insufficiently or insufficient fan blast. Excessive quantities of green material also cause this type of grain loss.

Maintenance and storage

The combine may only work a few weeks in the year. It is essential that it receive adequate maintenance during this very arduous time. Lubrication must be carried out according to the instruction manual, however inaccessible some of the grease nipples may be. The engine air cleaner has to receive careful attention as a dirty air cleaner can reduce engine revolutions (some diesel engine governors operate *via* the depression in the manifold), which reduces the cylinder speed and leads to a host of baffling troubles. Similarly, the radiator grill should be kept clean to avoid overheating. It is advisable to carry a fire extinguisher.

At the end of each season, careful attention is necessary to prevent deterioration of the machine before it is next required. The cutting and threshing mechanism should be carefully cleaned and treated with rust preventative. The knife and sieves should be removed and stored separately. The engine oil and filter should be changed and the batteries removed and given a booster charge every month. Finally, the water should be drained off and the wheels blocked clear of the ground.

Root harvesting machinery

Potato harvesting equipment

The susceptibility of potatoes to mechanical damage creates many problems for both machinery designer and operator, as damage reduces the keeping quality and the saleability of the crop. Many makes of harvester are available to the grower. The simpler and better established potato diggers lift the potatoes and separate them from soil, leaving them ready for hand-picking on the surface of the ground. Complete harvesters, which make an attempt to remove stones and clods, prior to final hand-selection on the machine, deposit the tubers in bags or a trailer running alongside.

Potato diggers can be divided into two main types, the *elevator digger* and the *spinner*.

Elevator diggers (Fig. 122). These may lift one or two rows at a time. They consists of broad A-shaped shares which lift the drill. The contents of the drill are raised by the forward motion

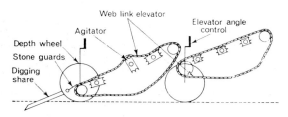

Fig. 122. Section of an elevator digger (web split)

and deposited on an endless rod link elevator or web. The soil falls through the links and the potatoes pass off the end of the elevator to the ground. To separate the maximum soil and trash from the potatoes, various means of controlling the degree of agitation on the web are used.

1. Oval sprockets of various sizes can be fitted under the web, between the two end sprockets, to increase agitation.

2. The elevator can be split and run in two sections, the potatoes and soil falling from the first to the second section.

3. The angle of the elevator can be altered, thus varying the speed at which the potatoes and soil pass over the web, hence the agitation they receive.

4. The drive to the elevator is by landwheel *via* a gearbox or

by tractor p.t.o. With both, the elevator to forward speed ratio can be varied.

Operation of an elevator digger. Tractor wheel settings must fit the row width and if the elevator is semi-mounted, the lift arms should be adjusted to the same height. The depth of the share is generally controlled by two screw adjustable wheels (Fig. 123). The share should be set as shallow as possible, to

Fig. 123. Two-row elevator digger (guards removed)

reduce the amount of soil lifted and hence the agitation necessary, while still deep enough to lift the whole crop without slicing the tubers. The degree of agitation depends on the soil type and conditions, but the aim is for the potato to be cushioned on the elevator by a layer of soil up to the last 0·15 m of its journey. This combines maximum necessary agitation with minimum opportunity for damage and a slight reserve of empty web, should it be needed.

Spinners (Fig. 124). These have the advantage over elevator diggers, in that they are capable of working under quite wet soil conditions. They are liable, however, to cause more damage to the crop, due to the method of lifting and separating.

A typical machine consists of a share running under the ridge and lifting the contents into the path of a series of rapidly rotating tines, fixed to a hub, driven from the tractor p.t.o. or by landwheel. The tines may be single or arranged in pairs and should be rubber-covered at the tips to reduce tuber

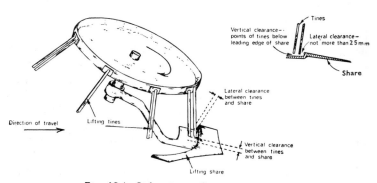

Fig. 124. Side view of potato spinner

damage through impact. The tines on some spinners are kept in near-vertical position by a linkage mechanism. These are called feathering tines and do less damage to the potatoes. These tines shatter the ridge and throw it sideways against a rope net, which allows the soil to pass through and the potatoes fall to the ground in a row. The potatoes may be partly covered up by clods or trash and are never left in such an even row for the pickers as with an elevator digger.

Operation of a potato spinner. After hitching to the tractor, adjust the share so that the points of the spinner run just below and about 25 mm from the back of the share, so that they cannot cause damage to the potatoes. The depth of the share should be just below the deepest potato. In work, the lowest spinner speed should be used, sufficient to break up the ridge, so as to ensure maximum separation with minimum damage.

Complete potato harvester. The complete potato harvester, although limited in the conditions under which it works satisfactorily, has increased in number, to overcome the peak labour demand associated with hand-picking. The types of machine vary widely in design but most have an A-shaped share which raises the complete ridge on to a mechanism designed to separate some of the stones and clods from potatoes. This mechanism is made up of an endless rod link elevator, which agitates the contents of the ridge as it rises, or a rotating spider wheel, which throws the contents of the ridge against a grid. On both, some of the soil passes through and some of the clods are broken and separated out. A platform carrying the pickers is fitted above the lifting mechanism and the soil and potatoes are raised to a picking table by endless rod link elevators or by a cage wheel. The pickers remove either the potatoes or the stones and clods from the table, according to the design of the machine and field conditions. The potatoes are then conveyed to a trailer running alongside or to sacks.

The separation of stones and clods from potatoes provides the biggest problem in the harvester. There are no mechanical devices able to separate stones from potatoes properly at the high rate required, although recently expensive electronic controlled mechanisms have been developed for this purpose. Clods can be broken by severe agitation but this generally causes considerable damage to tender potatoes. Tuber damage must naturally be kept to a minimum, so many parts of the machine are rubber covered or are designed so that a layer of soil remains to provide protection for the tuber.

A large weight of soil, some 1000 to 1500 tonnes/ha, passes through the machine. The separating mechanism is therefore of a considerable area. This makes a heavy machine and often it cannot be pulled in wet conditions. Some types of land, being stone and clod free, are suitable for the operation of potato harvesters. Husbandry techniques are being developed to help reduce the formation of clods produced during cultivation.

Sugar beet harvesters

The problem of harvesting sugar beet is simpler than that of harvesting potatoes. The beet is more tolerant of mechanical damage and saleability is unaffected. Also, beet grows in very straight lines, with similar root and crown shape.

It is harvested in two operations: topping and then lifting. These are usually combined in one machine, a row being topped in one bout of the machine and lifted in the next bout.

Topping mechanisms (Fig. 125). A series of serrated discs

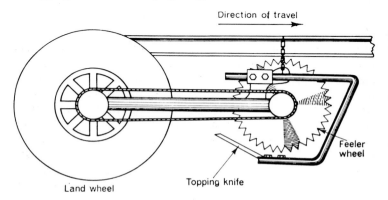

Direction of travel

Feeler wheel

Land wheel

Topping knife

Fig. 125. Topping unit on sugar beet harvester

known as the *feeler wheel*, driven by the axle of the harvester at a speed slightly greater than if it were rolling over the ground, pierces through the tops into the crown of the beet. This wheel is free to float over the line of beet and carries a knife for removing the crown of the beet, below the last leaf scar (Fig. 126). The knife is adjustable up and down, fore and aft. It is set to cut the crown parallel with the ground and just below the lowest leaf scar. The tops can be collected by a top saver and placed in a windrow or left scattered on the ground.

A series of rubber flails follows the topping unit and removes any trash or dead leaves from the row. This reduces blockage possibility in the lifting mechanism.

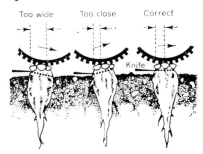

Fig. 126. Lateral setting of topping knife

Lifting mechanism. The commonest type of lifting mechanism is a pair of V-shaped shares, inclined slightly into the ground and depth-controlled by a screw-adjusted wheel. They squeeze the beet out of the ground and transfer them to a web elevator from the tractor p.t.o. The next mechanisms are designed to remove soil from the beet and carry the beet to a tank on the machine or a trailer being drawn alongside. The cleaning devices may consist of elevators with oval agitators or an elevator rolling the beet against a fixed web. A weight-loaded gate at the end of the elevator slows down the passage of the beet, until sufficient has accumulated to raise the gate. The beet may then fall on a cross-elevator and be carried by rows of widely spaced fingers to allow stones to drop through to the ground.

Another lifting mechanism consists of two large wheels, inclined towards each other. They rotate due to contact with the ground and lift the beet out of the ground. They have a low draught requirement and raise the beet clean, but tend to ride out of the ground in stony or hard conditions.

Operation of a sugar beet harvester. Tractor wheel settings must suit the row width. The centre of the topping unit should be exactly one row width from the centre of the lifting unit. The topping unit is set by driving down a row. The balance spring is adjusted so that the topper floats along the ground yet still bites through the leaves and into the crown. The knife is set as described above.

The lifting share should run as shallow as possible, yet still harvest all the beet. If the soil be hard or stony, the pitch of the shares can be increased a little, to aid penetration. The degree of agitation on the elevators depends on the type and condition of the soil, also on whether the beet is going to be cleaned again before being transported to the factory. Adequate cleaning reduces carriage costs and may, in the future, avoid penalties on dirty beet.

Maintenance of root harvesting machinery

1. Grease daily.
2. Check and adjust tension of chains.
3. Check shares for wear.

Storage

1. Remove, clean and treat all chains with rust preventative.
2. Spray all bright surfaces with rust preventative.
3. Block wheels off ground.
4. Replace all worn parts.

Field machinery safety regulations

1. *Mowers.* The cutter bar must be covered by a rigid guard when not in use.
2. *Combine.* It is not permissible to:
    (a) set a combine in motion, unless in the driving seat;
    (b) get on or off a combine while it is in motion.
3. *General*
    (a) All belts and chains on field machinery must be guarded at run-on points over pulleys, sprockets or tensioners. Wherever an operator is positioned on a machine, it should be suitably guarded to prevent him from being in contact with any moving part. It is the duty of the operator to report damaged and missing guards to his employer.

(b) It is not permissible to remove or adjust guards while the machine is in motion.

(c) No one under 16 years of age may remove or adjust the guarded parts on a field machine.

(d) All field machines must be maintained in a safe condition.

17. Grain Drying, Storage and Processing

Grain drying

All living seeds or grains respire. They take in oxygen and give off carbon dioxide, water and heat. The amount of respiration which occurs depends on the grain moisture content, the grain temperature and the amount of oxygen present in the air between the grains. In order to store grain safely it is necessary to control the rate of respiration and maintain it at a low level. If this is not done the heat and moisture will create conditions for fungal spores, ever-present on the surface of the grains, to grow. This growth will affect the germination and the musty smell will make it unpalatable for stock feed. Excessive heat and moisture may also cause seed to germinate and will encourage reproduction of insects whose eggs may be present in cracks in the store or in or on the grain.

The rate of respiration is normally controlled by drying the grain down to a moisture content at which heat production is so low it can easily be dissipated by convection without causing damage. These moisture contents depend on the method of storing grain and are as follows:

Crops	Storage Period	Maximum safe moisture content (%)
Wheat, barley, oats	1 year in bulk	14
Barley	Up to 6 months in sacks	15
Wheat, oats	Up to 6 months in sacks	16
Wheat, oats	Sacks for early dispatch	18

Grain drying is the process of reducing the moisture content of grain to a safe limit. Air is blown through the grain and it removes the water vapour in the air trapped between the grains. Further water moves from the grains into the air spaces and as this is removed the moisture content of the grains is reduced. The rate at which drying takes place depends on the rate of movement of moisture from the grain to the air. The flow of air can be increased by means of a fan and the air may also be heated. This not only increases the capacity of the air to absorb moisture but it also speeds up the movement of moisture from inside the grain to the surface.

In low-temperature driers it is important to be able to measure the potential of the air to absorb moisture. This is indicated by its relative humidity. It is then possible to determine the temperature rise, if any, required to reduce the relative humidity to the level required for drying.

A maximum safe working temperature has to be observed in high-temperature driers to avoid damage to grain which may affect its germination, milling or malting properties. The maximum safe drying air temperatures are indicated in the following table:

	Maximum air temperature (°C)
Feeding grain	82
Milling wheat	66
Malting barley up to 24% moisture	49
Seed grain up to 24% moisture	49
Malting barley over 24% moisture	43
Seed grain over 24% moisture	43

High-temperature driers

These driers usually operate on a continuous flow principle where moist grain enters the drier at one point and dry cool grain is delivered at another. The grain is dried by hot air which is directed at right angles, by a fan, through a thin layer or bed of steadily-moving grain. The grain may fall vertically or at an angle of about 60° or be moved horizontally by a conveyor. The rate the grain flows through the drier is regulated according to its moisture content.

An oil-fired furnace normally provides a source of heat for drying air. Under the control of a thermostat the furnace will heat the air to between 46°C and 84°C according to the moisture content and purpose to which the grain is to be used. Hot air is conveyed from the furnace and blown through the grain by a fan via a series of ducts.

As the grain dries it becomes hot and, if it were allowed to cool naturally in bulk, it would absorb moisture from the atmosphere and become mouldy. To prevent this happening cool air is blown through the bed of grain before it leaves the drier.

Moisture is removed quickly in these driers enabling a high throughput of grain. The capacity of continuous driers is usually expressed in tonnes/h throughput for a reduction of moisture content in the grain from 21% to 15% at a drying temperature of 66°C

Setting the drier is a very critical task requiring experience and knowledge of the moisture content of the grain and its intended use. The drier temperature is set to the maximum permissible for the type of grain being dried. The output of the drier is regulated carefully so that the grain is dried down to the required moisture content. Very wet grain may be put through the drier twice as it is not practical to remove more than 6 to 7% of the moisture each time the grain passes through the drier. Some driers are now fitted with an automatic controller which once set will make minor alterations to accommodate variations in the moisture content of incoming grain.

Low-temperature driers

These driers usually dry grain in bulk or in batches and it is essentially a slow process. The grain is ventilated with air at a relative humidity which will absorb moisture from the grain until eventually the moisture content of the grain is reduced to the desired level. If the relative humidity of the air is 70% the grain will eventually be dried down to approximately 15%.

In wet or damp weather it may be necessary to artificially heat the air to reduce it to a relative humidity of 70%.

These driers are of three main types.

Floor-ventilated bins. This type of drier involves the use of solid-walled grain storage bins fitted with an air chamber below a flat or nearly flat air permeable floor. Drying air is blown through the floor and permeates upwards through the

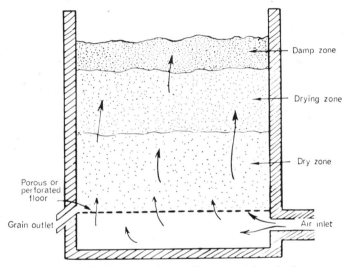

Fig. 127. Drying zones in floor-ventilated silo

grain. The drying zone (see Fig. 127) moves slowly up the bin. The maximum depth of wet grain for drying is 3 m, but where grain is over 24% it should be limited to 2 m. Some bins are designed with pneumatic emptying facilities.

Radially ventilated bins (Fig. 128). These bins are cylindrical in shape and have air permeable walls. Ventilating air is blown through a centrally situated permeable cylinder and the air, after passing through the grain, escapes radially through the bin walls. Drying begins around the central cylinder and gradually proceeds outwards.

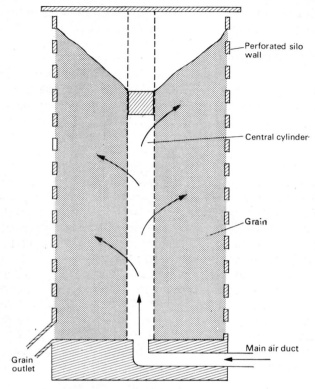

Perforated silo wall

Central cylinder

Grain

Main air duct

Grain outlet

Fig. 128. Radial flow ventilated silo

On-the-floor drier. This system is very similar to the ventilated bins, the main difference being that the grain is generally dried at a depth not greater than 2 to 3 m and the ventilating equipment can normally be removed to leave a clear floor for emptying and enables the building to be used for other purposes afterwards. The air is ducted via a central or side duct above or below ground level which is connected to a series of inverted A- or U-shaped lateral ducts. These lateral ducts are often made of open mesh wire (weld mesh) covered with light hessian sacking. Grain is heaped over these and is dried by the air blown along through these ducts from a fan.

Alternative methods of grain preservation

In order to avoid the cost of drying grain, alternative methods of treatment have been developed. These provide conditions which control or inhibit the rate of respiration by regulating either the temperature or the availability of oxygen rather than the level of moisture.

Grain chilling

In this system the grain is stored in bulk and air chilled by a refrigeration unit is blown through. As the incoming cool air lowers the grain temperature, the rate of respiration is reduced. The chilling ceases once the grain has reached a sufficiently low temperature. During storage the temperature of the grain may rise and will then need further chilling but two factors help to keep extra chilling to a minimum. The first is that grain is a poor conductor of heat, particularly when stored in bulk. The second is that, during the normal period of grain storage, the ambient temperature is generally fairly low. Some recommendations of safe storage temperature and moisture content are given below and it can be seen that, as the grain moisture content increases, so the maximum safe temperature decreases.

| | Maximum temperature for safe storage |
Grain moisture content (%)	Storage temperature (°C)
16	13
18	7
20	4
22	2

Low-volume aeration

A cheaper and simpler system of grain storage employs a small fan which blows a very low volume of air through a bin of grain. This air removes the heat produced by respiration but does not lower the grain moisture content. The fan produces an airflow of 0·5 to 0·6 m^3/min and is used for several days each month depending on the grain temperature and the ambient air temperature. The aim is to keep the grain temperature below 18°C to control insect activity. The table below shows how moisture content can affect the number of days per month the fan may be required.

Grain moisture content	Fan operation days/month
16	2
18	4
20	8

Grain stored under this system is only suitable for animal feed as the germination capacity of the grain is reduced.

Sealed storage

When moist grain is placed in a sealed container some respiration will take place. When all available oxygen has been used up the respiration will cease and the grain will gradually cool down. No further deterioration will take place providing the container remains sealed. This principle is used for storing grain which is to be used for stockfeed. A common type of storage container is a metal tower. The grain is blown in the top which is then sealed. As respiration takes place a greater amount of carbon dioxide is evolved than the original amount of oxygen present. A simple valve allows the surplus carbon dioxide to escape to the atmosphere.

The grain is removed from the bottom of the tower using an auger. This prevents entry of oxygen which would cause respiration to re-start.

This technique is suitable for grain at moisture contents of 15 to 25%. The resulting grain is free flowing and of normal colour, but has a smell due to the initial fermentation. It remains palatable for livestock.

Chemical preservation

If each grain is coated with a suitable chemical it will have the effect of sterilizing the grain and inhibit respiration and the growth of mould and insects. The grain may be stored in an open container and will be preserved for a considerable period of time. The chemical normally used in this technique is propionic acid. It must be added as soon as possible after harvest in the correct quantity in relation to the grain moisture content. It is essential that each grain is evenly coated and to achieve this a special applicator is used in the conveying system. It is suitable for grain up to 30% moisture content.

Grain processing equipment

Most farm livestock are unable to make efficient use of whole grains, so before feeding the grains are processed by rolling or grinding.

Rolling mills. These consist of two large steel rollers, one driven by a motor, the other turning through contact with the driven roller, although in the latest machines both rollers are driven. The pressure between the rollers can be controlled by an adjustable spring. Grain is fed between the rollers by a fluted feed roller and the pressure exerted on the grain should be such that it just crushes it and makes it more digestible. The optimum grain moisture content for rolling is 18 to 19% as the grain is then flattened without becoming shattered and dusty. Drier grains result in a dusty product.

Grinding mill. This is used when a fine floury consistency is required. One flat circular steel plate rotates against a fixed plate. Grain is fed through the centre of the fixed plate and emerges at the periphery as a fine grist. The fineness of the product is controlled by altering the clearance between the plates.

Hammer mills (Fig. 129). These are replacing the plate grinder as they are smaller, cheaper and are usually automatic in operation. They consist of a housing containing up to eight swinging flails or hammers on a rotor, with a circular screen fitted about 12 mm from the hammer tips. The hammers are driven up to 1500 rev/min. This creates a suction effect which is used to draw the grain through the centre of the rotor. By a combination of the action of the hammers and the screen, the grain is

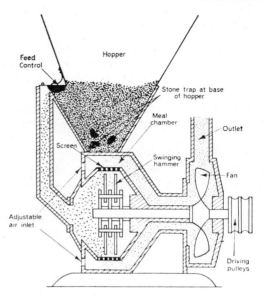

Fig. 129. Section through a hammer mill

reduced to a fine grist. The size of the grist is controlled by the size of the holes in the screen. There are no metal parts in contact with each other, so that wear is slight. The hammers are generally made double sided and reversible.

Mixers (Fig. 130). The commonest type of mixer mechanism consists of an auger running in a tube. This is fitted in the centre of a circular hopper with a capacity of up to 1 tonne. The lower part of the auger protrudes below the bottom of the hopper and round this is built a small intake or feeding hopper. In operation the auger draws the grist up the tube and it falls in the hopper. The constituents in the hopper are mixed by being circulated from the bottom to the top. After the mixing is completed, the hopper is emptied by connecting the top of the auger to an external chute by means of a valve or by gravity from the base of the hopper.

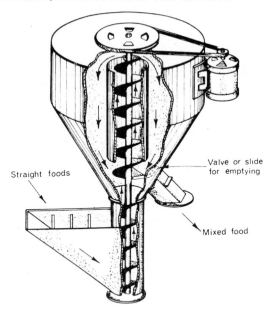

Straight foods

Valve or slide
for emptying

Mixed food

Fig. 130. Section through a vertical mixer

Safety regulations for stationary machinery

1. All belt and chain drives must be completely guarded.

2. All stopping devices must be readily accessible, clearly marked and positive in operation.

3. The worker must report damaged and missing guards to his employer.

4. No one under 16 years of age may remove or adjust guards.

5. It is not permissible to remove or adjust guards whilst the machine is in motion.

Safety regulations for work-places

1. Guards over openings in floors and walls may only be re-
    moved for the movement of feeding-stuffs or other
    materials.

2. Employers and workers share responsibility in the use of a ladder and they must make sure:

    (a) it is strong enough for the purpose for which it is being used;

    (b) it has no defective rung;

    (c) it is securely placed or held in position;

    (d) the top of the ladder extends above the point at which the worker has to get on or off unless another suitable handhold is available.

3. A worker must report any defects in a ladder.

18. Dairy Equipment

Mechanization of the milking routine has proceeded at great pace in recent years and the bucket machine is now being replaced by pipeline milking systems which convey the milk direct from the cow to a bulk tank for cooling and storage. This has been accompanied by the development of different types of milking parlours in an attempt to increase the number of cows which a man is able to milk. The most recent of these is the rotary milking parlour in which the cows are slowly rotated in front of the operator, so reducing the movement of the man to a minimum. Cleaning and sterilization of the milking equipment are also becoming automatic processes.

The milking process

When a calf is suckling a cow, it frequently releases the suction on the teat which allows the blood to circulate in the udder. The first milking machine applied continuous suction to the end of the teat with resultant udder damage, but modern machines follow more closely the principle of the calf, by alternating the period of suction and period of release.

It is necessary to understand how this suction, or *vacuum* as it is more correctly named, is measured. Atmospheric pressure is measured by an instrument called a barometer, which consists of a tube filled with mercury (Hg), closed at one end and the open end submerged in a bowl of mercury. Normal atmospheric pressure on the bowl of mercury maintains the column of mercury in the tube to a height of 750 mm above the level of the mercury in the bowl. This pressure is said to be equivalent to 750 mmHg. When the atmospheric pressure falls below normal a *partial vacuum* exists. This condition may be created by a vacuum pump. For the milking plant to function effectively a vacuum of 325 to 380 mmHg should be maintained. This is indicated on a *vacuum gauge* within easy view of the operator.

Vacuum pump

The *rotary vane* type of pump is the most popular type for creating the vacuum for milking. It consists of an eccentrically-mounted rotor with four or more longitudinal slots carrying cast iron, fibre or carbon vanes. During operation these are thrown out, and provide a seal against the side of the cylinder in which the rotor turns, due to centrifugal force. The inlet to the cylinder is located where the vanes project furthest, due to their eccentric mounting, and the exhaust port is located directly opposite. Air from the milking units is drawn through the inlet port of the pump, and conveyed around between the vanes, becoming compressed as it reaches the exhaust port. Under pressure the air is expelled via the exhaust port to the atmosphere. Lubrication is provided where necessary by continuous drip feed into the cylinder. The oil is expelled as an oil mist through the exhaust to the atmosphere.

The power to operate the vacuum pump is usually provided, through a V-belt, by an electric motor. Correct alignment of the pulleys is required to avoid abnormal belt-wear. In order to maintain the correct vacuum it is also important to keep the belt tension correct. It is wise to arrange an alternative source of power and many installations allow for the use of an engine or a tractor p.t.o. in the event of electrical supply failure. In any milking plant the vacuum pump should have a capacity in excess of that required to maintain the correct vacuum level when all units are operating. This excess capacity, or vacuum reserve, is required to deal with air which enters the vacuum system when the milking units are changed.

Sanitary trap

This consists of a large capacity bucket or container sited in the vacuum line near the vacuum pump. Its purpose is to prevent any liquid which may have entered the pipeline accidentally entering the vacuum pump. Some empty automatically when the pump is switched off while others should be checked after each milking and emptied if necessary.

Vacuum controller (regulator) and vacuum gauge

It is essential to maintain the correct vacuum in the pipe-lines (325 to 380 mmHg), irrespective of the number of milking units being used, for rapid and efficient milking. This is achieved by the vacuum controller which usually consists of a weight-loaded valve connecting the pipeline to the atmosphere. In order to maintain the correct level of vacuum the valve lifts to allow the air into the pipeline and prevent the correct level being exceeded. The level of vacuum in the pipeline is indicated by the vacuum gauge, the reading being given in millimetres of mercury (mmHg). If the correct vacuum cannot be reached or maintained, there may be an air leak in the system or the pump may be of inadequate capacity or be too badly worn to cope with the number of units being used.

Milking unit

A typical milking unit consists of four *teat cups*, a *claw* and a series of *pulse* and *milk tubes* (Fig. 131). The teat cups com-prise an outer *shell* and a rubber *teat cup liner*. Each teat cup is connected to the claw by two tubes, the *small milk tube* from the end of the liner to the milk chamber in the claw and the *pulse tube* from the shell to the air channel of the claw. The space between the shell and the liner is called the *pulse chamber*. The claw is connected to the recorder jar or milk line by the *long milk tube*. The milk tubes are always under vacuum whilst the pulse tubes alternate between atmospheric pressure and the required vacuum (Fig. 131).

Milk is drawn from the udder in the following way. When there is a vacuum in the pulse chamber, the teat cup retains its normal shape and the vacuum in the milk tube draws the milk away from the teat into the milk line. After a short period of time air is admitted via the pulsator or relay into the pulse

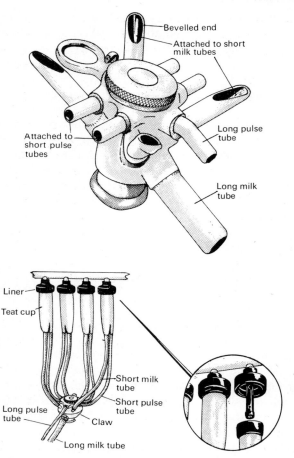

Bevelled end

Attached to short milk tubes

Attached to short pulse tubes

Long pulse tube

Long milk tube

Liner

Teat cup

Short milk tube

Short pulse tube

Long pulse tube

Claw

Long milk tube

Fig. 131. Milking unit: (a) Clawpiece; (b) milking unit attached to jetters

chamber and as a result the lower part of the liner collapses due to the vacuum inside it. This cuts off the milk flow and reduces the vacuum on the teat to an extent that it allows the blood to circulate yet holds the teat cup on. There are thus two distinct phases in the milking process; the *suction phase* when the milk is drawn from the teat and the *release* or rest phase when the liner is collapsed (Fig. 132 (a) and (b)). These phases are determined by the *pulsator*. This might be described as a valve which connects the pulse chamber alternately with the vacuum line and the atmosphere. The pulsator may be operated electrically,

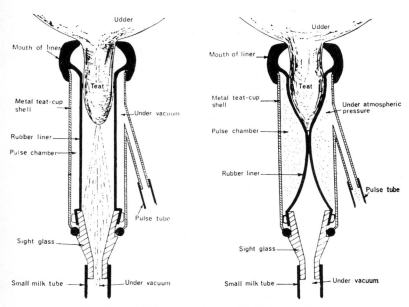

Fig. 132. (a) Suction phase. (b) Release phase

mechanically or pneumatically. Each milking unit may have its own pulsator or alternatively a *master pulsator* may be used. The master pulsator sends impulses to a *relay* which then acts as the valve alternating the phases of vacuum and atmospheric pressure to the milking unit.

The length of the suction phase related to the release phase is known as the *pulsation ratio*. In most machines this is between 3:1 and 4:1; the suction phase being 3 or 4 times longer than the release phase. The number of times the whole cycle is completed a minute is called the *pulsation rate* and is usually between 50 and 60 cycles min. It is interesting to note that the four metal tubes of the claw to which the short milk tubes are connected are bevelled. This facilitates fitting the unit to the cow. The operator holds the unit by the claw and as the teat cups hang down the bevelled end automatically cuts off the vacuum preventing it being lost.

In further attempts to minimize the labour involved in the milking process automatic cluster removal mechanisms have been designed.

Pipeline milking installations (Fig. 133)

Milk is drawn from the teat cups into a recorder jar to enable records to be kept of individual cow yields. The recorder jar is fitted with a tap to allow small samples to be taken and is usually fitted with a method of drawing off contaminated or otherwise unsuitable milk. From the recorder jar the milk is drawn into the milk-line.

Milk meters

These provide an alternative to the recorder jar for speedy recording. They are rather expensive at present but are continually being improved and are likely to be more widely used in future.

Milk pipelines

These are normally made of borosilicate glass or stainless steel and carry the milk to receiving jars. They are joined by sleeve joints of fat resistant synthetic rubber for easy dismantling and cleaning. The milk in the line is under vacuum and has to be transferred to the churns or bulk tank without affecting the vacuum level in the milk-line. This is achieved by the incorporation of a receiver jar into the system.

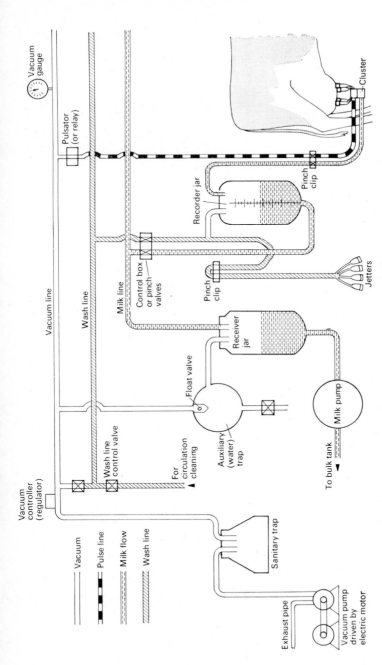

Fig. 133. Pipeline milking installation

Receiver jar and milk pump

Milk from the milk-line passes into the receiver jar. When the milk in the receiver jar reaches a predetermined level the milk pump is activated through an electrical switch. Similarly when the milk level in the receiver jar falls to a predetermined level, the milk pump is switched off. The milk pump is usually of the rotary or diaphragm type and is constructed to permit easy cleaning *in situ*, the pump being incorporated into the circulation cleaning system.

Auxiliary trap (water trap)

This is tapped into the vacuum line between the receiver vessel and the vacuum controller. A float valve in this trap prevents liquid being drawn into the vacuum line. It may also have a valve fitted at the base to permit liquid to drain away when the vacuum pump is switched off. The pipelines are also fitted with automatic valves which allow moisture to drain away when the vacuum pump is switched off. These should be fitted at the lowest points in the pipeline.

Circulation cleaning

Most milking plants incorporate a circulation cleaning system utilizing the components of the milking plant to circulate the cleaning fluid. To achieve this the milk circuit is connected to the wash-line by placing the teat cups in the *jetters* allowing the cleaning fluid to follow the same direction as the milk. During milking the wash-line is under vacuum and the section of the wash-line to the jetters is closed by a pinch clip. The control valve is then set for circulation cleaning and the cleaning fluid drawn from a reservoir. The discharge from the milk pump is either connected back to the reservoir or allowed to drain away.

Concentrate feeding

In addition to milking in modern parlours, provision is often made for concentrate feeding. Storage hoppers are pro-

vided which enable each cow to be fed a predetermined quantity of concentrate. The concentrate may be fed manually or
automatically using mechanical or electrical controls.

Cooling of milk

In order to improve the keeping quality of milk, it should be
cooled as soon as possible. Cooling may be done in bulk, in the
milk churn or the bulk tank, or by continuous flow over a surface cooler, through which cooled water or brine solution is
passed.

With in-churn cooling, cool water is circulated through rotating pipes immersed in the milk. The rotation of the pipes

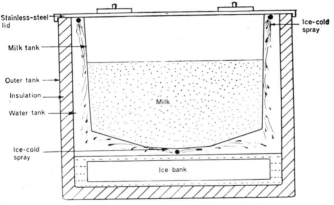

Fig. 134. Section of a bulk milk tank

brought about by the water leaving the top of the cooler, causes
the milk to cool evenly. This method of cooling is often used in
conjunction with a refrigeration unit, which cools the water
before it passes to the cooler and collects it again afterwards.
Cooling in a bulk tank occurs because the tank containing the
milk is surrounded by a layer of ice or cold water (Fig. 134).
Large paddles circulate the milk against the sides and the heat
passes through to the ice or cold water on the other side. The

ice or coolness of the water is maintained by a refrigeration process. Bulk tanks cool the milk very rapidly to 6°C and store it at that temperature until collection.

Electric fencer

An electrified fence controls stock with the minimum of fencing materials. This system is widely used for strip or paddock grazing of grass and other forage crops because it is relatively cheap and more easily moved than other types of fences. With one electrified wire for cattle and two wires for pigs and sheep, the stock are confined by the fear of the shock they will receive if they touch the fence. Some battery-operated fencer units work on the same principle as a coil ignition system (Chapter 8). It consists basically of two circuits, a primary and secondary. In the primary circuit, current stored in the battery flows from one battery terminal through the primary coil to earth and back to the other battery terminal. One end of the coil in the secondary circuit is earthed to the metal mounting pole of the unit, and the other end is connected to the bare wire of the fence which is to be electrified (Fig. 135). The fence wire is

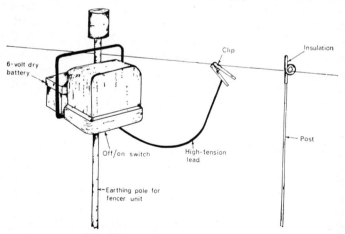

Fig. 135. Electric fencer unit

supported on insulators fixed to posts or, alternatively, the top of the post is looped and covered with plastic or rubber to carry and insulate the wire from the ground. Therefore, this secondary circuit is only completed and the current able to flow through it when the fence wire is earthed.

The current flow through the primary circuit is controlled and only occurs once per second, lasting one hundredth of a second. This is indicated by the tick of the fencer unit. An increase in the rate of the tick is an indication that the battery is becoming weak. During this one hundredth of a second, the current flow in the primary circuit is interrupted. This interruption causes the collapse of the magnetic field around the primary coil and induces a high voltage (9000 V) but low current in the secondary circuit. As already mentioned, a current flow in the secondary circuit is only possible when the fence wire is earthed and this happens when the fence is touched by an animal. The animal acts as a return wire in the secondary circuit, the high-tension current passing through the animal's body to earth, giving the animal a shock. The shock does not cause the animal injury because the electrical energy (watts) is minute.

When using an electric fence, it is important that the unit itself should be well earthed and this is best achieved by mounting it on a metal post driven well into the ground. Also the fence wire must be well insulated from the ground which means keeping grass and tall forage crops away from the wire and keeping the insulators on the posts in good condition.

19. Materials Handling

During farming operations large quantities of materials are moved from place to place. Indeed most production operations are solely concerned with the movement of materials. Fertilizers, seed and spray chemicals are moved from buildings to fields while harvested crops and straw are moved from fields to buildings. Inside the buildings, crops are moved for drying and processing and then for feeding to animals or effluent from animals is returned to the fields. Animal products such as milk and eggs are moved from their point of production to a processing area and are then finally moved off the farm for sale. Distances of movement vary from a few metres inside buildings to several kilometres between buildings and fields. Many systems have been developed to reduce the amount of manual effort required and a knowledge of the principles involved is necessary to enable the optimum selection of a system and its components to be made.

Most systems of materials handling can be placed into one or two distinct categories based on their principle of operation.

Continuous systems

The principle of these systems is one of continuous flow. Materials from one point are moved to another in an uninterrupted manner. In order to move or convey in this manner the material must have certain characteristics which enable it to flow. Few materials, in fact, have these characteristics and, in order to utilize a continuous system, they may be conveyed by adding them to a fluid which is used purely as a carrier. At the end of the system the material is usually separated from the fluid.

The fluid used is either liquid or air. In each case energy must be provided continuously to cause the process to occur.

Gravity is used wherever possible but a power source is necessary to provide a flow horizontally or uphill. Fluids are most conveniently transported in pipes and examples of continuous flow are found in the movement of effluent and in pipeline pig feeding systems. These use water as a fluid but air is used for milk and grain conveying. In some cases the form of the material is modified to give it improved flow characteristics. The pelleting of powdery concentrates improves their flowing ability. In each case consideration must be given to the importance of maintaining the quality of the material by the avoidance of damage and keeping the cost of the movement to within economic limits.

Despite the many varied systems in operation some common elements can be recognized in each. These elements are the basis of the system and a knowledge of their principles is necessary in order to be able to obtain maximum efficiency from the system. They provide the energy which give the movement to the fluid.

Pumps

Pumps are used for conveying liquids. From the handling aspect, the important characteristics of liquids are that their volume does not change with pressure and that their density enables them to flow under the influence of gravity. Many types of pump are available each having a special characteristic for the application required. Some of the performance characteristics are as follows:

Output. This is the volume of liquid which can be moved in a given period of time and is normally expressed in cubic metres per minute (m³/min) or per hour (m³/h).

Total head. This is given as a total vertical distance but it comprises a number of separate components. The *suction head* is the vertical distance from the liquid level to the pump inlet. This should be kept as small as possible for efficient operation. The *static head* represents the vertical distance from the pump to the outlet or highest point of the pipe. The *friction head* is a measure of the loss due to friction of the liquid against the pipe as it is being pumped. This will be affected by the length, diameter, type of pipe material and volume and type of liquid being pumped. The *pressure head* describes the equivalent vertical distance required to convert the flow to pressure as when forcing it through a sprinkler.

The heads are converted from volume, pipe diameter, length and pressure measurements to equivalent vertical distances by means of tables.

Different designs of pump have different output and head characteristics. *Centrifugal pumps* operate by drawing liquid through to the centre of the impellor and accelerate it rapidly down the impellor vanes to be thrown at high speed through the pump outlet. Some pumps are designed to produce high outputs at high heads or pressures. These are suitable for sprinkler irrigation systems. Others, designed for pumping slurry, produce high outputs at medium pressure whilst those in liquid feeding systems produce high outputs at low pressure.

Piston pumps differ from centrifugal pumps in that the flow is intermittent or pulsed as a result of the action of the piston. To overcome this a reservoir, or balancer tank, is incorporated on the output side of the pump to even the flow. These pumps are often used in situations where a low output and a high head or pressure is required such as in a pressure washer.

Other types of pump have been referred to in a previous chapter. *Gear* pumps, *Roller vane* pumps and *diaphragm* pumps in Chapter 15, pp. 194–6.

The performance characteristics of a pump in terms of output and head must be equal to or slightly greater than that required by a particular task for it to be carried out effectively.

Fans

Air as a fluid is a compressible medium and, unlike liquid, changes volume according to pressure. Thus its characteristics are described in relation to both volume and pressure. Some fans such as those used for grain drying and building ventilation are required to move large volumes of air at relatively low pressures. The volume is normally measured in cubic metres per minute (m³/min) or per hour (m³/h) while the pressure being low is expressed in length of water gauge (mm w.g.) by using a manometer. This is a U-shaped tube half filled with water with one side connected into the duct in which the air is flowing and the other open to the atmosphere. The difference between the water levels is measured to describe the pressure. The factor affecting the pressure is the *resistance* to airflow and, in the case of grain or hay drying, this is altered by the depth of the drying bed. When this becomes excessive the airflow is reduced and this may reduce the rate of drying.

Axial flow fans consist of propellor-like blades operating in a housing. They accelerate the air in the same direction as it was originally moving and are used for moving large volumes of air at low pressures as in the ventilation of buildings.

Centrifugal fans have a series of radial blades which may be straight or curved forward or backward. Air is drawn in at the centre, accelerated down the blades, then discharged at right angles to entry. These fans can exert higher pressures and are used for grain drying.

Very high pressure types are used for grain conveying. In these the air is blown through a *venturi* (see p. 74) and this causes the grain to be sucked into the stream of air moving at high speed. It can then be conveyed horizontally or vertically and is separated from the air by a cyclone.

Vacuum pumps are a special type of fan used mainly in milking systems. They produce a pressure lower than that of ambient air and generally operate on a low volume. They are discussed in detail in Chapter 18.

Conveyors

The movement of materials from one part of a building to another may be carried out by mechanical conveyors. Depending on the ability of the material to flow the system may be automatically controlled or may require manual loading and unloading. Materials with reasonable flow properties such as grain, fertilizer or pelleted feedstuffs are suited to automatic systems while those formed into sacks or bales are loaded and unloaded manually.

The type of conveyor mechanism selected will depend on the material being handled and the angle through which it is required to be moved. Some conveyors are designed for near-horizontal operation while others can operate through any angle from the horizontal to the vertical. Other qualities they should possess include self-cleaning and non-damaging action to the conveyed material. They should be capable of being started and stopped under load and should have a reasonable power requirement per tonne of material being conveyed.

Granular material conveyors

These are used for grain, fertilizer, pelleted and milled feeding stuffs.

Augers. These consist of a helical screw in a closely fitting tube. The screw projects at the inlet end of the tube and there is a slide to control the amount exposed. A motor at the other end drives the screw at a speed of 1000 to 1500 rev/min, depending on the size of the screw which may be 75 to 200 mm diameter.

Augers convey material at any angle from the horizontal to the vertical but the throughput depends on the angle. A horizontal auger will have about twice the throughput of a similar vertical auger. The moisture content of grain affects the throughput being reduced as the moisture content increases. High moisture-content grain will increase the power requirement and may burn out an electric motor unless the inlet slide is carefully adjusted. Augers have the advantage of being self-cleaning except for the intake screw area.

Chain and flight conveyors. These consist of an endless horizontal chain with cross bars or flights running in a rectangular trough. The material is carried between the flights. This type of conveyor is suitable for horizontal use or at very slight angles and is relatively cheap and durable. It is not self-cleaning and, therefore, may cause some contamination due to carry over.

Endless belt. A flat, endless rubber conveyor belt is supported by angled rollers which cause it to form a shallow trough and prevent loss of material. The material being conveyed can be removed from the end or anywhere along the length of the belt by deflecting it with an angled piece of metal. These are used for conveying horizontally or on slight angles and are self-cleaning and efficient, but the initial costs are relatively high.

Bucket elevator. A series of small metal containers is fitted to an endless canvas belt. The buckets dip into the material at the foot of the conveyor, raise it to the top then flick it out as they turn over the top. They are only suitable for vertical or near-vertical conveying and are not greatly affected by the moisture content of the material. They are not self-cleaning as a certain amount of material always remains at the foot of the conveyor.

Pneumatic conveyors. Material is fed through a venturi into a fast-moving stream of air produced by a fan. The main feature of this type of conveyor is its suitability to convey through any angle from the horizontal to the vertical and also around corners. Moist grain will reduce the conveying capacity due to its friction with the tube. It is self-cleaning, but in this respect it is essential that the feed-slide to the conveyors is closed and the system allowed to empty itself before being switched off. Damage to the material can result during the conveying process. The high power requirement makes it a rather costly system of conveying.

The separation of the material from the air is normally carried out in a cyclone. The material on entering the cyclone travels around the walls and slowly falls to the outlet at the base, whilst the air escapes through an opening in the upper part of the cyclone. Dust carried in the air may be filtered out by passing it through cloth sacks.

Non-granular material conveyors

These are designed for materials which do not flow easily and may also be susceptible to mechanical damage. Sacks, bales and loose potatoes are examples, and the conveyor or *elevator*, as it is generally called, is used for this operation. The main component is an endless chain or belt with various types of bar connected across. Sides may be added to prevent loss of loose material.

The most common type is a portable machine with its own power unit and various attachments are available to convert it for use with different types of materials. The angle of conveying is adjustable but it is limited by the angle at which the material rolls back down the elevator.

Unit load systems

Where distances are considerable it is uneconomic to install continuous flow systems for materials handling. Also many types of materials do not have the required flow characteristics to enable them to be moved continuously. Some materials, such as potatoes and apples are susceptible to mechanical damage and require special treatment. For these reasons the unit load system of handling is used. This system involves packaging the material into a suitable size bundle or into a suitable container and then moving the package or container. Four distant stages can be recognized; packaging, loading, transporting and, finally, the unloading stage. The process takes place intermittently.

1. *The packaging or forming stage*—each of the units must be assembled or formed. In the case of crops this is done in the field as part of the harvesting operation. Hay and straw are baled and the bales collected in groups; potatoes may be filled into sacks or pallets.

2. *The loading stage*—the assembled units are loaded on to the transport system. This is generally a trailer but in some cases mounted attachments at the front or rear of a tractor are used.

3. *The transport stage*—this is the movement of the transport from the field to the farm.

4. *The unloading stage*—the units are removed from the transport stage by hand or mechanically.

Forming the unit

The natural size, shape and volume of most agricultural commodities makes them unsuitable to be handled as unit loads without first giving them packaging treatment to make them into units of a suitable size to be handled manually or mechanically. The maximum size of unit which can be handled manually is one of about 50 kg, but units handled mechanically may be up to 1·5 tonnes.

Packaging

The treatment given will vary according to the material and the handling system which is to be used. Some examples of the more common treatments are given:

Sacks.—These are the most common containers used for packaging and are suitable for a wide range of granular materials such as grain, fertilizer and potatoes (which are being handled manually). The filling, weighing and sealing of sacks, together with their subsequent manual handling, requires considerable labour and they are too small a unit to be handled individually by mechanical means. For these reasons packaging into larger containers is gradually superseding sacks. The sack is still used as it is an easy means of accurately discriminating between small quantities.

Bales.—This treatment is universally applied to hay and straw as its normal characteristic is to lock together when laid in a large heap. It is then difficult to separate the individual units for handling. The normal bale is between 15 and 25 kg, and was developed for manual handling. It is too small, like the sack, for efficient mechanical handling, so attempts are being made to develop larger bales, systems of packaging small bales or gathering groups of small bales.

Pallets and slings. In order to increase the efficiency of sack handling, pallets or slings may be used. Fifteen to 30 sacks are laid on a wooden frame or placed in a plastic sling by hand. The frame or sling is then moved as a unit by an attachment mounted on a tractor.

Box. This is a larger unit load designed entirely for mechanical handling. It is normally made from wood or metal with a capacity of 300 to 1000 kg. It is used particularly for handling potatoes and apples. These products are very susceptible to mechanical damage, and in order to keep the effect of this to a minimum, they may be loaded, transported and stored in the same box.

The trailer

This is the most common form of container for all types of materials both loose and packaged by any of the previously described methods. It is used as a container for transport of materials and to increase its versatility it is available in many different forms and with different attachments. It may be two- or four-wheeled for extra carrying capacity. Most types are tipped hydraulically for emptying materials which flow. Some are specially designed for tipping on high heaps using a double ram and tipping mechanism. Various types of side are available with extensions for grain, roots or silage. Carrying capacity ranges from 1 to 10 tonnes.

Some specialized types of trailer are fitted with self-unloading mechanisms. These enable their load to be emptied in a controlled and progressive manner.

Those used for spreading farmyard manure have an endless chain to convey the material to the rear and a flail-type spreading mechanism for shredding and distributing. One type spreads from the side of the trailer using a set of chains as flails which rotate on a shaft down the length of the trailer.

Trailers for forage conservation and handling discharge from the side by means of a cross conveyor. This is used to feed a blower to a pit or tower, and it may be used for direct feeding of livestock.

Where the material being handled is slurry the trailer may be a sealed container with a p.t.o.-driven air pump, which creates a vacuum for filling and pressurizes the trailer for emptying. Other types are open containers and use a pump for filling. Emptying may be done by gravity or the use of an auger to move the solid material. In most cases provision is made for using the pump to agitate the contents of the collecting tank and the trailer to prevent the settling out of solid material.

Equipment for loading

The most common means of loading and unloading units is the tractor and loader fitted with an appropriate attachment. Many types of loader are available but the most common is the fore-loader as it provides the best visibility for the operator. However, its disadvantage is that, when large loads are lifted, much weight is transferred from the rear driving wheels and traction can become a problem in wet conditions. To overcome this, weights may be carried on the three-point linkage. Rear-mounted loaders overcome this problem but do not have such good operator visibility and tend to restrict the versatility of the tractor when attached. Where traction is a serious problem as in the field loading of sugar beet or farmyard manure, a slew loader may be used. This enables the loading to be carried out with the tractor stationary and when it moves to a fresh loading position it can do so without traction problems.

Fittings or attachments are available for front-end loaders and some rear-loaders to enable them to perform a wide range of tasks. Muck and root forks and earth buckets are the most common but others enable them to handle stacks of bales and boxes of potatoes. The latter may have a tippling valve for controlled emptying of potatoes into a trailer or store.

The choice of handling system

The decisions made by a farmer on the handling system he will select for a particular situation are made after considering many interacting factors. The result is frequently a combination of continuous and unit load elements and is a compromise between the speed of the operation and cost. It is essential that the speed of each operation is matched in order that, for example, a rapid loading operation is not hindered by a slow unloading operation. Many factors such as the size of the labour force and distance of conveying have to be considered together with the suitability of the equipment for other farming operations.

There is also a continuing change in both the type and level of production together with the decreasing labour force and the introduction of new handling techniques and equipment. Most handling systems on a particular farm develop over a number of years and comprise a series of replacements and improvements on the existing system. It is only occasionally the opportunity arises to install a totally new system.

Index

air clearner, 79
alloy, 33–5
ampere, 20
annealing, 36
anti-freeze,103

babbit, 38
baler, 220
    components, 220–3
    operation, 223–5
    storage, 225
ballasting, 115–6
battery, 85–7
battery charger, 88–9
bearings, 53
belts, 13, 58
bolts, 40
brakes, 112–4
brake power, 5
brass, 37
brazing, 31
brittleness, 31
bronze, 38
buckrake, 229
bush, 53

case hardening, 37
chain, 13, 56
chisel, 47
chisel plough, 156
clutch, 108–9
    slip clutch, 60
combine harvester, 229
    basic settings, 234–6
    components, 230–4
    grain losses, 236–7
    maintenance, 237
    storage, 237
conduction, 16
contraction, 15
convection, 17
conveyors, 271–3
coolong systems, 100
    air, 100
    frost precautions, 103
    maintenance, 103–4
    water, 100–3
copper, 37
corn drill, see drills
cultivating equipment
    selection, 155
    use 171
cultivators, tined, 157–8
    rotary, 162–3
current, 20
    alternating, 25
    direct 25

differential, 111
discharge tester, 90
draft, 3

drawbar power, 6
    pull, 3
drills, 182
    calibration, 185
    feed mechanisms, 182–5
    maintenance, 188
    operation, 185–7
drills (twist), 50
ductility, 31

efficiency (machine), 8, 22
electric fencer, 266–7
electrical system, 81
    battery, 85–7
    battery charger, 88–9
    battery charging system,
        86
    coil ignition, 81–4
    discharge tester, 90
    fault-finding, 120–4
    fuses, 87
    magneto, 84
    maintenance, 87–8
    spark plug, 82
    starter motor, 87
electricity, 20
    circuits, 22
    conductor, 20
    earthing, 26
    fuses, 23
    generation, 24
    insulator, 20
    measurement, 20
    power, 21
    transmission, 25–6
    unit, 22
energy, 1
    chemical, 1, 62
    electricity, 1, 21
    heat, 1, 14, 112
    kinetic, 2, 112
    mechanical, 1, 2, 62
    potential, 2, 62
engine, 62
    components, 62, 68–70
    compression ratio, 65
    four-stroke, 63–5
    timing, 70–1
    two-stroke, 66–8
expansion, 15

fans, 270–1
feeler gauge, 51
ferrous metals, 32
    identification, 36
fertilizer distributors, 173
    checking, 178
    maintenance, 129–80
    operation, 173–9
    types, 173–9
files, 48–9

forage harvesters, 225
    types, 225–8
    operation, 228–9
force, 2
    compressive, 29
    shear, 29
    tensile, 29
    turning, 3
four-stroke cycle, 63–5
friction, 9, 60
fuel systems, 73
    air cleaner, 78
    components, 73–8
    fault-finding, 120–4
    maintenance, 79–80
    storage, 80
    fuse, 23, 87

gearbox, 109
gear, 12, 55
    driven, 12
    driver, 12
    types, 55
grain
    chilling, 251
    conveying equipment,
        269–74
    driers, 246–51
    drying, 246–53
    drills, see drills
    preservation, 251–2
    processing equipment,
        253–5
grass seeding equipment,
    192

hacksaw, 49
hammer mills, 253
hammers, 46
hardness, 31
harrows
    disc, 159, 167
    dutch, 167
    reciprocating, 164
    spike-tooth, 163
hay conditioning machinery,
    217–9
heat, 14
    latent, 14
    transference, 16
hoes, components, 167
    setting, 169–70
    types, 170
hydraulic principles, 9
hydraulic systems, 116–9
    draft control, 117
    position control, 117
    external application, 118

ignition systems, 81–4
iron, 32

iron—*cont.*
   alloy, 33
   cast, 32
   chilled cast, 33
   galvanized, 38
   malleable, 34
   pig, 32
   wrought, 34

key, 57–8
keyway, 57–8

lead, 38
lever, 7
locking devices, 52
lubricating systems, 91
   classification of oils, 96–7
   deterioration of oils, 97–8
   fault-finding, 120–4
   filters, 9–5
   maintenance, 98–9
   principles, 91

machines, 7
magneto, 84
malleability, 31
mass, 4
materials, 29
   characteristics, 30–1
materials handling systems,
   268
   choice of system, 277
   continuous, 268–74
   unit load, 274–7
mechanical advantage, 8, 11
metals, ferrous, 32
   joining, 31
   non-ferrous, 37
milk cooling, 18, 265
milking machine, 257–65
mills, 253–4
mixers, 254–5
mowing machines, 208
   components, 208–13
   field operation, 214–7
   preparation for work,
     210–4
   rotating disc, 216–7
   storage, 216

normalizing, 36
nuts, 40
   lock, 52
   slotted, 53

ohms, 21
oil, classification, 96
   deterioration, 97
overload protection, 59–61

plastics, 38
plough, 126
   adjustments, 132–7
   chisel, 156
   components, 126–31
   disc, 135–7, 158

   faults, 151
   maintenance, 153
   reversible, 134
ploughing in lands, 137,
   146–9
   reversible, 150
   round and round, 149–51
potato harvesters, 237–41
   maintenance, 244
   operation, 237–41
power, 5
   brake power, 5
   drawbar power, 6
precision seeders, 188–91
   operation, 190
   types, 188–90
pulleys, 13, 18, 58
pumps, 269–70
   diaphragm, 196
   gear, 194
   roller vane, 194
   vacuum, 258
punches, 46

Radiation, 17
refrigeration, 17, 233
relative humidity, 18, 247
rolls, 159, 166
row-crop equipment,
   167–71
rubber, 39
rules, 51

safety regulations
   for field machines, 244
   for spray chemicals, 207
   for stationary machines,
     255
   for tractors, 124–5
   for work places, 255–6
screws, 11, 44
   Allen, 45
   Phillip's headed, 44
screwdrivers, 45
seeding equipment,
   180–92
setscrew, 40, 45
shaft, 56
shear bolt, 59
single-phase electricity
   supply, 26
solder, 31, 38
spanners, 42–4
spark plugs, 79
spline, 56–7
sprayer, application rates,
   198–201
   band sprayer, 205
   calibration, testing,
     201–3
   chemicals used, 199
   cleaning, 206
   components, 193–8
   field operation, 203–5
   safety precautions, 207

   storage, 206
sprocket, 13, 56–7
steel, 34
   alloy, 34–5
   heat treatment, 36
   high carbon, 35
   medium carbon, 35
   mild, 34
steerage hoe, 167–71
strain, 30
strength, 29–30
   compressive, 30
   shear, 30
   tensile, 30
stress, 29
stud, 41
sugar beet harvesters,
   242–4
   components, 242–3
   maintenance, 244
   operation, 243–4
   storage, 244

tedder, 218
temperature, 14
   Celsius, 15
tempering, 36
thread types, 41
three-phase electricity
   supply, 26
tin, 37
torque, 3, 55
toughness, 31
traction, 115–6
tractor, 105
   aids to traction, 115–6
   brakes, 112–4
   fault finding, 120–4
   hydraulics, 116
   maintenance, 79, 87, 98,
     103, 111, 114, 115,
     119–20
   safety regulations,
     124–5
   transmission system
     106–11
   types, 105–6
   tyres, 114–5
   wheels, 114
two-stroke cycle, 66–8

universal joint, 57

velocity ratio, 8, 10, 13
volts, 20

washers, 52
watts, 21
welding, 32
   bronze, 32
   fusion, 32
white metal, 38
work, 4
wrenches, 42–4

zinc, 38